Issues in African Law

CHANGE AND CONTINUITY IN AFRICA

MONOGRAPHS UNDER THE AUSPICES OF

THE AFRIKA-STUDIECENTRUM · LEIDEN

MOUTON · THE HAGUE · PARIS

J.F. HOLLEMAN

Issues in African Law

MOUTON · THE HAGUE · PARIS

This publication of miscellaneous papers is presented to their author by the Afrika-Studiecentrum in grateful recognition of his pioneering efforts as Director, 1963-69.

ISBN 90 279 7571 X

Library of Congress Catalog Card Number: 73-81812

Jacket-design by Jurriaan Schrofer

Printed in the Netherlands

Foreword

This collection of papers owes its publication to a very kind gesture of the Board of the Afrika-Studiecentrum when I laid down the directorship of that institute after some six years' tenure.

In the Dutch academic world the presentation to a scholar of a publication comprising his own *verspreide geschriften* or miscellaneous writings is a tribute usually reserved for an esteemed colleague and teacher when he becomes emeritus. Being still many years removed from this venerable status I felt duly flattered; but having been asked to select the material myself I was also faced with a personal problem. However loath to look a gift-horse in the mouth, I was forced to cast a critical eye upon products bred in my own stable over a period of many years and for a wide variety of purposes. The bulk of my published work had appeared in book form and was still available or in the course of being reprinted; but a volume of *verspreide geschriften* aims at bringing together shorter and less accessible pieces of writing. Of the latter I could find a fair number, some of which had appeared in print but most of them not. They covered many and widely divergent topics, and ranged from research reports to popular talks and even political commentaries. In fact, the only thing they seemed to have in common was that they had *not* originally been written for the express purpose of being published in learned journals.

In these circumstances I felt in need of an authoritative and more impartial opinion than mine, and submitted the material to Professor Schapera, whose critical judgment I have learned to respect. The present selection, its arrangement and collective title are the result of his scrutiny and advice, which I have gratefully accepted.

The political essays and two fairly lengthy research reports[1] have been excluded because they dealt with European rather than African problems; and only those pieces were selected which, with some good will, may be con-

1. These reports are published separately under the title *White Mine Workers in Northern Rhodesia, 1959-60* (African Social Research Documents No. 6), Leiden/Cambridge.

sidered to fall within two broad fields: African tribal law, and family problems of transition. This is also the basis on which they have been grouped, though in each case the date(s) of writing and some other particulars have been mentioned in a footnote, introductory passage or postcript.

I stated that these writings, including those that have previously appeared in print, were not originally prepared as contributions to learned journals. To be exact, the present collection comprises:

nine talks I had been asked to give, most of them to lay audiences in southern Africa on topics believed to be of public interest;

two extensive case reports which I have used with my students as comparative material at seminars on dispute settlement in tribal societies.

Having originated like this their style is therefore popular rather than academic, and although they were composed with due care they were presented either without references to other literature or with but a minimal number. Extensive editorial treatment would have remedied this omission but would also have involved a considerable amount of rewriting. This, it was felt, would have run counter to the idea underlying this kind of publication. I have therefore confined myself to minor text corrections (including two changes of title), one large and several small deletions of redundant matter, and the addition of some explanatory notes.

Though I have, on one or two occasions, drawn attention to the fact that some statutory provisions which I had criticized have since been changed, I have generally refrained from 'updating' these writings. But the reader will of course bear in mind that a good many other things are likely to have changed and that the facets of African law and life here presented, and which I observed and reported between the middle 'forties and early 'sixties, may be somewhat differently coloured or shaped today.

Leiden
August 1972

J. F. H.

Acknowledgements

Kind permission to reproduce previously published material in this volume has been given by:
the Institute for African Studies, University of Zambia, Lusaka, (successor to the Rhodes-Livingstone Institute);
the Editor of NADA, Ministry of Internal Affairs, Salisbury, Rhodesia;
the Institute for Social Research of the University of Natal, Durban, South Africa;
the South African Institute of Race Relations, Johannesburg, South Africa;
Max Reinhardt Ltd, London.

Table of contents

FOREWORD V

ACKNOWLEDGEMENTS VII

SOME CHARACTERISTICS OF BANTU LAW
(with special reference to Shona law) (1948) 1

INDIGENOUS ADMINISTRATION OF JUSTICE (1954) 16

THE CASE OF THE TROUBLESOME FATHER (1946/1968) 22

I. *Case report* 22
Introduction 22
Background of the case 22
Preliminary proceedings 24
The trial 27
II. *Analysis of certain aspects* 37
The communal element 37
The concrete element 40
Postscript (1968) 44

THE CASE OF THE IRATE HEADMAN (1951/1970) 48

I. *Case report* 48
Introduction 48
Background of the case 52
The process 54
II. *Analysis* 66
The venue 66
Procedure 69
Conciliatory aims and formal acts of reconciliation 78

MARRIAGE, BRIDEWEALTH AND WOMEN IN AN AFRICAN SOCIETY (1951/1953) 84

Preface 84
I. *The significance of the Lobola system* 87
I. *Some other aspects of marriage* 101
III. *The position of women* 112
IV. *The dissolution of customary marriage* 123

CASH, CATTLE OR WOMAN: A CONFLICT OF CONCEPTS IN A DUAL ECONOMY (1962) 133

AFRICAN MARRIAGE AT THE CROSS-ROADS (1960) 150

I. *Customary marriage* 150
II. *Statutory recognition of customary Bantu marriages* 150
Civil and Christian marriages 159
III. *Urban marriages* 161
Urban lobolo 165
Urban 'customary unions' and the application of the law 168

THE CHANGING ROLES OF AFRICAN WOMEN (1956) 171

WORKS CITED OR CONSULTED 177

Some characteristics of Bantu law*
(with special reference to Shona law)

When a person with a Western background sets himself to explore the peculiarities and characteristics of a non-Western society, he is inevitably inclined to compare the two societies, their peoples and their modes of expression. It is often a dangerous method of analysis because the points in question may not be comparable (being founded on entirely different bases), but it does serve this purpose, that in attempting to compare the two some sort of contrast emerges which, even if the comparison itself is not altogether valid, reveals a difference of social action and expression more vividly than would a mere description. And so I shall succumb to the temptation and give you three aspects in which I compare Bantu (especially Shona) and the West.

I submit that, generally but not unreservedly speaking, Western man is *inclined* to express himself individualistically rather than communally; abstractly rather than concretely or tangibly or realistically; and his actions and reactions are dictated by rational and causal (or, if you wish, commercial) thinking, rather than prompted by emotional or magico-religious considerations. With the Bantu, on the other hand, the communal element tends to dominate the individual element; he is *inclined* to express himself concretely, tangibly and realistically rather than abstractly, and his reasoning is still heavily veiled with a cloak of magico-religious beliefs.

These are not absolute contrasts as between black and white, and I certainly do not mean to say that Western society lacks the communal, or concrete, or emotional elements, nor that in Bantu one does not find individualistic elements or examples of abstract and rational thinking. But I do mean that, when comparing the two societies, and assuming that all the above-mentioned elements are present in both types of society, the West leans towards the individual, abstract and rational, while the Bantu leans towards the communal, tangible and emotional.

* Paper read at a staff conference of the Rhodes-Livingstone Institute at Salisbury, December 1948. Originally published under the title 'An Anthropological Approach to Bantu Law', *Rhodes-Livingstone Journal X* (1950), 51-64.

Let me give some examples:

Western man, knowing himself both as a private individual and as a member of the community in which he lives and strives, regards himself in the first place as his individual self, holding and exercising his individual rights and protecting his individual interests, and in the second place he also acknowledges his position as a member of a wider and widening community, accepting (simetimes very reluctantly) his obligations, responsibilities and privileges as such. In Bantu society a man knows himself in the first place as a member of his community (whether small or big) with duties, responsibilities and certain privileges in connexion with this communal body, and in the second place he is an individual anxious to protect his individual sphere of interest and to pursue his individual aims.

In any orderly society in which so many individuals make up the community, it is obvious that individuality cannot go unchecked lest it conflict with the legitimate interests of other individual co-members and with the interests of the community as a whole. There has developed, therefore, an accepted body of rules (or system of law), through which some sort of flexible balance is maintained between these seemingly opposing factors, and which thus prevents the essential community from disintegrating. In the *Western* system we find the problem approached from the *individual* point of view, and emphasis is placed upon the safeguarding of personal (individual) rights and interests. In the *Bantu* society the approach is undoubtedly *communal,* in that not only do the interests of the community naturally rank first, but that, a person being in the first place a member of the community, the infringement of individualized interests by other individuals affects the community *itself* more directly than it would in the West.

With us, the adjudication of conflicts between individual persons is brought to a recognized, impersonal and impartial forum (an organ of the state community) which is concerned with the question of right and wrong, strictly according to the rules of law, between the parties only (one of the parties may, of course, be the State). Amongst the Bantu it is not only a question of right and wrong between parties, but the conflict inevitably affects the community with which the parties, as well as the adjudication body, are identified in a closer unity than we conceive it in our society. Both with regard to the informal arbitration in legal disputes by a subordinate headman, and regarding the more formal administration of justice in the higher instances, one cannot expect the kind of impartiality (one would be inclined to say, aloofness) that one finds in our impersonal courts of law. Instead, one finds displayed a deep interest in, or even anxiety about, the wider, communal aspect of the conflict.

A correct decision as to right or wrong, arrived at after a logical, impersonal and impartial deduction of clearly defined legal principles, will (usually) suffice in our courts and is, in fact, our professed ideal of a judge's duty and integrity. But it will not do in tribal society where the court is not merely concerned with the question of right or wrong but also (and I would say, especially) with the effect of the judgment upon the future relations between the parties, which are so vital to the life of the community itself.

A Shona chieftain (not even to speak of an inferior headman) will hesitate to pronounce judgment unless he is reasonably certain that the parties will abide by his decision or settlement. He will ask both parties if they are satisfied, and if they are not, renewed efforts are made to bring about a solution acceptable to both. This takes time, which is an essential element of tribal litigation. It lapses into stages in which the court seems to disintegrate into a free-for-all debating society without rules of precedence, speech or conduct. Everyone chimes in and gives his opinion – and the one who sits back, seemingly powerless to keep order, is the chief himself. It may strike us as a sign of weakness and lack of authority on the part of the chief and his court. But is it? Isn't this rather the very nature of indigenous jurisdiction, a direct consequence of a predominantly communally-adjusted frame of mind? A case in which every personal matter brought before a public forum is of public interest, that is, not merely as a matter of curiosity regarding the affairs of one's neighbour, but in a very real sense a conflict that belongs to the community itself and which has to be thrashed out and settled, not only in public but by the public, that is, by the *community itself?* The answer seems to be in the affirmative, because whenever there is a question of public reconciliation of parties by means of meat killed and eaten, or snuff taken, *all present* partake in the act of reconciliation: chief, parties and public alike.

But, one may ask, in former days when (according to informants suffering from nostalgia) a chief had 'jurisdiction over life and death' and the administration of justice seemed to have been so much stricter and sterner – in those days, did the character of African litigation differ so fundamentally that a chief would decide according to strict rules regarding right and wrong and enforce his decision regardless of the consequences they would have on the future relations of the parties in their community? Certainly informants are fond of saying that, 'If a man disobeyed the chief's judgment or failed to pay up immediately, his cattle and belongings would be seized, his village destroyed and he himself chased out of the country'. There is no reason to doubt that under certain circumstances the chief had such jurisdiction and could enforce his judgment by such stern measures, provided, of course, that he could count on the general support of his people. But if one asks for actual case material regarding these dramatic manifestations of a chief's power, memory (otherwise so keen) usually fails: only a very few isolated examples or none at all can be given. Let us then consider the abounding evidence that, in those days, a chief's authority was judged by the extent to which he *followed*, rather than *led*, the wishes of his people. He depended upon them, and as a sane and responsible person he would not risk dissatisfaction and unrest amongst his people. The old chiefs, too, would settle rather than decide, appease and reconcile rather than enforce. I should be inclined to regard examples in which a Shona chief has strict discipline in court, takes a leading part in the proceedings and summarily disposes of a lot of cases per session by concise interpretation of the relevant points of law and snappy judgments as *innovations* rather than renovations of Shona procedure.[1] Because in the traditional manner he should be personally detached from the process up to the very end, when the case is given to him for his judgment. But he should keep his eyes peeled and ears wide open, to watch and listen to his henchmen conducting the case, to the questions, arguments and interjections from the side of the public, to the behaviour, mood and changing attitude of the parties, as the conflict, with the so often amazingly numerous side issues, is finally laid bare. By the time the chief is supposed to act and 'cut the case', the issue and side issues are clear – and so are the sentiments of the parties and the public. Knowing from which direction the strongest wind blows, he gives his judgment accordingly. He is a good chief when he knows how to listen patiently and watch faithfully. If he can do this long and diligently enough, the initial turmoil and stubbornness may very likely spend themselves, and the solution emerges as the common product of many minds. The chief's decision is then as undramatic and uneventful as a fullstop after a long paragraph. Acting as a representative of the community, he formally pronounces its verdict.

Let me give you another example of the preponderance of the communal element. Undoubtedly Bantu law recognizes individual rights and interests. Take for instance the strongest of these rights, that of *bantu*-ownership in connexion with fields under actual cultivation, or to a man's cattle standing in his kraal. The question now arises: are these rights individual in the sense we know them? They are not. You will find, first, that as a rule the holder is not an individual but *a small collectivity respresented by an individual* who acts as *bantu*-owner on behalf of it. Amongst the Shona, *bantu*-ownership relating to land is apparently *controlled* by the village headman, but

1. See also p. 78 ff. below.

actually *held* by the village community which he represents. Regarding cattle, the *bantu*-owner will be the single family and usually even a bigger agnatic unit; but active *control* will be exercised by the representative of the unit. Even when an unmarried young man or woman acquires livestock, ostensibly in his or her own name, there is so little freedom of action in connexion with this property that one cannot, in such a case, assume a right of ownership independent of that of the family. *Bantu*-ownership therefore is not an individual right but an *individualized* right in the sense that it tends towards the *individual* (and this tendency is usually accelerated in modern times, through contact with the individualistic European), but is still essentially communal.

But the second observation regarding this right is just as revealing. With us, ownership is as sharply defined as a blot of India ink. In Bantu society it lacks such strict definition and the edges are heavily blurred. For it remains embedded in the dominant communal right[2] which may exert its pressure at any time when this is dictated by the common interests of the community. In Shona land tenure this condition can be clearly observed. As a member of the community (*dunhu* – tribal ward) and as a representative of a collectivity capable of exercising a right of *bantu*-ownership, a man can reclaim an available tract of land held by the community of which he is a member. By his cultivation he wrests his holding from the communal right and vests upon it, on behalf of the collectivity he represents, the individualized right of *bantu*-ownership. Through these lawful individual efforts the land becomes 'his', i.e., he has the right to cultivate the land and reap the benefit of his cultivation undisturbedly for himself and his dependents. He can subdivide his holding and apportion it to members of his family. He can lend his field to others, though usually such others must be co-members of the same community which exercises the communal right over the area. As long as he stays there and uses his fields, or as long as he stays in the vicinity while temporarily abandoning his fields so that the presumption arises that he will, at some time or other, resume his cultivation, it remains 'his land', and his rights will be respected. But once he goes away, preferably outside the boundaries of his community, or even within the same boundaries but a good distance away from his first place, so that the resumption of his original cultivation is impracticable or unlikely, the legal position changes. His *bantu*-ownership weakens: in some cases it subsides into a pref-

2. Here I still used 'communal right' for the right of an autonomous community to avail itself of the resources of the total territory under its jurisdiction. I later employed the term 'right of avail' as a more satisfactory rendering of this 'bundle of rights' held by the community and its rights-sharing members. – J. F. H.

erential right to return to it, in other cases even this right becomes an academic question which may be hard to defend. What has happened is that the communal right has automatically resumed its latent grip and become stronger as *bantu*-ownership weakens, like the flow of high tide over a low-lying island. In African parlance it would be said that the land again belongs to the headman (or chief), by which is meant, of course, to such an official as the representative of the community and *not* in the headman's own right. In due time it can be allotted again to another holder.

This, surely, is different from our unshakable ownership.

Apart from this, there are the *seasonal lapses* of *bantu*-ownership: for instance, after the fields have been reaped, the individualized fields become common grazing area for all the cattle of the community. It is not a condition in which, until the start of the next ploughing season, *bantu*-ownership ceases to exist, but this right becomes, so to say, *latent*, until such time as it is revived by actual cultivation. If, for instance, a man wishes to prevent the seasonal resurgence of the communal right he takes specific steps to safeguard his interests. For *legitimate* reasons (e.g., the protection of a vegetable plot situated there) he will put a fence around it. Such a measure is a lawful act of *bantu*-ownership, a sign that the holder, at a time of a general resurgence of the communal right, wishes to lift his holding from what has now temporarily become 'commoning' again, in order to preserve his specific, individualized interests.

This brings me to a small but significant side issue, that of fences generally. So obviously and closely (to the mind of the Shona) does the communal right embrace *bantu*-ownership that the erection of *permanent* fences, or an undue emphasis on individual boundaries, strikes them not only as ridiculous, but as suspicious. Even when the land is under actual cultivation, and *bantu*-ownership is most evident and indisputable, the division between the individual and the communal is not so absolute as a surrounding fence would indicate. Certainly, in years where game abounds and may damage crops, thorny bushes are often thrown around a field as a protective measure. But this is not meant to put a stop to the trespass of one's neighbours who still can, and do, enter through a slightly covered opening in the hedge.

I have taken these illustrations of the communal element out of a host of others, which can be found wherever you turn in Bantu life and law. You will find it in the position of chiefs and headmen, in marriage law, in the succession to property or obligations arising from actionable wrongs. Everywhere you will find, without denying the individual, a preponderance of the communal.

I now turn to my second point, that, given the contrast between abstract as against concrete, realistic or tangible thought and action (of which we can find examples in both our own and Bantu society) we shall observe that the Western mind is more adept in abstract thinking and the Bantu is naturally more inclined to express himself concretely. The difference is again clearly shown when we compare Western and Bantu law and institutions. Let me give an illustration. In the relations between boy and girl, tender feelings and affections may be expressed with gifts which may take the shape of a love token: with us a delicate golden ring with a heart-shaped shield; with the Shona a bead necklace (*cuma* or *nduma*). The difference does not appear to be great. We would say, 'This is a symbol of my love'; the Shona boy says, 'Now I know that you truly love me.' Yet there *is* a difference. The Western girl would, normally, accept her beloved's oral declaration of love also without a ring; the Shona youth would very definitely feel doubtful without his *cuma*. I go further. Imagine the type of Western girl who insists on being given a tangible thing before she believes that her boy friend really loves her. It would be inconceivable that, if he were to pull a button from his shirt or coat and offer this to her with the words, 'With this button I tell you that I truly love you', she would accept him. She would think him mad. A cut-glass powder set might do the trick as a symbol of love, but not a shirt button. In Shona society such an action *is* conceivable. The girl who knows that her confession of love should be crystallized into something (anything) tangible may, lacking the customary bead necklace, give him a hair pin, or a piece of her skirt, or a button, *anything* small and handy and concrete, and he would accept this, not as a 'symbol' of her love, but as the tangible earnest of her words. The difference is that the love token to the Western girl has become a symbol, the abstract representation of love; in Shona it is the necessity that words of love (like many other words of special importance) should be reduced to substance, something you can keep in your hands, feel and see, and put into your pocket. This being the aim, anything concrete will do, and if not beads, then any other thing belonging to her.

In case you think that the above example is merely an isolated one and not an illustration of a general tendency, and if you prefer to stick to the ordinary generalization that tokens or concrete actions in African law are just so many 'symbols' or abstract representations in the same or similar manner as we so often find in our own society, I will develop my argument. To the African mind, as to ours, actions and deeds are more real than words. To *see* an action or thing is more acceptable than to hear about it. To hear that a title deed on a plot and house has been passed in your name may tell you that you have become the owner; the actual possession of that document may make your sense of ownership more acute. But even this paper and description of your property (which suffices in our law to give you a title) is a mere abstraction of the real thing, i.e., to occupy the house itself, to potter about in your garden and to take some of your own soil into your hands. We can still appreciate the difference, but *legally* we have learnt to work with abstractions and be satisfied with them. And so the right to property is transferred by scraps of paper describing the property and through signatures representing the parties. But Bantu law has not developed that far yet. As a rule *bantu*-ownership in land is vested only through actual occupation and cultivation. And the man who wants to have a real right in a heifer which he cannot yet take home with him gives the previous owner (if he hesitates to pay the full purchase price without being able to accept simultaneous delivery) a concrete thing – a token payment in hard cash, a bicycle pump, a walking stick or pocket knife – as *cibato,* something to hold on to, as tangible proof of his fixed intention to take actual possession of the animal at a later date.

In the marriage contract we find a classic example of our different inclinations. In the West, the abstract marriage contract before an impersonal marriage officer, the oral statement that they accept one another as husband and wife, legal proof of which is a document bearing the signatures of the parties, marriage officer, witnesses, is the legal contract; and without these abstractions the marriage is not valid. Amongst the Bantu, the consensus of the individual parties and their famlies is *enacted* and finds tangible expression in the sending and acceptance of specific tokens. The marriage contract itself is *enacted* realistically by the physical delivery of the bride by her family and the physical delivery of the marriage cattle by the groom's family. This is not a symbolic act (as with us, when the bride is 'given away' by her father), it is the *performance of the marriage contract itself.* With the Shona, at this stage of the proceedings the marriage is still a communal matter, the bride having been delivered as a wife to the husband's *family.* It is not yet an individual marriage between spouses. This happens later, when the head of the groom's family formally directs the family's new wife to her individual husband. This order, too, is reduced to substance, nowadays a one-shilling piece which is given to the bride. This is not 'symbolism'. It is but one more example of the urge that words of special significance should be reduced to substance in order to make them real and undeniable.

For the same reason, the first approach to a girl's family with a view to opening marriage negotiations should be couched in a concrete object (a hoe; nowadays an amount in cash); and the latter's willingness or unwillingness to consider the matter should be expressed by their *action* (acceptance or refusal of such token) and not merely with words. In elopement marriages, when the boy's family employ an intermediary to tell the girl's family where she can be found so that parties may meet and discuss a marriage agreement, the intermediary shouts out the girl's whereabouts and then runs for dear life. But he leaves behind a small object as material proof of his message. Husband and wife may have a violent quarrel and shout that they want to get rid of one another. But these threats need not to be taken seriously until the husband gives his wife a sixpence or shilling or any object in which his 'I don't want you any longer' is crystallized. Showing this to her family gives them legal evidence that her husband is *seeking* a divorce (and not, of course, that he has 'divorced' her, as is sometimes believed). Or she may have a lover and wants to make it absolutely clear that she no longer loves her husband. She should do this concretely, not merely with words. So she refuses to have intercourse with him, and if he regards this as a whim, she may dish up his food in a broken vessel, or run away to her lover. Is this symbolism? We might associate a broken plate with broken love, and quite possibly a poetically minded Shona will appreciate the same association. But to the ordinary Shona husband this means a slap in the face – the lord of the family getting his food on a broken plate!

Let us turn to court procedure, a subject which, perhaps more than any other, reveals the essential character of law. With us, the drawing up of an indictment or plea is such a complicated and important business that failure to copy faithfully the correct set of abstract legal definitions or to present the documents relating to the case in the correct order or failure to affix the correct amount of revenue stamps to it may paralyse the process. Only professional lawyers know their way through the maze of court formalities and even they are sometimes found quibbling about points of procedure, apparently forgetting that the issue of the case is not found in statutory regulations exemplified by learned textbooks but in the very real conflict between living people who go to court to hear about *their* case, and not their lawyers' case. Shona procedure is less abstract. There is a conflict and the parties have failed to settle the matter amicably between them. So they go to a higher instance, and I actually mean 'higher', i.e., more important, superior. They acknowledge the higher level of the court through the payment of an initial hearing token, *gwiro* (from *ku-kwira,* to climb), which is *not* a court fee, but the request to be heard, wrapped in a concrete token, a sixpence, a button, a pin. (The importance of this token becomes doubly clear when it is explained that, if at any stage during the formal process either or both parties feel that they can reach a satisfactory solution without the court, another token, *dururo* – from *kuturura,* to get down – must be given to the court in order to nullify the *gwiro*.) The *gwiro* token ensures the complainant a hearing for which he, of course, also has to *pay* something. In traditional Hera procedure the defendant now also has to give something tangible to signify his submission to the court's jurisdiction so that he will answer the questions which will be put to him. Nowadays the subtle distinctions between tokens given and fees paid have often fallen away, but in many courts it is established practice that both complainant and defendant hand over the court fee (5*s*.) to the court, the one losing the action forfeiting his money. Apart from the obvious advantage that the chief is at least certain that he gets his due, the action still implies that both parties have concretely pledged themselves to submit their case to the court.

When the court is ready to listen, the complainant may tell his story – as the Hera saying is, 'The one who has eaten most is the one that first opens the door', and he is invited to unburden his heart. He does so freely and uninterruptedly, often emotionally, always in great detail, which may strike us as 'irrelevant' but which is essential not only in his view, but also in that of the court and public. As he unfolds his story, the conflict emerges in the natural and realistic setting of the overall relations between the parties and is given greater depth and scope by the defendant who is allowed to speak after him, with the same verbosity and attention to detail and background. Then the matter is discussed in open court. Questions are asked and opinions given, by court assessors, members of the public, sometimes the chief or headman himself. At this stage court formalities are reduced to a minimum, and the impression one gets is of a sometimes heated performance of a debating society. But one rule is strictly observed: there is *no direct communication between the parties*. Having chosen to put their case before the court, they cannot address one another personally but only through an intermediary. This, too, is a concrete manifestation of the fact that they have become socially estranged and separated by the conflict.

There comes a stage when the defendant is convinced that he has been wrong and that he must acknowledge his guilt and responsibility. If he, initially, has fought the action stubbornly, his oral admission of guilt may not be sufficient. Something more is needed to convince the court and public that his change of attitude is genuine. Very often I have noted a public clamoring for a tangible expression of guilt. 'We have heard you say that you have been wrong, but we must *see* it, too!' The defendant then produces a small coin or other object belonging to him and hands it over as *matatendendava* or *rutenda mhoswa* (admission of guilt): 'With this thing I admit that I am wrong in the matter.' The token is handed to the court, shown to the public and given to the complainant. In the remote areas of the Hera country (Southern Sabi Reserve) a further token may then be required from the defendant as concrete evidence of his willingness to compensate the complainant.

The complainant states the amount and the court will ask the defendant if he is prepared to pay it. If the demand is unreasonable the court will try to persuade the complainant to lower it, pointing out that the defendant has now admitted his responsibility but that he should not, on account of his mistakes, be reduced to poverty. If the complainant is adamant, they may openly ridicule him or bluntly tell him that they will withdraw their support unless he becomes more reasonable. Public pressure exerted upon an obstinate party may be enormous and only a fool is prepared to risk a wave of public disapproval. In the discussions and bargaining which follow it becomes fairly clear what amount will be ultimately acceptable to both parties. If the case has reached this successful stage, it is handed to the presiding chief or headman for a formal judgment. He pronounces his judgment, after summing up the case, reiterating the main arguments, and he finally admonishes the parties to live peacefully together again.

Sometimes the nature of the conflict is such that the mere payment of compensation is not enough to restore normal relations between parties and harmony in community. In cases like adultery, or others in which one party feels grievously insulted or his reputation seriously impaired, the court may, if it fears further trouble between parties (especially when they live in the same village or immediate neigbourhood) insist that they be publicly reconciled. There are various ways in which this can be accomplished amongst the Shona. For instance, the guilty party is made to produce a goat or fowl which is killed at the court. The chief has a piece of meat prepared which he divides between the parties, making them eat together. Or they are required to take snuff together. The inference is clear. One does not take food or snuff together with one's enemy. [3] The action is, therefore, a concrete manifestation of friendly relations. After this has happened neither party can, with justification, belie his action and show himself hostile towards the other. I have mentioned the other interesting feature of public reconciliation, namely that the members of the court and public themselves partake in the eating of the animal or in taking snuff as an expression of the communal element inherently present in any individual conflict.

It is not difficult to provide many more examples of the concrete element in whatever subject of law, but I hope that the ones I have given are sufficient to establish my point. I must repeat again that I do not deny the Afri-

3. *Cf.* p. 82 below.

can's capacity for abstract thought and expression. I do not say that unless a particular legal action or institution is reduced to or accompanied by something concrete, it cannot be good Bantu law. But I do say that, compared to our Western state of mind with its capacity for abstract thought as it is revealed in our legal institutions and requirements, there is in Bantu a general and natural tendency towards a more tangible and realistic way of thinking, formulation and expression which is reflected in their law. Superficially, some of these expressions might be regarded as examples of some sort of 'symbolism' (that is, as abstract associations instead of the closest approach to the real thing), but if the phenomenon recurs again and again in the most variegated forms, lending a peculair colour to African law as a whole, we have to regard them in terms of a fundamental difference between their law and ours.

The third difference I wish to discuss is that, given the contrast between rational, causal, unemotional or commercial thinking on the one hand and emotional or magico-religious thought on the other, the West is inclined to follow the first line and to express itself accordingly, while Bantu thought and action tend to be dominated by the second line of thought. I must confess that this is a subject with which I feel very little at home, and I find it difficult to give you more than a few, as yet unco-ordinated, impressions. But because I think it is important, and because I have been struggling with the material, I mention it. In general I would state the problem like this: confining ourselves to law as one aspect in which man's mind, as moulded by his particular social environment and heritage, is expressed, I wish to draw your attention to our jurisprudence, the science of our law. In this we find – neatly systematized into chapters and definitions, whether stored in statute books and regulations or in common law textbooks of a general or topical character, or in recorded judgments carrying the weighty authority of a legal precendent – the tabulated abstractions of an actively functioning legal system. It is a science according to which human conflicts with rules of law are measured in a rational, unemotional manner, the various aspects coldly analysed and treated according to the prescribed formulae. It is a work of intellect in which the principal difficulty lies in the occasional question of interpretation, when the case under consideration does not exactly fit the established jurisprudential abstractions. Once you have found the right pigeon hole, the results are predictable, because our reason leaves us very little discretion. The emotional element is not entirely cut out; it plays a part in the acceptance or rejection of evidence, in the criminal sentence or civil judgment you have to pronounce. But even here you have to rationalize the emotional, you must explain by sound and sober reasoning why and to what extent you were forced to recognize the emotional element. So that in our day and society and under normal circumstances the course of justice is determined by *reason*. Things have to be *proven* before they can be accepted: this seems to be a basic rule in our law.

Now let us turn to Shona law. There is no African jurisprudence, no systematization of legal institutions, not even a clear distinction between what we term civil and criminal law. You will find no tribal African, however intelligent or experienced, who can even venture to give you a systematic and critical exposition of a particular legal subject, let alone a review of the salient principles or classifications of the law of his people. He may quote a number of legal maxims and present these as if they were strict legal definitions, rigid rules of law. But when it comes to actual practice it becomes evident that these maxims are too generalized or too vague to permit strict interpretation. They lack the power of law because they are *not rules of law*, but traditional *expressions relating to law*. They are important because they represent certain broad guiding principles or approximations or isolated beacons or land marks by which a general direction can be found. But they are certainly not strict, charted roads from which one cannot deviate. And so the course of Shona law is a flexible one and, to our mind, often unpredictable. Although, undoubtedly, a fair amount of rational thinking and sober analysis is found in African process, the law can never be divorced from the specific conflict at hand. To settle the conflict matters more, in fact, than a correct interpretation of the law in question. Abstract and unemotional analysis is strongly modified by an emotional element. And in Bantu process the emotional is often swayed by considerations of a mystical or religious character. The crudest examples of the latter are cases arising from the accusation of witchcraft. The allegation may have been made in a heated argument. The party so accused tries to get hold of something belonging to the accuser as concrete proof of the accusation uttered. The accuser likewise gets hold of something belonging to the other, as proof of his denial. With this 'material evidence' of *accusation* and *denial (not* of the alleged act of witchcraft) the parties approach the court where they deposit these tokens as a sign that they submit the matter to the jurisdiction of the court. The court then refers them to a diviner, sending an official witness to report on the result of the consultation. The court will abide by these metaphysical findings without doing a stitch of rational thinking. The accused may, in case he privately doubts the findings of the witch-doctor, employ another one, but if this one, too, pronounces him guilty, he will meekly surrender to the decision of the 'bones'.

In cases of unlawful sexual intercourse the lover-defendant may obstinately deny that he has cohabited with the woman, or even that he has seen hei alone. And when he leads evidence to show that she is a loose type of woman, now seeking a scape-goat to cover an illegitimate pregnancy, it may be very difficult for her to prove her case – until she resorts to a last, desperate act. Taking off her front skirt she slaps him over his face or shoulders with it (*kupuma*). With that one stroke she invokes the intangible, irrational and emotional, against which no reason can avail. The court at least is satisfied that this man is the responsible party, and the defendant will not even try to establish his defence. The European research worker may now stupidly try to be rational and ask: 'But what if she acted out of spite and slapped the wrong man?' The only answer will be: 'That is impossible, she will never do a thing like that unless he has been her lover.' Or one may suggest that a man with a stout heart might even then deny. And the reaction is almost one of consternation. How could he possibly deny? When making love to her he has touched the very skirt with which she struck him!

A woman in childbirth will confess any act of infidelity and mention her lover's name. The only evidence required and adduced in court is that of the woman and midwives *concerning the confession*. Once this is established, her act of adultery with the man whose name has been mentioned is accepted by the court as a fact. Usually the defendant does not even try to put up a defence, but if he does, he will only hear the old maxim *mukadzi ngangga* – 'a woman is a diviner'. It is useless to refute a confession uttered under such circumstances.

One finds the emotional and magical or religious element dominating in cases of homicide; or when a man's food supply is threatened or destroyed by arson; in cases of incest; or of adultery with one's brother's wife or father's younger wife; in illicit intercourse during a period of mourning; or when a woman sues her lover for the return of her love token when she fails to become pregnant by her legal husband. In all these cases special compensation has to be paid by the wrongdoer, but the amount is unpredictable because the matter is judged on an emotional, and not a rational basis.

There is perhaps no subject on which I found greater unanimity than the *principles* of succession to a person's name and dignity as well as to his estate; but when it came to the *practical application* of these principles as revealed through actual cases, the diversity was so great that it was sometimes hard to acknowledge the existence of any principle at all. For in these matters the surviving members of the family have to consider not only so many conflicting claims and ambitions amongst themselves, but also the often unpredictable whims of the ancestral spirits.

I have not tried to systematize the communal, the concrete and the emotional elements in Shona law, and I certainly do not suggest that a systematization and classification of Bantu law should be attempted along these lines. But I do think it essential that in any systematic treatment of Bantu law one should be constantly aware of these particular tendencies. When one becomes sensitive to these peculiarities, the study of Bantu law becomes something more than an abstract classification and tabulation of rules of conduct and of law, modelled upon the ill-fitting frame of our own legal system. It becomes an absorbing search for flexible, guiding principles and conceptions which express the legal conscience of the people. For the sake of comparative jurisprudence these principles should be abstracted in a faithful and orderly manner, but these will give you only the lifeless and incomplete skeleton of Bantu law. For the sake of the administration of justice in Bantu territories, and the practical understanding of Bantu law as a flexible and highly effective instrument in human relations, emphasis should be placed on the collection and preservation of a vast store of actual case data. This material will give you the true index of Bantu law. The sometimes perplexing 'deviations' from well-established principles may give the Western jurist, with his sense of precision and order, grey hair, but they are nevertheless essential for a deeper understanding of such principles.

The question that really matters is not in how far Bantu law conforms to, or falls short of, our legal standards, requirements and classifications, but what it really *is*, and how it fulfills its essential function in Bantu society.

Indigenous administration of justice*

In government circles plans are being prepared for a reorganization of the native administration of justice.[1] If these plans are realized on the basis of the new Howman report on Native courts, tribal officials – chiefs, headmen, etc. – will officially be given a far wider scope of jurisdiction than they have at present. The new scheme will then be founded on the best elements of the indigenous system, while adequate provision will be made for a gradual introduction of the not too cumbersome aspects of our own law and legal process.

Since the most important factor in this new scheme will be a thorough understanding of tribal administration of justice, and since the merits of the tribal system have been seriously doubted, especially by those who have never attended a tribal process, I thought it might be useful if I gave you an idea of some of its principal characteristics.

First of all, its aim and approach, which are different from our idea of administration of justice. In our society, government, legislation and administration of justice are separate functions, and of these the administration of justice is probably the most aloof. Law to us is an abstract discipline, and a supreme body of rules which must be obeyed. The judge has to interpret these rules to the best of his ability. Once he is satisfied that he knows what the law wants, he has no choice but to give his decision as to right or wrong as directed by the law. It is virtually only in the weighing of evidence and in determining the sentence that he has a measure of discretion or, to put it differently, that he may allow himself to take the human element into consideration.

In tribal society there is, as yet, very little differentiation between government, legislation and administration of justice. They are three indivisible aspects of indigenous government, and of these the administration of justice

* Address given at a luncheon of Rotary International, Bulawayo, 19 February, 1954.
Published in NADA No. 23 (1955), 41-46.

1. [No major change was effected until many years later, with the passage of the *African Law and Tribal Courts Act, 1969*. – J. F. H.]

is by far the most important and very close to the heart of the people. Moreover, although the African has clear concepts of certain aspects of his law, law is not formulated in rigid rules, but consists of a number of guiding principles which serve as beacons by which the administration of justice is steered and certainly not as narrow charted fairways outside of which justice may not venture. Putting it broadly, the African approach to justice is a realistic one. He knows that the relations between man and his fellowmen are not governed by law alone. Hence, in the determination of a lawsuit law is not taken as the only determining factor. The whole social setting and relationship of the parties and their position in the community are taken into consideration; and in the interest of justice, 'legal rules' are sometimes thrown overboard.

To understand the inevitability of such an approach one must understand the dominant principles of rural African society. In our society we have learned to live as individuals, and the contact we make with others is largely a matter of our own choice. The necessity of 'getting on' with others exists to some extent in the sphere of our employment, but outside this sphere we have progressed so far in our individualism that we happily think we can live our lives without the help of others. We think so merely because the multiple help we receive from our butcher, grocer, tailor, garage mechanics, civil servants and farm hands is no longer considered as help but as impersonal, paid services. Although without such services we would not be able to live, they lie outside the sphere of our social relationships.

Our law reflects this individualistic tendency. If you study our civil law, you will notice that most of it has been written from the point of view of the individual.

In rural African society all this is quite different. There the life of the individual is still very much wrapped up in the life of the community. Although there, too, you will find the concept that every man's home is his castle, this castle is very small and its walls are not impervious. Save for the most intimate aspects of a person's private life, his entire social, religious and economic life is still more or less shared with that of his neighbours, with whom he lives in an intricately woven fabric of kinship and other relationships. There is still a very strong feeling that everyone is actually or potentially in need of the help of everyone else.

You can now understand that in a society where this spirit of interdependence between members of a village or other community dominates, a legal dispute of any consequence cannot be regarded as a matter confined to the individual parties. A split between two means a cleavage between many and a potential danger to the essential collective activities in social, religious and economic life. Such a conflict is something in which the community as such must and does take a vital interest. You can also easily see that under these circumstances a decision of a lawsuit strictly according to the rules of law is completely unrealistic and inadequate, unless such a decision has the effect of *removing the cause of the conflict* and of *reconciling* the litigating parties, which in our own legal practice it rarely does.

In short, therefore, indigenous administration of justice aims at *solving* the conflict between the parties rather than *deciding* its legal aspects in terms of law. Justice, instead of the rational and impartial application of abstract rules of law, then becomes a process of persuasion with the accent on the reasonable behaviour of all concerned in a spirit of give and take. The rules of law hereby serve as a broad and flexible basis for discussion and consideration, but are not inviolate and imperative as we know our laws to be. The successful end of a tribal process is a judgment which both parties formally agree to accept and observe.

Is there, in this system of 'justice by persuasion', a question of a 'sanction enforced by law'? Yes and no. It is a fact that even in the old days before our administration curtailed the traditional powers of chiefs and headmen very few tribal courts would resort to a forcible execution of judgment. Judicial seizure of property was very rare indeed, although (and this is important to the theorists) no one denies that the higher tribunals did have such powers. Nowadays the knowledge that Native Commissioners' courts may confirm and enforce a tribal court's judgment, is, of course, of great importance, but this is a most erratic kind of sanction from a African law point of view. For government support of tribal courts is seldom constant and in practice often arbitrary. Native Commissioners' courts undermine the prestige of tribal courts as often as they bolster it. What then constituted, and still constitutes, the principal indigenous sanction? A short description of indigenous procedure will give a clue to the answer. I shall base it on the Mashona procedure because I know this well from personal experience. Basically, however, it is similar to procedures among other African tribes and, indeed, among many tribal folk everywhere.

Court convenes at any suitable place, usually outdoors: under a shady tree in summertime, on a nice warm flat rock in winter time. It is a public affair, and there are always a fair number of people from nearby villages in attendance. Their role, as you will see, is very important. The presiding officer is the chief or headman, assisted by two or more assessors, kinsmen or commoners who are well versed in law and elocution. There is also a court officer who acts as an intermediary between the parties and between the parties and the court. This is because the parties are socially, if not mystically, separated by their conflict, and the court is, on account of its authority, thought to be a good deal 'higher' than the parties. Both these cleavages have to be bridged by the intermediary, who becomes the clearing house of everything that is said during the formal stages of the trial. Everything is, therefore, said twice, although everyone present has heard perfectly well the first time.

Usually both parties deposit a hearing fee at the opening of the trial. This is their concrete token of submission to the authority of the court. The party that loses forfeits his fee to the court; the winning party gets his back.

The complainant is given the first word. He speaks without interruption, officially addressing the intermediary, but loud enough for everyone to hear. He starts off with a fine show of deference and humility to the court, but with a fine dramatic sense builds up his case until he ends with wide and despairing gestures and a wounded voice, the picture of a man deeply wronged. The intermediary gives a summary of his statement to the court, often pouring into his words the same sentiments as displayed by the complainant.

After him comes the defendant, giving his version, again usually as fine a piece of dramatic eloquence as you could hope to hear anywhere. Then come the witnesses for the parties, who are often no more than 'secondants', that is, they often do no more than reaffirm what their party has said. With all the relevant facts now known, the first stage of the trial is over. The case is now as the Vahera say 'thrown to the dogs to chew on'. Now comes a vital, lively, if sometimes a bit chaotic, stage, during which court formalities are reduced to a minimum and any member of the public who feels that he can ask a question, make a statement or express a sentiment that may help clear up the conflict can have his say.

This is the time of cross-examination, of the most searching questions, of asking for further evidence and, especially, of trying to get a clear idea of the background of the case, not so much the legal side (which seldom remains obscure for long) as the personal relations between the parties. Although this debate has an informal and sometimes riotous character, it is the most crucial stage of the process, because it is during this stage that the public, having a vital interest in the successful outcome of the case, voices its opinion with the utmost candour. Unfaithful wives are scolded, inconsiderate husbands are rebuked, undue obstinacy and false pride are ridiculed, rebellious youth is upbraided. But always the necessity of taking a reasonable attitude of give and take is stressed. Among the Vabudya of the northeast of Mashonaland this public participation has developed into a most remarkable institution, which they call *mumanjemanje* ('giving a hand'). Here, after the parties and their principal witnesses have spoken they are no longer allowed to take part in the debate. Instead, any one who feels like it presents himself as an advocate *pro deo*, assuming for a particular point of debate the identity of one of the parties and challenging anyone else to answer his arguments. The result is that, at any moment during this stage, there are two neutrals trying to out-argue each other. At the end of the debate, when every conceivable point has been threshed out, it is pretty clear which party's case is the better. It is no coincidence that in this area (and even elsewhere in Mashonaland) the term for trying cases is *kutamba mhoswa*, to 'play cases'. The beauty of this system is that if a man has, on one point, taken the side of party A, he is free to take the side of party B on a subsequent point of debate. So the best lawyers and most eloquent speakers give their services freely to both parties during the same process.[2]

At last, sometimes at very long last, something like a responsible public opinion as to the merits of the case and a suggested line of action becomes crystallized. At this stage the case is 'handed back to the court'. The assessors sum up the case, then give it to the chief or headman for a decision. A good chief and a wise judge is he who knows how to listen and how to frame his judgment in accordance with the predominant view of the public. He gives his judgment and asks the parties whether they agree. Sometimes they disagree, and then a strenuous argument may follow between chief and party, usually with regard to the exact amount of compensation or fine to be paid, in which the public sometimes joins in order to help find an acceptable solution.

In some cases, especially in adultery cases, even the agreement by the defendant to pay a stipulated amount of compensation does not clear the air. The parties still show signs of hostility, and their strife remains a potentially disruptive element in community life. It is then that the court, and very often the public, insists on an overt act of reconciliation between the parties. This may be done by persuading them to share a piece of meat or take a pinch of each other's snuff. Such an act is no mere symbolic formality. The realistic basis is that no one will eat the food or take the snuff of an enemy for fear of being poisoned. The very fact that the parties are persuaded to do this in public is, therefore, regarded as realistic proof that they have overcome their mutual prejudice and are friends again. An interesting aspect is the fact that usually all present, chief, assessors, members of the public, participate in this act, which thus becomes a communal demonstration of the fact that all is well again in the community.

2. In the 'Case of the Irate Headman' (p. 48 ff.) this kind of process is fully demonstrated.

We are now able to answer the question posed earlier: whether there is a sanction of law behind indigenous process. Largely theoretical, it is the knowledge that the court can, if necessary, insist on forcible execution of judgment, which in practice it hardly ever does, because the conflict has been threshed out in public and by the public – i.e., the community. The party who has agreed to a decision or solution which seemed fair to the majority of the people will not subsequently lightly refuse to fulfil his commitments. Failure and bad faith would mark him in the eyes of the community. And if you will remember how closely interwoven the life of an individual is with the life of the rest of the community, and how interdependent all are in their social, ritual and economic life, you will admit that the fear of losing the goodwill and support of one's neighbours is a very effective sanction indeed.

European lawyers will probably argue that this is a moral and not a legal sanction, because it is not applied by what we consider the recognised instruments of law. But then remember that in African society there is no clear distinction between legal and other rules of conduct; that the maintenance of law and order (to use this hackneyed and ambiguous phrase) is not solely the responsibility of especially appointed officers; and that, if in a formal legal process the community as of right takes a hand, a potential communal sanction by such a community is as much rooted in the legal consciousness of the people as would be a formal sanction which is enforced by the appointed authorities.

Time does not permit more than this very summary sketch of only a few aspects of indigenous administration of justice, but there is one question which I have often been asked, especially by people who are convinced that there is nothing finer in the world than the system of 'British justice'. They ask, 'Which do you think is better, the native system or the British system?' The best way to answer this would be to think what kind of answer an engineer would give if he were asked, 'Which is better, tungsten steel or chromium steel?' He would tell you that it is really a silly question because it all depends on the particular purpose for which you want to use the steel.

Well then, the British system is a fine system, gradually developed and adjusted to suit the people living and thinking the British way of life. But do not be shocked when I tell you that imposed upon a people who do not live and think the British way of life this fine system is capable of doing as much harm and injustice as the African system would do in our society.

The case of the troublesome father*

I. CASE REPORT

Introduction

This paper is, in a sense, an experiment.[1] It attempts to catch the spirit of indigenous litigation as well as some of its basic principles by a detailed description of a single case. The emphasis is hereby shifted from the bare analysis of legal principles and the strict application of rules of law to the conflict of human relations and the community's concern about the maintenance of goodwill and peace amongst its members.

Having selected my case, I am obviously limited to the particular aspects and legal issues involved. Many of these are, however, characteristic of Hera (and, indeed, Shona) law and procedure generally. A few may be especially mentioned: public participation in the process; a probing interest in the root cause of the conflict rather than in patent facts; the urge for a public reconciliation in the face (and fear) of enmity; the extensive use of concrete tokens in support of vital (verbal) communications; the slender division between (and partial merger of) 'criminal' and 'civil' aspects in indigenous jurisdiction; and finally, the importance attached in the judicial process to much that would be considered 'irrelevant' in a Western court of law.

Background of the case

In the south-eastern corner of the Hera tribal territory (Nyashanu Chieftainship, Sabi Reserve, Southern Rhodesia) are two neighbouring *matunhu*

* Case report, 1946. First published as 'Hera Court Procedure' in *NADA* (1952), 26-42. *Postscript* added in 1968.

1. See *Postscript*, p. 44 ff.

(tribal wards). One is controlled by Capanduka, a high-ranking Hera headman of the ruling Shava-clan; the other is occupied by a homogeneous group of kinsmen, the descendants of an immigrant Moyo settler whose name, Nemadziva, is now the hereditary name of the headmanship of the *dunhu*. The Moyo people acknowledge allegiance to their Hera overlords, but enjoy a considerable measure of domestic autonomy. The relations between the two groups are, on the whole, good, but occasionally there is a friction and tension, for instance when the Hera believe that the Moyo do not behave respectfully enough or when the Moyo think that the Hera are unnecessarily overbearing.

From time to time individual members of the Moyo group, with their wives and children, were given permission by the Hera headman to settle outside the area originally allotted to Nemadziva, and such people then fell under the direct control of headman Capanduka.

A number of years ago Ciwedzo, one of the married sons of Swikepi (full brother of Nemadziva) and then a man of about thirty years of age, left his paternal home in the Nemadziva area and was given a site and a garden by Capanduka, because 'he wanted to be on his own and he did not always live well with his father'. A year later his father Swikepi, finding that his own lands were becoming exhausted, decided to follow his son to Capanduka's area where he built his huts so close to his son's homestead that they shared the same threshing floor,[2] around which each had his own granaries and store huts. Almost from the beginning the old man caused trouble with his son and other neighbours. The Hera liked the son, but intensely disliked the father, an overbearing man of uneasy temper who was apt to forget that he was 'only a *mutorwa*' (foreigner, commoner) in Hera territory. The Hera tolerated him for a number of years, mainly on account of his age and wealth, but their patience gave out when Swikepi began to assume the particular privileges and functions of a Hera headman. At beer parties, for instance, when Capanduka was late or could not be present, the Moyo immigrant would claim the *cifuro* (calabash of beer especially reserved for the head of the community) and give the sign to start the festivities. Having 'behaved as if he were a *mucinda* (member of the ruling lineage)' he was told to go back to his own area after he had reaped his crops. His son, Ciwedzo, could remain however.

The old man was furious and accused his son, who had openly sided with the Hera, of betraying him. Before he left, in a last effort to save his dignity, Swikepi prepared a beer party as a 'farewell'. Very few people attended and

2. *Mbuwa*, the type of floor laboriously prepared of a mixture of clay and manure.

even his son stayed away. This hurt the old man so much that, after he had removed his new crop and other belongings, he proceeded to make the place uninhabitable. Digging up a portion of the carefully prepared threshing floor, he proceeded to burn the chaff of his grain so close to his son's full storehuts that the fire threatened to destroy the newly reaped crop.[3] When the son asked a few people to help him repair the floor, Swikepi chased them away. And after a heated argument, during which the son threatened to hit his father with an axe, Swikepi pulled down his storehuts and made a bonfire in the middle of the threshing floor which rendered it useless. He also cut down trees with bees' nests and a number of wild fruit trees 'from which the children used to eat the fruit'. As a final act of spite he pulled up the seedlings of his own tobacco plants, lest his son or anyone else make use of them'.[4]

Preliminary proceedings

The son, Ciwedzo, now complained to Capanduka, the Hera headman under whose jurisdiction he resided and in whose territory his father had misbehaved. After much hesitation – formal litigation being disliked by these people – it was decided to bring action against Swikepi, who by this time was living in the Nemadziva ward where he had started to build a new home. The charge against him was of dual nature:

a. Ciwedzo accused his father of destroying his threshing floor and trying

3. To set fire to one's property without adequate reason (e.g., getting rid of a lot of junk) is considered abnormal; if this is done when the owner is moving to another *dunhu*, it is an offence; when, in so doing, the property of others (esp. food supplies) is threatened, it becomes *makazhi* (arson) which in Shona law is virtually the same as *vuroyi* (sorcery).

4. So long as a member of a *dunhu* community, including a foreigner accepted as a temporary settler, stays within its recognized boundaries and submits to the lawful local authority, he has a right to the homestead he has built, the garden he has cultivated and its produce. Should he desire to move his kraal elsewhere but within the same *dunhu*, he can pull down his huts, use the material for his home and retain his right to his abandoned garden should he later wish to cultivate it again. But if he moves outside the *dunhu* boundaries, his homestead and fields revert to the headman in his capacity as head of the community. He must therefore leave everything intact, although he will always be allowed to reap his standing crops and remove a few items (wooden doors, stamping block, etc.) which he might find difficult to replace.

The natural resources of the tribal territory, such as waterholes, wild fruit trees and wild bee swarms (unless caught in individually made 'hives') can be used by anyone to satisfy his reasonable requirements, but can be never individually appropriated. To cut down fruit trees or destroy a bee swarm is, therefore, an offence against the community.

to prevent its being repaired and of attempting 'to kill his children' by threatening to burn his storehuts.

b. Capanduka, as headman of the *dunhu* community, wanted to prosecute Swikepi for 'destroying the food of the people' by cutting down (wild) fruit trees and 'trees in which bees made honey, which was food for the people', for pulling down and burning his buildings upon leaving the *dunhu,* for *makazhi* (arson), threatening to burn another's food supply, which he regarded as *vuroyi* (sorcery).

In Western terms, the proposed action had both a 'civil' and a 'criminal' character.

Because Swikepi now lived under the direct jurisdiction of his own headman, Nemadziva, Capanduka sent a messenger (*mudzimbahwe*)[5] to Nemadziva, asking him 'to pass the word' to his younger brother Swikepi to appear before the Hera headman at a certain date.

Two days later the first meeting took place. Amongst those present were:

Capanduka, the Hera headman and 'judge' (*mutonggi*) in the case;

Tapamba, the *cigwende,* deputy (no kinsman) who would act as spokesman for Capanduka and intermediary between the parties;

Ciwedzo, the complainant;

several members of the Hera ward, who had come to witness the case.

On the other side were:

Nemadziva, headman of the Moyo group of kinsmen;

Swikepi, the defendant – accused in the case and a brother of Nemadziva;

ten or twelve Moyo kinsmen, amongst them Gava, the second in authority (*nevanje*) in the Moyo *dunhu* and a classificatory son of Nemadziva.

The parties were grouped as follows: Capanduka sat on a stone; to his right were Tapamba, his deputy, and other members of the Hera party (including the complainant), as well as some people residing in neighbouring wards; to Capanduka's left were Nemadziva, Swikepi and the other members of the Moyo party. All, except Capanduka, sat or sqatted on the ground.[6]

Before the proceedings started there was the customary exchange of

5. The less formal term *munyai* is often used in the same connexion.

6. The way litigation parties are grouped on either side of the judge expresses the cleavage between the parties ('They cannot see each other'). There is also a distance between the judge and the parties. His being on a higher level is visibly manifested by his sitting on a stone, i.e., actually higher than any other. Hence, the initial token given by the complainant is called '*gwiro* (climbing up)'. Should, once a formal process has been started, the defendant think that he could settle more satisfactorily out of court, he asks permission to bring down the case, giving a *dururo* token (*kuturura,* to bring or put down).

greetings, accompanied by the rhythmic clapping of hands. Since Capanduka was superior, the Moyo section started to 'honour' him (*kuvucira*), after which the Hera reciprocated.

Then the proceedings started. Capanduka ordered the deputy to tell Ciwedzo to state his complaint. Ciwedzo first produced a sixpence which he gave tot he deputy, who handed it to Capanduka. This was the customary *gwiro* token (from *kukwira* – to climb) with which every complainant *a.* 'climbs (to the higher level of) the court' in order to obtain a hearing, and *b.* thereby submits himself and his case to the court's jurisdiction. He sat down close to Capanduka and told his story, first calmly, but later on passionately. There were no interruptions. He finished by clapping his hands in honour of the judge and sat back again. The deputy then gave a summary of the complaint to Nemadziva, calling upon him 'to pass the words (*kupfuwudza mashoko*)' to the defendant, Swikepi. But Nemadziva was unwilling, saying that he 'had no brother', thereby refusing to accept the responsibility for the action of his kinsman. Court formalities were now temporarily abandoned and an excited general argument followed in which Nemadziva was supported only by the defendant himself.

Sample arguments:

Capanduka (flourishing a small branch cut from one of the trees felled by Swikepi) to Nemadziva: 'You, who are the father of your people, you, who are the elder brother (*mukoma*), do you then think he did right when he burned down his place and cut down the trees from which the children get their food? Is this the way you leave a place where you have been staying for a long time?'

Nemadziva, dramatically and pathetically, as if he were addressing his brother (who sat behind him): 'Be quiet, my brother, and listen. Listen how they accuse me. They are against me. They say that I am guilty!'

Some others threw in old legal phrases, such as these:

'Don't fear a crocodile when your legs are already in the water (*usatye nggwena makumba ari mumvura*) – it is too late to try to dodge the issue when it is upon you';

'The spirit who allowed you to be wounded also allowed the flies to eat you (*mudzimu wakuparire cironda wati nhunzi dzikurye*) – as you have made your bed, so you must lie on it.'

Finally Gava, second in authority over the Moyo group, stood up, clearly annoyed with his kinsman. Crossing over to the Hera group he rebuked Nemadziva: 'You must not refuse to pass the word because we then seem to be suppressing the case. We all commit adultery, we may all steal, we all may be accused of sorcery (i.e., anyone may go wrong at some time or other); but there is no such thing that matters which have gone wrong should not be put straight again.'

Nemadziva then became more reasonable.[7] He drew himself up and addressed Capanduka: 'Shava, I have heard. I am present! When the honey falls off the chin it must be lapped up (*vuci bgwire cirevu hwati bgu nanziwe*).' He then turned to his brother and sternly addressed him. The defendant, who had been lying on the ground, pretending not to be interested in the matter (and, strictly speaking, he had not yet been formally informed), now respectfully squatted in front of his headman and brother. He listened attentively to a repetition of the charge, punctuating every other sentence by clapping his hands and uttering Moyo praise names: '*Cirandu* (their sub-clan name)!' '*Nzombe huru* (big bull)!'

When Nemadziva had finished, the defendant was asked by the deputy to produce the *ruvundzo* token, formal submission to the jurisdiction of the court. But Swikepi refused, displaying a frenzy of indignation, digging into the soil with his nails and beating the ground with his fists.

He was cut short by Gava Moyo who told him sharply that 'this is not the right manner to behave'. Contempt was clearly shown in the faces of all present, but instead of ridiculing the defendant one after the other of his own people tried to reason with him. The defendant then calmed down but found another excuse: a few of his sons were not present; he 'could not speak without my sons', who could testify that the complainant had tried 'to cut my skull open with an axe, and had threatened to throw me into the river'.

The deputy repeated his words to Capanduka, who agreed to adjourn the proceedings until three days later. All would then meet at an old kraal site of Capanduka's, near the place where Swikepi had lived, 'so that all might see what had happened to the trees and threshing floor, should defendant deny (*kuramba*) what was said against him'.

7. Headman Capanduka could 'contact' the defendant only through the senior representative of the community of which the latter was a member. If the defendant had, at the time the action was being taken against him, been living in the Hera area, the matter would have been an internal affair of the Hera *dunhu* (ward) and the defendant could have been sued directly, being the head of an independent family living under the jurisdiction of the Hera headman. Even then, however, Nemadziva would probably have been invited to attend as the head of the wider kinship grouping to which defendant belonged. Once Nemadziva had established contact between defendant and the court, he could 'withdraw' without disrupting the proceedings, as in fact he later did.

The trial

On the appointed day the parties met again, this time under a huge baobab tree at Capanduka's kraal site. The people were grouped in a similar manner as before.

After the customary exchange of courtesies Capanduka nodded to his deputy, Tapamba, who announced that 'The one who has eaten too much is the one who first opens the door (*muzimbirwi ndiye muzaruri wesuvo*) – the complainant, being the person most anxious to unburden his heart, is the first to speak'. Ciwedzo got up and squatted near Capanduka. He produced four bundles of tobacco leaves and handed them to Tapamba as *marime*, court fee (not to be confused with the *ruvundzo* token), informing him that he did not have ready cash. Capanduka assessed the value at four shillings. Court fees being ten shillings, Tapamba told Ciwedzo that he owed the court another six shillings, which the latter promised 'to look for (*kutswaka*)'.

The deputy then called upon Nemadziva to tell the defendant that he was required to give the *ruvundzo* token.[8] Nemadziva replied that he had three days ago agreed 'to pass the words' to Swikepi and he had done so. Having secured the defendant's attendance at the court they could expect no more from him. He said he was an old man and that it was bitter to see at the end of his life that a child of his family had become so bold as to accuse his own father in open court. This was a bad thing and he did not wish to have anything to do with it. It was now 'the case of Capanduka, Ciwedzo and Swikepi'. He would allow them to pass the words directly to Swikepi. He, Nemadziva, would only listen, not speak. He stood up and sat aside, closing his eyes.

The deputy now addressed Swikepi: 'We want you to give something for the case. Your son has given something, so now you must also give something.'

Defendant: 'The other day I heard about a case in which my son Ciwedzo was against me. I also heard about a case in which Capanduka was against me. How do I know for which case I must give?'

Headman Capanduka, addressing the meeting in general: 'You remember the matter for which I brought you all together the other day. It is the same matter for which I have called you together today. There is a case between Ciwedzo and his father, Swikepi. So Swikepi must first give *ruvundzo* for this case. Then there is *my* case (i.e., of Capanduka representing his *dunhu*),

8. Also called *vukumpira mashoko*, see p. 32 below.

in which I wanted Nemadziva to be present so that he could *see* (Capanduka waved a twig he had cut from a wild fruit tree felled by Swikepi) what his brother did when he left the country of the chief where he had been living a long time . . .'

Defendant, interrupting Capanduka: 'I laugh at that. The other day you said . . .' He was cut short by one of his own sons: 'Do not speak like that, my father, we do not like endless talking. There is one who has given *gwiro,* so now you should also give something for that case. You should think of what is coming later. First finish what is already here (i.e., limit yourself to the issue before you).'

After a moment's deliberation Swikepi produced a half-crown piece. Handing this to the deputy, he said he wanted to give only two shillings and that he expected a sixpence change. Tapamba promised 'to look for a sixpence' and handed the money to Capanduka.

Complainant then gave an account of his case, even more fully and passionately than three days before. Again he was allowed to speak uninterruptedly. With typical verbosity he recalled how he had attended a *doro* (beer party) and had there found three women who had borrowed grain from him and how he had therefore asked those women to help him repair the part of the *mbuwa* (threshing floor) which his father had broken up; how they had later reported to him that they had been chased away by his father, and how he had looked for Capanduka at another beer party to bring his complaint; Capanduka had not been there and he had told the wife of Capanduka all about the matter. He had invited all present at the beer party to come and see what his father had done to his home. He also told how his father, even before he had seen Capanduka about his complaint, had accused him of stealing tobacco, a plough share and other things. 'And now I have come to complain because of my grain which my father wanted to burn. I want the *civara* (court) to find out for me why it is that my father did all these things to me, because I have a wife and children and I am his son; and my family is his family, and I want to feed his family.'

He finished by clapping his hand respectfully and sat back.

Tapamba, the deputy, retold the story in his own words to Swikepi. The defendant then turned to his brother, Nemadziva (although the latter had previously 'withdrawn' from the process): 'Hear, Cirandu (Moyo praise name), since you are my father and since you have come to listen, hear what they have said against me?' He then gave a long summary. Nemadziva replied: 'We hear it, Cirandu!'

Defendant then addressed the deputy: 'Yes, I did all this, but even now I do not like to tell all the reasons why I did it. But I must tell that at some time, my son (Ciwedzo) accused me of *makona* (sorcery).[9] I also remember that once my son chased the people away from (wild) fruit trees which were standing near his fields and even from a *tsime* (communal water hole).'

Swikepi must have realized that his wantonness could easily be interpreted as a spiteful action against the Hera headman who had ordered him to leave the territory, and he must have heard (as I did myself) the rumour that Capanduka intended to fine him a head of cattle for his misbehaviour. He therefore addressed the meeting in general: 'I wish to say that I do not disagree with Capanduka (i.e., I bear him no enmity). If I have done wrong, I have done it solely because I hate my son.' He then referred to a previous occasion on which he had had trouble with his son, a case which the court apparently had decided in his favour. 'I remember that once I complained to the chief (Capanduka) because of something between my child and me, and he had to pay me compensation, but I refused to accept his payment because I only complained in order to find out why my son had wronged his father. All he had to do then was to pay back to me the *marime* (court fee) I had paid to the court; but even this he has never done. And now I observe my son's cleverness! He is much more clever than his father, for today I am here, a guilty man (*ndaka parendava*) while he is innocent! Yes, I did all the things he has said I did. I do not deny it.' He paused for a moment, then turned around to his son behind him: 'Did I speak well?' He sat back without clapping hands.

Tapamba, the deputy, to Capanduka: 'Have you heard what he said? He says he is against his son and not against anyone else!'

Capanduka repeated to all present: 'Have you all heard?'

As both complainant and defendant had been given an opportunity to state their case, the matter was now opened for general discussion. (Tapamba: 'The bones are now thrown to the dogs to make them eat – *kukandire mbga hona kuti dzirye.*')

So far the session had been of a formal character. It is true that the headman, Capanduka, had rolled and smoked a cigarette; that Nemadziva had found a comfortable niche between two roots of the baobab tree and had pretended to be asleep; that most members of the public had made themselves comfortable on the ground, cutting axe handles or doing some other trifling work, smoking or passing snuff occasionally. At least three times during the proceedings a newcomer had sat down amongst them and courteously 'asked the health' of Capanduka, Nemadziva and other acquain-

9. Lit.: the container in which an African doctor keeps his tools.

tances, always accompanied by rhythmic clapping of hands by all present. These traditional courtesies, although they completely stop the legal process for at least four or five minutes at a time, are, however, so much part of daily life that they cannot, strictly, be regarded as 'interruptions'.

But from the moment the case was opened for general discussion virtually all formalities ceased. Many asked questions and voiced opinions, and often two or more people were speaking at the same time. It was also evident that the parties could be examined without the deputy acting as go-between. Only between the parties themselves no direct communication was permitted.

Several persons asked the defendant whether he 'agreed (*kutenda*)' with what was said against him, and every time Swikepi 'agreed' that he had done wrong, adding that he had hated his son. Some asked what he had meant by his remark that he did not want to reveal all the reasons for his behaviour.

It was an aged visitor from elsewhere, Ngandini, who finally addressed the complainant: 'You have heard that your father has agreed (admitted his wrongs). Now you must say what is to be done' (i.e., complainant should now state his claim for damages).

But Ciwedzo was not yet satisfied.

'Why does my father say that he does not want to tell everything? What does he mean by that? Why did he quarrel so much before? Why doesn't he speak his mind? Are you really convinced that he admits (his guilt) with his whole heart?'

Others interrupted him: 'But you, too, do not speak clearly. You must say what you want to be done. The hen has laid an egg at the *civara* (court) and it wants a nest to be made.'[10]

Swikepi impatiently shouted across the court to his son: 'I have said I am guilty. You should say what you want!'

The complainant meant to answer his father directly, but was promptly stopped by some elders: 'You cannot speak to your father. You brought your case to the *civara*, so you must tell the *civara* what you want.'

Complainant: 'I do not wish to ask (claim) anything from my father. I'd rather that the matter be finished.'

For a better understanding of the issue at stake and of the confusion which occurred during the ensuing stage of the debate, the following notes on tokens and fees must be inserted here:

10. '*Huku yakandire zai pacivara, vati denere rurukwe*' – meaning that, formal proceedings having been instituted, it is the duty of the court to settle (*kuenzanisa*) the matter.

Gwiro is given by the complainant at the beginning of the process as a token that he desires to be heard and thereby submits to the court's jurisdiction. The counterpart is:

Ruvundzo (or *civundzo* – from *kuvundza*, to ask). This token must be given by the defendant or accused before he can be questioned. By handing it over he, too, formally submits to the court's jurisdiction and agrees to being questioned. It is also known as *vukumpira mashoko* (to invite words).

Matatendendava or *rutenda mhoswa* (from *kutenda*, to agree, and *ndava*, dispute, matter, and *mhoswa*, lawsuit, guilt). This is the formal admission of guilt, a token which the defendant has to produce to satisfy the court and complainant that he fully acknowledges his guilt.

Sometimes, and especially in cases in which the defendant has to pay compensation to the complainant, the defendant may produce a further token, *maviri* (*kubata maviri*, to hold the two, also called *nhema muripo* (lit: cutting the fine or compensation). This token (*a*) invites the complainant to state his claim for damages, and (*b*) signifies the defendant's willingness to pay compensation for his wrong. If the complainant *accepts* this token, he is obliged to state his exact demands for compensation – which the court can always turn down at its discretion.

In the centre of the Sabi Reserve I have found that the *rutenda mhoswa* (= *matatendendava*) and the *nhema muripo* tokens are clearly distinguished; but elsewhere (*e.g.*, in the Nemadziva area) there is a tendency to give only one token, which may be called either *matatendendava* or *maviri* (= *nhema muripo*), but which embodies the functions of both. In the present case this difference in usage led, as will be seen, to a serious misunderstanding and confusion.

The last–mentioned two tokens (*maviri* and *matatendendava*) should not be regarded as 'court fees'. They may consist of any small object belonging to the defendant (such as a pin, coat button or ring). Nowadays, however, usually a coin (sixpence or shilling) serves the purpose and it is afterwards given to the complainant.

The two other tokens mentioned so far, *gwiro* and *ruvundzo*, *are retained by the court*. Because coins have also in this connexion become increasingly common they are often (but incorrectly) referred to as 'court fees' (*marime*).[11]

11. It is here sufficient to say that, in Hera procedure, the complainant is in the first instance responsible for *marime* (court fees) but he may claim a refund from the defendant if he wins the case. Nowadays a standard payment of five to ten shillings has become common. Of this amount a few shillings are regarded as 'messenger's fees' (*cimangaro*; or *makumbo omudzimbahwe* – legs of the court's messenger). Elsewhere, both parties may have to deposit *marime* at the start of the proceedings, the successful party subsequently recovering his money.

Ngandini, the old outsider, now rose: 'Both you and your father do not speak clearly (*a mu revi pa cena*). Your father merely says that he's guilty, and you merely say, "Let it be finished", but you speak no further. So we cannot see the case clearly. Therefore *your father has to give something, and if you then refuse we can see what is what.*'

Defendant: 'I have said I am guilty, why should I give *matatendendava* (token of admission of guilt)?'

Members of the public: 'But we must see it, too! We must see that you have admitted your guilt.'

One of Swikepi's sons, to his father: 'You cannot say this, you cannot stop here. You should give *matatendendava.*'

Defendant finally agreed to give something, but he told the court: 'I gave a half-crown wanting to give only two shillings. So you can keep the sixpence as *matatendendava.*' At this several people protested. 'No, it is better to give back the half-crown to him (defendant) so that he may make it small. He will then be able to give the sixpence.'

This incident is highly revealing. The court and the public insisted that the admission of guilt be given as a separate token, physically distinct from the money the defendant had paid as *ruvundzo.* As it happened nobody had small change and the deputy came to me with the half-crown. I gave him a two-shilling piece and a sixpence. The two-shilling piece was given back to Capanduka. The sixpence was first given to Swikepi, who formally handed it to the deputy, announcing: 'Here is my sixpence which I meant to give as *matatendendava.*' He then added, by way of apology: 'For it is said that if you enter (a house) without clapping your hands, you can clap afterwards (*kupinda musa embera munobva mukayembera*)', i.e., one may always rectify what was omitted earlier.

Ngandini again addressed the complainant: 'You have now seen that your father has paid the *maviri*(!) Will you now say what you want your father to do?'

But the complainant refused. The token was now being interpreted as *nhema muripo*, a specific demand for the complainant to state the amount of damages he wants the defendant to pay. He did not want to be *materially* compensated by his father and therefore refused the token. He repeated, sullenly: 'I do not want my father to pay. Rather let the whole matter rest.'

Capanduka, a bit impatient, asked him: 'Now you have said the matter had ended, are you going to talk happily with your father? Are you going to invite him to your beer parties?'

Complainant: 'It was not I who refused to come to my father's beer parties (*doro*); it was my father who does not like to come to my *doro.*'

Tapamba, the deputy: 'It seems that he does not like his father to pay. Is this so, Ciwedzo? Or what else do you mean?'

Complainant: 'I only want to thresh my grain in peace. I do not want my father to set fire to my grain. That is all I want.'

Ngandini: 'But now you seem to forget that it is a matter of *makazhi* (arson), and that it (the grain) is now (vested) in the *civara.* If you want to thresh it you could ask permission from the *dzimbahwe* (court) to do so.'[12]

Complainant: 'That is true, but I did mean to ask the court's permission to thresh it.'

There was now again a deadlock in the proceedings, and an excited free-for-all discussion followed, in which almost everyone tried to find out or to explain why the son refused to accept his father's token, the interpretation of which was now evidently confused. Ngandini suggested that the son first pay back the amount of money his father had stated Ciwedzo owed him from a previous case 'to calm the heart of Swikepi'. Once this was done, he thought, the son might feel free to put forward his own claim. But others disagreed and doubted if this would clarify the issue which, they suspected, went far deeper than a mere debt of money.

Capanduka now ordered the deputy to give the sixpence back to the defendant. The deputy: 'Your son wants the sixpence to be given back to you, *because he does not want you to pay.*' (i.e., the token was being interpreted as *nhema muripo.*)

Capanduka: 'We have *seen* that Swikepi has given *matatendendava* (interpretation of the token as admission of guilt), and I should like to regard the case (*mhoswa*) as finished. Yet I doubt whether the matter (*ndava*) is really finished, because the son has not yet spoken clearly.'

At this moment one of Swikepi's sons, who sided with his father, said: 'I know now the answer (i.e., I could explain everything), but Swikepi is my father and Ciwedzo is my *mukoma* (elder brother) and I do not want my answer to be remembered by them!' A roar of laughter followed this announcement. When it had subsided, the deputy called upon Nemadziva as head of the group of kinsmen to which defendant and complainant belonged: 'You, who are their father, should tell Swikepi that his son does not want his father to pay. You should tell them that they must now go happily together.'

Nemadziva, who apparently thought that a reconciliation at this stage was unlikely, made an impatient gesture: 'Ah, how can I do this?'

12. *Cf.* footnote 4.

The complainant: 'I want you, my chief, to ask my father if he will come to my *doro* (beer parties) when I invite him. I have often been to his parties but he has never come to mine.'

Swikepi spoke in an undertone to Nemadziva, who then announced: 'It does not enter the heart (we are not convinced of his sincerity) when he says he does not want his father to pay. We do not understand the way in which he talks of his father. Should he really have forgiven his father, he should have spoken thus: "My father, who has begotten me (*bereka*), who has moulded me in the womb of my mother." We have not heard you speak like that.'

The deputy and Ngandini talked to the complainant, apparently trying to persuade him to show a more lenient attitude, for after a few minutes Ngandini addressed Swikepi: 'Your son says that he does not like his father to pay, the father who has slept on one mat with his mother, who moulded him in his mother's womb and who later gave him a wife!'

Nemadziva: 'Does he truly mean that we are his fathers? Did he really speak of us in those words? Say it again so I may hear!'

Nagandini: 'If you wish to doubt my words you had better brace yourself!'

Swikepi: 'My child says that I am his father. He does not like to make me pay. That sounds all right!'

At this stage public despondency gave way to general relief. Several voices called: '*Forya*! (snuff tobacco)', evidently wishing to see the traditional overt proof of reconciliation at which the parties partake of snuff or food together at the conclusion of cases in which personal hatred (*daka*, *bundu*) had been revealed. In the words of the outsider Ngandini: 'Merely saying with words that everything is well, is not enough. They should take snuff (*forya*) together.'

But Swikepi protested: 'If I say that all is well, this should be enough. Why do you want us to take snuff? What I want is this: if he is my child as he says he is, and I am his father, then let him follow me to my homestead, and we will discuss everything there. Should he then find that I drive him away, he will know I hate him. But he must come to my place and find out what is in my heart. He will then find that I shall not drive him away, but speak to him as my own child.'

Complainant: 'Those are words which I can understand, words which come from the heart (*a no bva pa moyo*).'

But the public insisted: 'Let them take snuff among us, so that we may witness. Let them take snuff so that we shall know that they are indeed reconciled (*kuyanana*)!'

Finally the parties gave in. Ciwedzo produced his snuff-box and shook a little snuff into the hands of the deputy. Capanduka took the first pinch, then Nemadziva, then Swikepi, then Ciwedzo himself, now siding with his father. Subsequently Swikepi produced snuff which the deputy distributed to Capanduka, the complainant and several members of the public. All snuffed happily. Old Ngandini sang an old song (which I failed to record), causing general merriment.

Nemadziva looked happy for a moment, but after he had snuffed remarked wearily: 'Oh, my son, it has come so far that your father and you had to take snuff together at the *civara*. Don't think, because I have been silent, that I have nothing to say. There is so much in my mind . . .'

But the others told him not to worry.

'It is all right now, there is peace again. People can always disagree, but later there is peace again. To stir up water is to make it calm again (*kubvonggodze mvura kuti iyerane*)' – it is sometimes necessary to face trouble in order to get things straightened out.

Swikepi now addressed Capanduka: 'I have given snuff to say that I no longer bear my son a grudge (*daka*). If he is truly my son, as he has said, let him follow me to my place and hear my words. If he prefers to live here (i.e., in Capanduka's country) he should come to me. I shall then take him to Capanduka and entrust my child to him, saying: "Look well after my child. If there is anything wrong with him or should he get sick, I ask you to send for me so that I may know." '

Capanduka to Ciwedzo: 'You have heard what your father has said. You two must from now on invite one another, and upon meeting you should be happy and laugh together. And we should now close this case by clapping hands together (*kuvucira*).'

The case of Ciwedzo against his father having been concluded, there remained the 'criminal' aspect of the matter.

Capanduka announced: 'And now there is this case of mine. I only want to know this: why has Swikepi cut down fruit trees and why had he burned his huts? Has this anything to do with his son?'

Swikepi: 'I did this only because I hated my son, and I did not want him to eat from it (the trees). I was angry with my child, but now I see that I was wrong.' He then quoted two old proverbs: '*Kurerembga inozukuruma* (if you rear a dog it will bite you)';[13] and '*Kurowe benzi rowa uciise mberi,*

13. Meaning: one may expect from those that are being taught to obey authority, that they rebel sometimes.

uka rowa uciise kunze rinoryiwa ngebere (freely rendered: chastise a child but do not cast him out, as he may then be lost).'[14]

He seemed genuinely moved when he turned to his son. 'My child, if I had died before this matter had been settled, I (i.e., my spirit) would have had an everlasting grudge against you. But all is well now, and so, my son, I tell you to come home with me. And if you want to live in Capanduka's country, we can arrange that, too.'

Capanduka appeared to be satisfied with Swikepi's explanation. The people were, moreover, gathering their belongings, impatient to go to a beer party which had been in progress near by. The headman hesitated a moment, then stated: 'I have nothing more to say. We have heard Swikepi saying that he had done all this because of his son. We have *seen* that he knows that he did wrong. So this matter is ended (*za pera*).' After a ceremonial clapping of hands the meeting broke up.

II. ANALYSIS OF CERTAIN ASPECTS

In the following pages I shall limit myself to a discussion of only two aspects: the communal element in the conflict and the concrete element in law and procedure. In both these aspects the case is typical of customary Hera law and a fair illustration of well-established principles of Shona law generally.

The communal element

At the outset the Hera court sharply distinguished 'two cases': one in which the individual complainant sued his father for certain wrongs committed against him and his property; and the other in which the community, as represented by its headman, Capanduka, accused Swikepi of certain offences against the community. The formal action against the wrongdoer had, therefore, its individual and its communal aspects. (I now purposely avoid using the Western distinction between 'civil' and 'criminal' actions.) In the course of the process, as we have seen, practically all attention became focused on the 'individual' case; the community's case, although never quite lost sight of,

14. The more literal translation runs: 'When beating a fool beat him while pushing him in front of you; do not beat him so that he is left behind, lest he be eaten by a hyena.'

being reduced to a secondary issue disposed of almost incidentally – though formally – at the very end of the trial.

It must be emphasized, however, that although the *communal charge* in the 'indictment' was never fully pursued in this case yet the communal element became the dominant feature in the conflict between the individual parties.

At the time the wrongs were committed both parties (at least temporarily) were accepted members of one tribal ward (Capanduka's *dunhu*). When formal action was brought against Swikepi, he was back in the Nemadziva ward. But the two wards adjoined, and their members almost daily combined in collective and social activities, thus constituting, in effect, a wider social and even political entity of which Capanduka (of the ruling Hera lineage) was the principal representative. Court and public therefore viewed the conflict between the parties as one between members of a single close community the social unity of which they wished to preserve. In spite of the defendant's assertions that his wanton actions had been directed mainly against his son personally, their conflict threatened normal communications, peace and harmony in the community and therefore immediately assumed much wider proportions. Against this threat the community itself reacted in order to protect its own vital interests. The nature of its reactions is clearly revealed in the course of the judicial process.

The case was submitted to a formally constituted court presided over by Capanduka who, as superior headman, represented his own tribal ward and the wider unity of Hera and Moyo groups. In the beginning of the process this formal judicial body had full control, but soon the public (i.e., the community itself) participated. In fact, from an early stage onwards Capanduka did little more then formulate public opinion. The communal element in the procedure was revealed in many ways. Every grown-up male present, including the visitor Ngandini, had the right to voice his opinion once the case had been 'thrown to the dogs to chew' and did so whenever he felt like it. But even before this stage was reached, spontaneous pressure from the side of the public arose whenever the formal proceedings seemed to reach a deadlock. For example, when Swikepi (to whom the whole process was deeply humiliating) proudly and obstinately maintained that his verbal assurance should be sufficient proof of his sincerity, the public insisted that concrete tokens be handed over. But its interest was not confined to matters of procedure. It had a deeper significance, as became clear towards the end of the trial, when the authoritarian Swikepi demanded that his son should first come to his father's place as an act of submission to paternal control. The old man evidently regarded this as essential to the restoration of his *family* unity, which to him was the primary issue. But the community insisted that their *public* reconciliation should precede this, thus shifting the emphasis to the wider communal aspect of the matter. It is significant that not only the individual parties and court officials but *all* present took snuff in unison, thereby turning the act of reconciliation between individual litigants into a public demonstration of general peace and goodwill in the community.

On more than one occasion the public chose to lead their headman instead of being led by him. Perhaps most revealing was its conception of the conflict, its persistent search for root causes beyond specific charges and admitted facts. It became more important to probe the hidden depths of the conflict between father and son. Both were called upon to 'speak clearly', to reveal what was truly in their minds and hearts. At this stage court formalities were reduced to a minimum: the parties were addressed directly, without the deputy as intermediary (only between the complainant and the defendant did his services remain essential). It was an informal, and often excited, free examination and debate. Most of it would, in an European court, have been considered 'irrelevant to the issue', but Capanduka listened attentively, without interfering. He then added formal support to the new turn the case had taken under public pressure, for he stated that, though he liked to regard the case as 'finished' he doubted if the conflict itself had been solved. A moment later the deputy reintroduced Nemadziva into the proceedings by asking him, as head of the group of kinsmen to which both litigants belonged, to use his influence in bringing about a formal settlement. The proceedings continued more or less formally until Swikepi refused to take snuff. His resistance was, again, overcome by spontaneous public clamour. After public reconciliation had actually taken place, it remained for the court formally to close the case.

What should have followed next was a formal prosecution of Swikepi as the accused in the community's case. It was evident that Capanduka had this in mind, but the public thought differently. It had satisfied itself that the offences against the community were related to and largely derived from the embittered relations between father and son. It had pressed for and witnessed their reconciliation, which would ensure the resumption of normal communications between them and the return of social harmony. The primary purpose of the case having been achieved, further prosecution might spoil this success and threaten this newly-won peace.

Capanduka sensed this general feeling and he dropped 'his' case.

Numerous other instances can be recalled in which the communal element is revealed: Nemadziva, representative of the Moyo group, having to 'pass the word' to the defendant before the action could be pursued; his kinsman, Gava, urging his family head that they as a group should face the charge or at least lend their assistance to make prosecution possible; Capanduka's insistence upon Nemadziva's presence so that 'he could see what his brother had done when he left the country...' There was Nemadziva's significant subsequent exclamation: 'Listen how they accuse me – ... they say that I am guilty!' – not a response to a mistaken personal accusation, but his ready assumption that he personified a community responsible for the wrongful deeds of one of its members.

Other examples illustrate the basic communal background of individual thought and actions. Swikepi – a more autocratic and individualistically inclined person than most tribesmen I have met – asked for the postponement of the trial because some of his sons were absent and 'he could not speak without them'. The same sense of solidarity was revealed by his question, 'Did I speak well?' to his son, after he had spoken in his own defense. For the same reason he continued to refer to Nemadziva, in spite of the latter having formally 'withdrawn' from the process. He regarded himself, naturally and obviously, as an indivisible part of his kingroup.

The inference seems clear: in spite of the fact that the cause of the conflict originated between two individuals and the wrongs committed were mainly directed by one individual against the other, the communal aspect became involved as a matter of course.

Not only because the dispute was formally submitted to a common tribunal but because, in the present [15] day, the sense of community still prevails in this tribal society. It is the natural and pervasive background from which no individual can wholly extricate himself in thought or action.

The concrete element

Frequent use was made of concrete tokens in support of the spoken word. So the complainant was required to give *gwiro* to obtain a hearing in court; the defendant had to give *ruvundzo* or *kukumpira mashoko* as proof that he acknowledged the court's authority; and he had to produce *matatendendava* to substantiate his oral admission of guilt.

Although in most instances coins were given, these should not be mistaken for court fees. As has been stated before, the principle of giving such tokens

15. That is, in 1946, when I recorded this case.

is quite different and should be sharply distinguished from the payment of actual court fees (*marime*). The underlying thought reveals a basic element in Shona law and life. It is the urge to reduce words (and sometimes actions) of particular significance to something tangible, to transform verbal non-material communications into something palpable, a concrete *thing* which can be handled, stored and made available at will by the party who has acquired it. Its application is widespread and often imperative. For instance: In marriage preliminaries the marriage proposal is invariably contained in a concrete token. Once accepted by the other party it is tangible proof that the marriage is, in principle at least, acceptable. In modern times, when it is considered advisable, if not necessary, to obtain proof of the willingness of the bride-to-be, she is required by the families to touch or take possession of a portion of the betrothal payment offered to her family. The husband-to-be in a *kuzwarira*-marriage agreement,[16] which so often implies a child betrothal, will give the girl a *rugadzo* token when she has grown up to reaffirm his acceptance of her as bride.

In cases of serious marital trouble the husband may return a recalcitrant wife to her people with a *gupuro* (rejection) token, substantiating his verbal statement that he no longer wishes to live with her. Likewise, an ill-treated wife may demand such a token from him before leaving him, to prove his attitude in terms more convincing than any verbal explanation she might give to her family for deserting him.

The judgment debtor, if he cannot immediately pay his debts, may leave (or be required to leave) his axe, coat or any other article belonging to him personally as *cibato* (something to hold on to), a token of his verbal promise to pay his debt – not to be confused with an actual *pledge* covering the debt, since the material value of the token may be insignificant in comparison with the debt.

Among unmarried lovers we find the *nduma*, a love token given through a go-between by the girl to the boy. It is more than a mere symbol of her love. It remains material proof of her affection, which she must recover from him should she subsequently marry another, and wish to avoid the risk of being thought unfaithful to her husband.[17] Love tokens given by boys are not as common among the Hera as among some other Shona tribes, but a woman committing adultery may, if she wants her lover to share the respon-

16. See my *Shona Customary Law*, OUP, Cape Town, 1952, pp. 115-120.

17. I have witnessed several formal court actions in which young wives sued former lovers, usually because their failure to become pregnant had been ascribed to their 'still being in love with the other man'.

sibility, induce him to give her a button, pin or sixpence as 'proof of his true love' which may (and will) be produced in court if he denies his guilt.

In cases of overt but erroneous accusation of theft or witchcraft the person accused may grab anything (knife, snuff box, coat) belonging to the accuser as *cibato* (also referred to in this connexion as *gakato*) thereby reducing, so to speak, the allegation to material evidence of having been maligned. Often the accuser, feeling certain of his case but meeting with a hot denial, likewise tries to get hold of a piece of property of the other as tangible evidence of the latter's denial. In the ensuing court case both objects are deposited as primary evidence of their owner's words (and not, of course, of the alleged offence).

All those tokens should never be regarded as mere 'formalities', in spite of their often formal character. The admission of guilt token (*rutenda mhoswa*), for instance, may be demanded even if the dispute is never tried before a formal court but settled between parties. Nor are they believed to be 'mystically charged' – although some, such as a love token held by a jilted lover, might indeed be used for magical purposes. Basically and essentially they are meant to reduce to substance what is insubstantial and abstract.

In Swikepi's case, his repeated oral admission of guilt would amply suffice in a Western court of law – although we would have required the 'mystic' sanction of an oath – but the Hera were not satisfied and demanded that something personal, tangible and visible be given in order to make it 'real'.

The case provided a striking illustration of this sense of reality. Swikepi had suggested that the sixpence still due to him after having given two shillings *ruvundzo* by means of a half-crown piece be *retained* by the court and *regarded as* his admission of guilt token. The public was indignant, as if its sense of reality had been insulted. The sixpence change had to be found, for it had to be handed back to its owner first. Only then could he give this personal bit of property as a materialisation of his 'I am guilty' to the court. This was direct, undeniable, palpable proof of this vital piece of communication.

The line of thinking behind this urge for 'concretization' seems to run somewhat as follows: I require from another a certain promise, concession, confession, agreement. He may give me this by word of mouth, but this communication gives me little real security, even if uttered in the presence of witnesses. For words are lost as soon as they are spoken. They are essentially elusive. Even if I or my witnesses may later remember and repeat them correctly, he may deny them, for they have lost their personal character and primary, direct value. So I want these words to be transformed and cast, as it were, into something tangible, something I can appropriate and keep with me, a material, imperishable thing, which I can produce at will, which is a bit of himself, the words he spoke, undeniable and irretractible. So I demand that he give me something palpable, *anything* small and tangible belonging to him, which I can hold, feel and see as a physical object. Only then do I have certainty.

But the 'concrete' element in Shona law is not confined to the giving of tokens. It finds a far wider and often less 'material' (in a literal sense) expression. As a basic phenomenon it rests on a general inclination to think and comprehend in terms of reality rather than of abstraction. In the abovementioned trial the very demand for taking snuff together in public, this insistence upon a customary and widely recognized act of mutual goodwill, is a good example. The public were not satisfied with a mere verbal (abstract) assurance that all was well again. They desired the *actual* performance of an *act* of goodwill. This presented reality and was therefore convincing. Likewise, the communal aspect was expressed realistically, by public participation in the act of taking snuff.

Numerous other examples could be found in Swikepi's case, for instance in the positioning of the opposing parties at the scene of the trial: the authority and relative kinship seniority being visibly revealed in the order in which the men were sitting. Nemadziva did not merely state that he withdrew from the trial, he *actually sat aside*. Gava, one of Nemadziva's people, when opposing his own headman, actually stood up and sat with the Hera crowd, thus *performing* his opposition to his own kingroup.

Many of the actual words used by the court and the members of the public either consciously or unconsciously expressed this sense of realism. Capanduka wanted Nemadziva to 'see' (not merely hear) his brother's offence and waved a twig cut from one of the felled trees as tangible evidence. The public clamoured to 'see' the defendant admitting his guilt, despite his repeated oral admission. For the same reason Swikepi actually wanted his son to return to his father's home – the *performance* of an act of filial obedience and loyalty – before he was prepared to state in which manner he would meet his wishes. A little earlier, Nemadziva had refused to believe that the complainant Ciwedzo truly respected his father. To the old patriarch, himself steeped in traditional etiquette, Ciwedzo's summary reference to 'my father' failed to convey a convincing attitude of filial respect. Only when Ciwedzo used the traditional form of address ('my father, who has slept on one mat with my mother, etc.') was the old man satisfied because, to him, this represented reality, or at least a big step towards it.

Then the trial itself, taken as a whole. The proceedings were formally conducted according to Hera legal practice, but in spite of formalities and the observance of traditional rules of procedure the general picture retained a relaxed, sociable quality.

Those present kept themselves occupied with trifling work; they sometimes smoked or gossiped; they were sitting or lying down comfortably. Occasional outbursts of emotion were allowed, and formalities were forgotten or temporarily suspended when necessary. On several occasions someone would get up for a private exchange of views with either of the litigants. In short, the whole process was a mixture of formal discipline and social leisure, of judicial order blended with the informalities of an everyday village gathering and with the pervasive reality of social intercourse.

Finally, there was the conception of the conflict itself, the realistic recognition of the actual cause of trouble and its implications in a community of interdependent neighbours. And when this matter had been satisfactorily settled, there remained the decision either to act according to formal law by prosecuting the accused for his offences against the community or to be satisfied with what had been accomplished and to accept this as substantial proof that the requirements of justice had been adequately met. Following a 'concrete' and realistic rather than a formal line of thought, the decision to drop the case was the more obvious and natural one to take.

Postcript (1968)

The increasing use of this case report as students' reading material makes it desirable that I should add a postscript. Except for some minor revisions the above piece was written in the field in November, 1946, as a preliminary exercise for a dual purpose: as a contribution to a meeting of fellow-workers of the (then) Rhodes-Livingstone Institute to which I was attached as a Beit research fellow; and also as one of a collection of elaborate case reports which I intended to incorporate in a full-scale study of the Shona judicial process. The latter purpose has not been fulfilled. My first major effort in writing up my field material went instead into a book on customary marriage and family law[18] at the urgent request of the Southern Rhodesian administration, and the hope of producing a comprehensive study of the judicial process vanished with the passage of time under the pressure of other commitments.

That the paper was published at all was due to a frantic appeal for copy from a hard-pressed editor of NADA in 1951. It was sent to him virtually

18. *Shona Customary Law*, OUP, Cape Town, 1952.

as I lifted it from my files, a hastily composed and analytically somewhat lopsided piece of writing. It seems to have found more favour in the eyes of others than in mine. I can only view it as a preparatory exercise of the larger study I had in mind.

For its present republication I have left it substantially unchanged. I have tried to correct some cumbersome English usage and to cut out undue verbiage. I have even retained the original opening sentences, in spite of their somewhat pretentious sound, for at the time I wrote the method I employed was still an early experiment in the analysis of the African judicial process (two much earlier reports, verbatim records though without further comments were published by Schapera in 1938).[19] Gluckman was the first fully to exploit the same method, more comprehensively and with superior results, in his *Judicial Process among the Barotse* (1955). He must however have collected his case material with a view of treating it in this fashion as early as, and even before, I did. Moreover, this type of analysis is but a fresh application of the method he employed[20] in 1940, the analysis of a social situation, structure or process, radiating from a single social event as spokes radiate from the hub of a wheel. Epstein, Bohannan, Mitchell, Gulliver, Van Velsen, to mention a few, have likewise used it with considerable success from the 'fifties onwards'. So much for the originality of my Hera experiment.

I must add some further critical comment. In retrospect I feel that I either attempted too much or did not complete what I set out to do. There is, at any rate, a lack of balance in the paper in that the analytical section fails to take account of several aspects to which I had given some prominence in the preceding descriptive part. Now to redress this omission would extend an already lengthy essay much beyond the space allotted to it in this book. Moreover, it may well be asked if such an extension, with its inevitable multiplication of themes, would not have overburdened the foundation of a single case report and have required instead the much larger and more broadly based study I had in mind.

Perhaps more serious, however, I consider my neglect to conclude with even a simple summary of what was purporting to be an analysis of the successive phases of customary formal Hera judicial process. This omission, at least, must now be rectified in a brief addendum.

In essence the formal traditional court procedure among the Hera and kin-

19. At the end of his *Handbook of Tswana Law and Custom*, OUP, London, 1938.
20. 'Analysis of a social situation in modern Zululand,' *Bantu Studies*, vol. 14, 1940; also in *Rhodes-Livingstone Papers*, no. 28, Manchester, 1958.

dred Shona tribes conforms with the classic model: thesis, antithesis and (whenever possible) synthesis, in that:

a. the aggrieved party states his case,

b. the defendant/accused opposes this case;

c. the tribunal tries to effect a solution or compromise acceptable to both.

In the customary formal process[21] there are three distinct phases which do not, however, fully coincide with the triple sequence mentioned above. These phases are:

1. The formal and strictly disciplined stage, during which first the aggrieved party states his case (often followed by one or two principal 'witnesses' testifying on his behalf, usually rather as 'moral supporters' than as independent sources of factual evidence), and subsequently his opponent (again often backed by one or two supporters) giving his version of the conflict. During this stage therefore both thesis and antithesis are invariably included.

2. The stage of participant inquiry, during which most formalities are suspended and all adults present have the right to examine litigants and (new) witnesses, and can freely express opinions on points of law, mores and social behaviour. Almost invariably this is the critical stage of the process, for in this free-for-all debate not only thesis and antithesis are exhaustively expounded, but there is a distinct if somewhat haphazard and fragmentary effort towards formulating a solution, an acceptable form of synthesis. This development is therefore closely guided by the trend of public opinion revealed during this stage of the process.

3. The final stage, when formal court discipline is resumed and the presiding officer (or his deputy) summarizes the conflict, interprets right and wrong with reference both to relevant legal principles and to the expressed community opinion regarding reasonable social behaviour[22] in the community concerned. The judgment or verdict by the presiding officer, whether it be merely an admonishment or with the additional imposition of a material 'fine' or 'compensation', should be (and in my experience almost invariably is) concluded with the pointed question to both litigants: 'Do you agree?'

Public reconciliation between litigants (as in Swikepi's case) is less common practice, but a desirable visible demonstration of this verbally acknowl-

21. 'Formal' as distinct from the less clearly defined and often 'informal' procedure of trying to solve a (legal) dispute with the help of one or more elders in informal and more or less private meetings. Formal procedure usually begins at the level of a tribal ward (*dunhu*) tribunal whence appeal lies to the chief's court. Informal procedure is rarely if ever maintained beyond the village (*musha*) level.

22. *Cf.* Gluckman's emphasis on the behaviour of the 'reasonable man', *op. cit.*, *passim.*

edged 'agreement' in cases in which personal enmity (hatred) has been revealed and its continuance would pose a threat to peace in the community.

Should either party signify 'disagreement' (*kuramba*, to refuse) with the judgment, the debate may either be reopened before the same tribunal immediately or after an adjournment, or – more likely – be pursued in a fashion similar to that described here before a higher court in the tribal hierarchy. In the traditional Shona system the Chief's court is the highest tribal tribunal. Colonial legislation, however, in particular the *African Law and Courts Act of 1928* (as amended from time to time),[23] has extended the judicial hierarchy to the District Commissioner's and African Appeal Courts and has removed most 'criminal' issues from the recognized field of customary judicial process. The latter aspects, however, fall outside the scope of this paper.

23. Now superseded by the *African Law and Tribal Courts Act, 1969*.

The case of the irate headman*

I. CASE REPORT

Introduction

The people of Careva live in the roughly triangular northern part of the Mtoko district in north-eastern Rhodesia. They were originally Korekore immigrants coming down from the north under their leader Noureka, a powerful rainmaker who, 'by the arrows of his magic', defeated Makate, then chief of the Budya tribe (one of the many Shona speaking peoples and culturally akin to the Korekore sub-group). Noureka established his spiritual supremacy by preventing his opponent's spirit to emerge (*kubuda*) after his death and assumed the latter's clan name, Shumba (Lion), in the place of his own (Nzou, Elephant). Having thus appropriated the clan name most closely associated with the *Mhondoro* (tribal spirit) cult and having established the fiction, staunchly upheld until this day, that his immigrant group and the Budya are 'of the same stock' (*rudzi* – kind, lineage), it was his (Noureka's) spirit which in time became the Budya *Mhondoro.*

The secret cult centre of this spiritual power lies in the valley behind Marapati Hill. Known as 'Careva' ('the Speaker') – the name Noureka is never mentioned in public and was long kept secret from me – and represented by an old female *swikiro* (medium) who shuns all public contact except with a few special functionaries, this Spirit is consulted in all matters concerning the Budya chieftainship of Mutoko (the senior one of the district), in the succession to which it traditionally had the decisive voice.[1]

The name Careva also applies to the senior tribal court in the area, which holds its weekly sessions at an open place within hailing distance of the

* Case report, 1951; part II added in 1970.

1. 'The Spirit does not recognize Government appointees not approved by it.' – Careva informant.

small homestead of the medium. It further serves to indicate the progenitor of the immigrant lineage whose five major branches (*dzimba* – houses) now represent as many recognized headmanships, each with its own following, hereditary name and defined territory (*nzwimbo*[2]). These are, in order of seniority, Cindenga, Kawazwa, Mudzengerere, Kadiki and Nyamakope. Together they form a political unity, in that all except one 'take the [court] cases that have defeated them to Careva before taking them to chief Mutoko'. Mudzengerere bypasses the Careva court 'because he [i.e., one of his forefathers] once quarrelled with Careva and the spirit prohibited him from coming to his place [i.e., the cult areal]'. He goes direct to Mutoko (or the District Commissioner) on appeal.

The extremely complex relationship and system of functionaries balancing Careva's spiritual supremacy and Mutoko's secular power do not concern us here, except for a few important facts.

First, the person who is the principal link between the two powers, the right-hand man of the spirit medium and the 'supreme judge' (*vutonga*[3]) at the court of Careva, though 'appointed by the Spirit', is not a member of the 'House of Careva', but of true Budya (Mutoko) stock.[4] Kaukonde was a very frail undersized old man when I was closely associated with him in 1951-52. Soft-spoken and almost self-effacing by age and nature, he amply had one quality the Shona expect a good judge to have: the capacity to listen well (even when he seemed to be asleep during a prolonged session) and to speak little. Yet when he did speak, to put an occasional question or to summarize a verdict, he was usually brief and to the point. His authority was immense. He could calm an excited audience with a slight hand gesture, and people would silently strain to hear his soft but unwavering voice.

Secondly, the *vutonga* was assisted by a small panel of regular 'assessors'

2. These political units are structurally the same as the common Shona *dunhu* (tribal ward); the latter term, though locally not unknown, is usually reserved for the whole Careva complex, which may thus be regarded as an agnatic cluster of tribal wards within the *nyika* (chiefdom, tribal territory) of Mutoko.

3. The prefix *vu-* for abstract nouns, coupled with the verb-stem (instead of the usual '*mutongi*', judge), denotes the much enhanced status accorded to this functionary.

4. Ironically, *vutonga* Kaukonde was unknown to the administration until I briefed them. They were vaguely aware of the importance of Careva ('a rather mysterious figure, a sort of priestess-chief who seems to have a lot of power in connexion with the Mutoko chieftainship'), but as she was 'not permitted by her religion to meet Europeans' they had given the official brass emblem to her 'representative'. This rather unhappy individual, however, fulfilled only a minor role in the Careva complex. Called '*Tsoka dzashe*' (the Feet of the Chief) or, even less dignified, '*mupurisa*' (policeman), he was regarded as a mere messenger between Careva and district headquarters or Chief Mutoko.

(to use official parlance) who, like he himself, were approved of by the Spirit and did not belong to the House of Careva. They were usually referred to as *masamakomo*, 'Keepers of the Mountains', a hereditary title which indicated that they were the heirs of the principal families or village heads who first settled in the area, when each of them used one of the imposing steep rock formations which abound in this part of the country as a basis and place of refuge for his settlement. Through intermarriage in the past, however, virtually all these functionaries are at present cognatic relations (classificatory sister's sons – *vazukuru* – or mother's brothers – *vasekuru)* of the lineage of Careva.

The only person acting fairly regularly as an official of the court of Careva as a 'messenger' (*munyai*) or occasionally as an assessor – and who was regarded as 'belonging to Careva' – was the 'Son of the Spirit', a vigorous, bright young man, actually the son of the present spirit medium,[5] upon whom the assumed clan names of his spiritual 'father' had been bestowed.

Together these functionaries constituted probably the best organized and most conscientious tribunal among the many tribal courts whose operations I have observed.

The judicial process among the Budya is essentially the same as that practised by all Shona traditional tribal courts whose sessions I attended. There are variations in terminology and in the use of certain tokens and 'court fees', but the principal characteristics are very similar to those I have described for the Hera. There is, however, one variation which merits some preliminary attention because it adds to the Budya procedure an element of 'stage-play' even in cases of the most bitter litigation. It concerns the institution of *mumanjemanje* during the second stage of the judicial process, when most formalities are suspended and the matter is (to use the Hera expression) 'thrown to the dogs to chew on'. The Budya call this stage simply *cibvunza*, 'question time'. It serves the same crucial purpose of enabling members of the community to probe into the nature of the conflict, to express their opinions about the parties' right or wrong behaviour and to suggest possible solutions. *Mumanjemanje* is the particular way in which it takes place. The term probably derives from *manja* (hands) and might be freely translated as 'giving [the parties] a helpful hand'. The essential feature of this institution is that any speaker who volunteers a question of opinion on

5. This old woman, shrouded in secrecy, must, at the time of my inquiries, already have been in office for about forty years.

any point first announces: 'I am So-and-so' – giving the name of one of the contesting parties – and then proceeds as if he in fact were the named party himself, using the latter's appropriate forms of addressing his opponent, relatives and others, and displaying the sentiments and convictions this party may be expected to hold. This performance and role-identification is a challenge to someone else to assume the identity of the opposing party in a similar performance, and so an often lively if not passionate debate is literally 'staged' with regard to any point of law, fact or behaviour which may be considered questionable or in need of further clarification. It is not necessary for a speaker thus identifying himself with either plaintiff or defendant in respect of one debated issue to assume the same role when another point crops up. In fact, the most skillful debaters may 'change roles' several times during the same process, moved by a keen desire to score a telling point in an evolving game of wits. The effect of this 'bipartiality' is not confusion; on the contrary, it leads to the most articulate expression of prevailing public views and sentiments with regard to all relevant aspects of the often complex pattern of conflicting interests which a law suit presents. An important corollary of *mumanjemanje* is that the litigating parties themselves are strictly prohibited from participating in this performance. They are mere spectators not permitted to speak or interrupt. Only very rarely, and then through the intermediary or another court official, may a litigant at this stage be called upon to supply a missing piece of information which only he (or she) is presumed to possess. Both plaintiff and defendant are therefore urged at the beginning of the hearing 'to speak openly so that nothing remains hidden'.

The institution of *mumanjemanje* removes, so to speak, the actual combatants from the arena of conflict at the very stage when, both having revealed their colours and armory, tempers might flare up during the searching and often provocative public debate and cross-examination. They are not merely, as is common in other Shona judicial processes, kept 'separate' from one another; they are actually disqualified from further active participation while their opposing roles are being enacted by successive pairs of personally non-involved actors on the judicial stage. In fact, it is this playful element which makes the phrase *kutamba mhoswa*, 'to play cases', a much more common usage when the Budya refer to their judicial process than the general terms *kutonga* or *kugura mhoswa* (to judge or 'cut' lawsuits).

All this in no way affects the quality of their administration of justice. The dialogues are usually sharp and purposeful, the actors seriously engaged and conscious of their responsibilities. The public is critical and, however faithful the performances, never forgets that these are not the real contestants who are waiting for justice to be done to real grievances. Clever questions, sharp and witty retorts, cogent arguments are enjoyed and may even be openly applauded. But any 'over-acting', purposeless chatter or frivolous fun making is likely to invite a reprimand from one of the court officials or derisive noises from the public. As much as people like a good show, they also expect a serious effort at dispensing justice. At this crucial stage of *cibvunza*, with its public participation by *mumanjemanje*, the delicate balance between the elements of play and serious inquiry is sometimes difficult to maintain. Yet only once or twice have I seen a process threaten to get out of hand and turn into a sheer ribaldry, and this was at a height of a hot summer's day when some participants had gazed too deeply into the cool beer pots to keep their wits and composure. Usually, however, public question time is an orderly but lively performance, a quick succession of verbal duels during which the litigating parties' behaviour, evidences and attitudes are scrutinized, analysed and evaluated with reference to accepted tenets of law and procedure and tested against such norms of conduct as would be considered reasonable in the particular circumstances of their conduct.

When *cibvunza* has ended, the functionary acting as official 'interpreter' or go-between (here usually merely called *munyai*, messenger) formally 'gives the case [back] to the court', for the final stage during which at least one assessor gives a brief summary of and comments upon its main issues before he, in turn, puts the matter into the hands of the presiding *mutongi* for judgment.

After these introductory remarks I shall now present first the factual background and then the judicial process relating to the 'Case of the Irate Headman', which was judged by Kaukonde, the old *vutonga* of the court of Careva, in July 1951.

Background of the case

The 'messenger' (*munyai*) of the court of Careva briefed me on the main background facts a few weeks before the case was actually submitted for a formal hearing. According to the notes I jotted down when he spoke, the story was, briefly, as follows.

There had been a public meeting at the *dare* (courtyard) of the ward headman Mudzengerere (House of Careva) of a number of African agricultural demonstrators who would teach the people how to improve their crop production. Dismayed at the poor attendance one A. D. publicly asked

Mudzengerere: 'Why have all your people not come here? Don't they obey you any longer?'

Katiyu, a young man teaching at a mission village school in the adjoining area of headman Nyamokope (classificatory 'younger brother' of Mudzengerere), stood up and said: 'It is like that nowadays in our country. We do no longer obey our *mambo's* (chiefs).[6] We regard them as we do our *masabuku* (village headmen). We even respect [lit: 'fear', *kutyira*] our *masabuku* more than our *mambo's.*'

Hearing this, Mudzengerere became 'very angry' and said he 'could not speak to a boy during this meeting' but would do so later. The young teacher was subsequently summoned to Mudzengerere's *dare,* where the headman severely 'scolded him'. Katiyu protested that he had not meant to be disrespectful; he had only 'answered the question of the *madumeni* (agricultural demonstrators)' by giving his honest opinion on a situation which he himself found deplorable. Mudzengere then calmed down and told Katyu that he 'had no case'. The young man was accordingly discharged without *muripo* ('fine') and went home. He did, however, feel that he had been unduly 'shamed' and went to his own headman, Nyamokope, to complain about the matter.

This apparently angered Mudzengerere again, for – I am again quoting my informant – he 'then wrote a letter which said that he no longer wanted Katiyu in his country, otherwise he [Katiyu] would die'.[7]

Thus threatened after he had been told that he had committed no offence, Katiyu became so 'angry and much afraid' that he went to the district headquarters at Mtoko to report the matter, 'begging the District Commissioner to call Mudzengerere and make him explain [the reason for his behaviour]'. But the District Commissioner was of the opinion that the case should first be taken to a competent tribal court – 'one that has the emblem'. This could only mean the court of Careva, where the functionary referred to as the Feet of the Chief (p. 51, note 4) was given this official token of recognition. Consequently the young teacher reported the matter to Careva who agreed to summon Mudzengerere and judge the case.

There was, however, one difficulty. Mudzengerere was, as I have related, not permitted by the Spirit to enter the valley behind Marapati Hill where

6. The Budya are more generous with '*mambo*' as a term of *reference* than many other Shona, who usually reserve this term for the chief of their tribe. As a form of *addressing* any superior it is, however, commonly and widely used.

7. It will be seen later that the letter contained no such explicit threat, but my informant, like so many others, readily inferred this from the fact that the letter was written in *red ink.*

the court of Careva habitually convened. He was prepared to send his grown-up sons – to whom the prohibition did not apply – as his representatives but 'refused to come himself'.

The court's officials considered that they could not judge the case in the absence of the defendant personally and decided upon a site just inside the territory of headman Cindenga, the representative of the most senior branch of the House of Careva and the (classificatory) 'elder brother' of Mudzengerere. The latter agreed to come to this venue.

These are the facts as I was told them beforehand. I need only add that my informant, who would be officiating as '*munyai*' at the forthcoming process, thought that 'it would now be for the court to decide whether it was a matter of abusing (*kutuka*) the *mambo*' and that Katiyu would have to show that he merely stated what he believed to be the truth, without meaning to be disrespectful. But even if he had been disrespectful, Mudzengerere (so the *munyai* confided to me) had been 'too harsh' in his letter, and the imposition of a 'fine' would have been more appropriate in a case like this.

The process

The court officials had asked me for a 'lift' to the appointed site (some 7 miles away from their usual venue) as the case would start 'early' – an outstretched arm pointing east had indicated the position of the sun to be at between eight and nine in the morning, a very early start on a winter's day. By half past nine they had gathered in my camp and my light truck reached the site a quarter of an hour later. There was a nip in the air and they selected an elevated flat and slightly sloping rock surface (clearly used as a threshing floor), well protected against the wind and overlooking a village close by. No one else had yet arrived, but after a while the village headman came, urging the court party to conduct their business in his village, because he was staging a big beer feast which, in his opinion, was an attractive setting in which to hold a serious inquiry. The young officials hesitated, but the old *vutonga* shook his head. 'When we have properly finished here, we can go to the beer afterwards.' The village headman courteously clapped his hands, spoke of the wisdom of the very old and promised that he would keep some beer in store.

The plaintiff, together with his ward headman Nyamakope and other supporters, arrived a little later; the defendant, Mudzengerere, together with a few of his sons and followers, unhurriedly climbed up to the site at half past ten. There was the usual exchange of courtesies before people had sorted themselves out and settled down.

The site was roughly shaped like a circle-quadrant, sloping down from its radial point where *vutonga* Kaukonde sat together with ward headman Cindenga, the 'owner' of the area (*muridzi wenzwimbo*). Masusa, the 'messenger' of the court of Careva, sat at their feet. A few yards away on one side of the quadrant were a couple of 'Mountain Keepers' (p. 52), regular assessors at Careva together with Jojo, the 'Son of the Spirit'. It struck me that their position was markedly different from their habitual one at the Careva site, where they usually flanked the *vutonga.* The official called Feet of the Chief or *mupurisa* by the Careva people (see note 4) had found a place on the opposite side, cutting a rather lonely figure. In the central area lower down, though clearly separated by an open space between them, were the plaintiff Katiyu with his *mambo* Nyamakope and two or three other close supporters, and the defendant Mudzengerere with his sons.

The public, whose numbers varied from about twenty to about forty during the course of the trial, occupied the broad lower fringe of the improvised courtyard (*dare*).

The proceedings opened at a quarter to eleven with an unusual overture which, considering the special circumstances of the case, was however entirely appropriate. One of the officials of the court of Careva (Jojo, the 'Son of the Spirit') moved forward, sat down and, after respectfully clapping his hands, formally asked why this site, and not the venue of Careva, had been chosen to hear this case. His question was conveyed to the judges by the *munyai* (who also fulfilled the function of intermediary[8] during the process). He was given a brief whispered instruction by the *vutonga* and then gave a lengthy account not only of the reasons why the defendant 'could not enter the area (*nzwimbo*) of Careva' but also of the fact that the District Commissioner had instructed the case to be heard by the court of Careva. Therefore 'the *vutonga* has chosen this place, where Mudzengerere can come without angering the Spirit, and this is why Cindenga, the owner of this place, is sitting with the *vutonga*'. His account struck me as being not merely informative but distinctly apologetic, as if the change of venue might wrongly have been interpreted as a sign of disrespect to (the court of) Careva. It also contained an explicit reference to the letter Katiyu had received from the defendant (causing him to go to the 'office') and casually mentioned the fact that it had been written in red ink – a detail which was still news to me at the time, but which did not cause an undue stir among the apparently better informed public, who merely exchanged some meaningful glances.

8. See p. 18-19, 25 ff.

The importance of his information was enhanced by the fact that the defendant himself in even greater detail corroborated the *munyai*'s account. Though omitting reference to the red ink, he mentioned that he had actually sent his sons to Careva, but they 'had been refused' because the 'office' had said that he himself had to be 'judged' (*kutonga*) by Careva. The defendant's story, audible to all, seemed to be addressed especially to the headman of the local village, who publicly conveyed his words to the *munyai*, who duly informed the co-judge Cidenga, who again informed Kaukonde, Careva's *vutonga*.

After this elaborate introduction, the *munyai* asked both plaintiff and defendant each to deposit five shillings as *rutongo* ('judging' fees), while the plaintiff had to pay an extra five shillings as *tsoka* ('feet') to the *munyai* 'for having summoned' the defendant. The first ten shillings were placed upon an old hat in the middle of the floor where, visible to all, they remained until the end of the process. Having announced that the winning party could receive back his deposit after the verdict, the *munyai* was told by the *vutonga* to call upon the plaintiff to state his case.

The young man faced the court, clapped his hands respectfully and, remaining in a squatting position, quietly told his story in very great detail, starting with the incident at the 'agricultural demonstrators' meeting (protesting that he had meant no disrespect, but had merely stated his honest opinion about a situation which he himself deplored), his subsequent 'trial' at Mudzengerere's *dare* (court) where 'the *mambo* himself told me that I had no case', then about the receipt of the *mambo*'s letter (duly produced and read aloud), his reaction to it and so forth. It was a good and restrained performance, to which all listened attentively and without any interruption. It was immediately repeated at length by the intermediary (*munyai*) for the benefit of the judges. It produced few material facts which I had not known before, but two things struck me. One was plaintiff's emphatic question to 'the *vakuru* (great ones) who are judging me', why he, an unmarried young man posted from outside the district to teach in this area, had been summoned to appear alone before Mudzengerere, that is, without the support of anyone (village- or ward-headman) who was 'like a father to me in a place where I have no family'. The other point concerned the letter itself. Its having been written in red ink had come as surprise to me, but also the fact that it contained no more than a prohibition to visit Mudzengerere's territory (*nzwimbo*) except by keeping strictly to the main road which ran across it. Remembering that a few weeks earlier my informant (the present *munyai*) had explicitly told me that the letter threatened death to the plaintiff should he trespass upon the headman's territory, it was clear that not the wording of the letter but its red ink, with its implicit association with *cishava* (ominous misfortune), or even *ropa* (blood), presented the main threat.

The *vutonga* now told the *munyai* to call upon the defendant who, likewise squatting down, clapped respectfully and addressed the court at length. He found his main defence in a fine show of barely suppressed indignation. At the agricultural meeting he had indeed at first believed that this young man, who 'comes from outside our country', was merely stirring up trouble against established tribal authority, as so many young people ('children') were beginning to do. Being in a sense a 'father' to him, because the young teacher was employed by the same church of which he (Mudzengerere) was an elder, he had called him to his *dare* to question him and teach him how to behave towards his tribal superiors. Surely, there could be little wrong with his course of action, even if plaintiff did live in the adjacent area of his 'younger brother' Nyamakope? He frankly admitted that, after hearing the explanation of this 'boy' (*mukomana*), he had 'found no case (*mhaka*) with him', but had merely warned him to mind his tongue in the future. Dramatically spreading his hands wide the defendant then said: 'But what did I hear next? This boy was complaining about me to his own *mambo* and telling many people that I had treated him harshly.' He paused and, looking at the people around him as if to solicit their support, then asked: 'What could I do? I had spoken to him as a father, finding no case with him; yet he was maligning me, threatening me with a grudge (*daka*) and he even went to the *ofisi* to complain to the *varungu* (European) about me.' Ignoring the fact that in his statement he had skipped an important link in the chain of events, he concluded: 'So I was mistaken after all when he abused me at my own *dare* the day the *madumeni* (agricultural demonstrators) were there. He does not want to obey a *mambo*; he wants to make trouble, that boy.' He paused again, then, as an afterthought, added: 'I did not want him to make trouble among my people. Yes, about this letter. I did write him, telling him only not to come to my place, and if he had to cross it he should not leave the big road that the Europeans of the *ofisi* have made. I did not even punish him, but sometimes I thought I should go to the *ofisi* to complain about him and other young ones like him. These are my words.' He clapped respectfully for the judges, but when he turned around his face was working with indignation.

The *munyai* repeated his statement fully and faithfully. The court then called, as part of the normal Budya procedure, upon each party to present his chief 'witness' (*capupu, mupupuri*). Headman Nyamakope appeared on behalf of the young plaintiff ('I am his *mambo* and therefore his father'); the old defendant had his oldest son to assist him.

From a functional point of view the term 'witness' is somewhat misleading, considering the roles played by these *capupus*. They seldom if ever give new evidence on behalf of their parties and it is certainly not common practice to subject them to cross-examination. They do little more than repeat in their own words what their parties have said – in fact, one of the meanings of *kukupura* is 'to repeat' – and there being no objection to hearsay evidence, they often openly state that they derive most of their information not from their own observation but from what their party has told them about the matter. But the mere fact of having a *capupu* unhesitatingly repeat a litigant's story at least serves to enhance its credibility. Moreover, it is common for a *capupu* either to extoll his party's virtues or to emphasize whatever grief he may have suffered through his opponent's wrongful behaviour. In short, the principal role of a *capupu* in a Budya process is that of a 'secondant' and character witness to his party, rather than that of a bearer of independent and first-hand evidence in support of his party's case or to refute his opponent's allegations.

Like the principal parties, their *capupus* were given an uninterrupted hearing. Nyamakope, for the plaintiff, dealt mainly with the fact that the young teacher was living in his area away from his immediate kinsmen, that he was but a 'boy' who should not have been summoned to a *mambo*'s courtyard without being supported by a 'father', and that he, Nyamakope, being the *mambo* of the plaintiff's domicile, should have been notified in the first place when Mudzengerere wanted to 'judge' (*kutonga*) him. He said that since he was 'not allowed to appear at Careva' he had agreed that the young man was right to report to the District Commissioner after the receipt of the letter 'which threatened him if he crossed the boundary [of Mudzengerere's territory]'.

The defendant's eldest son dwelt upon the fact that his father was an old man and an important *mambo*, that he had been insulted by a young man 'who is a *mutorwa* (stranger) whom we do not know' and that his father had shown great leniency by not 'fining' (*kuripa*) him. Yet this young man had gone home and complained to Nyamakope, accusing his [Nyamakope's] elder brother so as to distrust him', even going so far as to report to the *ofisi*, asking the District Commissioner 'to send a *mupurisa* (policeman) to arrest my father like a criminal (*munhu wakapara mkaka*)'.

The statements of both *capupus* were duly conveyed to the judges, and the *munyai* announced that 'The people should now speak clearly, one to the other, so that we may know the truth in this matter.' The parties were told to 'keep silent, for you have said all you wished to say, and it is now that others should speak.'

There were a few minutes of obvious hesitation as to who should open the debate; and even a suggestion (promptly turned down by the old *vutonga*) that it might be better to 'rest and see how the beer is'. (A few people left anyway, some of them coming back later.)

Then the first one stood up: '*I am Mudzengerere*, and I say that this boy had no right to speak to me as he did, abusing me by saying that people do not listen to me while they obey their *masubuku* (village headman).'

A young opponent rose from the crowd to meet the challenge. '*I am Katiyu*! The *madumeni* (demonstrators) were mocking the *mambo* and I wanted to tell the truth, for I have eyes to see and ears to listen. Yet I respect the *mambo*, knowing him to be the *mukoma* (elder brother) of *mambo* Nyamakope, who is like my father whom I greatly respect.'

A third one got up, and the other two sat down. '*I am Mudzengerere*, and I say that there were many others, men with wives and children who belong to this place and who know the truth. Why did you, an unmarried one (*jaya*) and a foreigner, tell these lies, trying to make me smaller than my *masabuku*?'

Then the fourth one, a middle-aged man, speaking with a fine smile: '*I am Katiyu*. If I spoke too soon and if I told lies, it was because of my youth and my ignorance. But I did mean to speak only the truth.' He paused a moment. Then, looking straight at Mudzengerere, he quietly added: 'Even you yourself, *mambo*, afterwards told me I had no case [against me]. So why should I now be accused for wanting to be disrespectful [*kushinyira*, lit: to disobey] to you?'

There was a murmur of approval among his audience. But no sooner had he sat down than another jumped up: '*I am Mudzengerere*! So you agree that you went away satisfied from my *dare*. I did not fine you on account of your youthfulness, and yet you complained afterwards, accusing me of harshness!'

'*I am Katiyu*! I was called by you without a father. I went like a child without fear because I had done no wrong, not expecting to be accused at your *dare*. You scolded me severely and threatened me. It was then that I became much afraid, for you are a *mambo* and I am but a little one (*mudiki*). That is why I told Mazengera [his village headman] and Nyamakope.'

'*I am Mudzengerere*! Am I not like a father to you, being an elder of the church which made you a teacher? Surely I had the right to reprimand you, telling you how to speak properly about your *vakuru* (seniors). Like a forgiving father I did not make you pay anything. Yet you complained afterwards, accusing me falsely. I wondered why . . . That is why I wrote you a letter telling you to avoid my boundary.'

'*I am Katiyu*! I agree you are an elder of my church, but my school and the place where I live are not in your *nzwimbo*. I am staying with [i.e., in the area of] *mambo* Nyamakope. He is my father, yet you failed to tell him, making me come without protection. I also greatly feared your letter warning me about your boundary.'

I have condensed the debate. So far, it had disposed of only one point of law: plaintiff's plea that his remarks at the agricultural meeting had not been insulting had apparently been accepted by the audience. But with regard to the defendant's action to summon the young man to his *dare* without notifying his headman (a point of procedure) the debate had been prolonged without being conclusive. The reason probably was that this issue could not very well be isolated from the subsequent course of events, which the plaintiff himself had provoked by his somewhat dramatic reaction to the relatively mild and not unfair ticking off the old headman had given him. Moreover, his going to the 'office', apparently without the prior knowledge of his headman Nyamakope, had invited a good deal of criticism – the proper procedure would have been first to report to his village headman, then to Nyamakope, 'who would then decide what to do'.

Apart from this, there seemed to be a reluctance on the part of the public to come to grips with the real issue: Mudzengerere's letter. Its verbal contents, though severe, would have been a readily accepted subject of debate. Its red ink, however, gave it a mysteriously threatening character, into the implications of which no one seemed anxious to be the first to inquire.

The debate so far had been a strictly orderly *mumanjemanje* performance, a succession of brief and restrained verbal duels. But tension was rising and after the last remark there was some visible excitement. Prodded by a few people with whom he had been sitting, a neatly dressed young man, a teacher himself (and probably a friend of the plaintiff), rose to his feet. After a moment's hesitation he announced in a clear voice:

'*I am Katiyu*, and I'll tell why I went straight to the *ofisi*. It was because of the letter warning me about your boundary. I was like a dog being left in a big forest, having no one to protect me, because you would no longer allow me to see my friends. *I might have been killed already*, and then someone would have to report my death to the *ofisi*. That is the true reason why I went to the *ofisi*.'

The site was buzzing with voices and the *munyai* had to call for silence. 'Let Mudzengerere answer', he called. One of the defendant's sons stood up and moved over to where the public sat.

'*I am Mudzengerere*, and I ask why you are afraid to be killed, as you say you have done wrong to no one. I merely mentioned a boundary to you, but you could still freely cross my country by the big road.'

Excitement now reached a high pitch and several people were on their feet, shouting questions without properly identifying themselves. 'What if I cross the boundary?' 'Who will protect me?' 'Who said I would kill you?' 'Anyone may die anywhere, but why should I be the one to have killed him?' 'Mentioning a boundary is not killing!'

The *munyai*, evidently unable to keep order, looked appealingly to the judges, but Kaukonde seemed to be asleep with his head touching his knees, and Cindenga merely looked around him. The judges were evidently not yet prepared to intervene. Then the tall, slender figure of Nyakanyanga, one of Careva's 'Mountain Keepers' and a regular assessor at the court of Careva, slowly moved from the place on the side where he had been silently listening all the time and went to the fringe area where the public sat. I knew him well, a quiet man of about forty-five who – unlike his younger friend, the 'Son of the Spirit', whose tongue was often too flippant – always bided his time before he spoke. He was the old *vutonga*'s right-hand man. Having heard him often at the court of Careva, I considered him one of the most balanced and skilful adjudicators I had ever met, soft-spoken, lucid, persuasive and, above all, a man of great integrity and moral courage.

Standing among the people he had but to lift his hand to obtain silence. 'We have not been speaking clearly,' he began. 'There has been too much talk about a boundary, and several times mention has been made of the letter written by Mudzengerere, warning Katiyu about this boundary and that he should not cross it but remain in the big road by which the motorcars and trucks go. We have all seen the letter this morning, for it was in Katiyu's hand and even Musasa [the *munyai*] has repeated the words written in it. The boundary and the big road are the things we heard about when the letter was read. No other things were mentioned. Yet we have heard people say that because he received this letter he is afraid of being killed by someone. This is not speaking clearly. There is too much darkness in this matter.'

He paused, looking at the tensely listening crown around him. Then, for the first time acting as a *mumanjemanje* player, he called out:

'I am Katiyu, and I want to ask Mudzengerere why he wrote to me with red ink while it is customary for other people to write with black.'

He did not wait for an answer but went quietly back to his old place, evidently knowing that he had broken the impasse and that people would now debate the one point they had carefully skirted so far. Even before he sat down a young man had taken over his role: *'I am Katiyu*! It was indeed the red ink which made me greatly afraid, for when I read about the boundary it was like seeing blood (*ropa*).'

The eldest son of Mudzengerere again moved to the fringe of the site. '*I am Mudzengerere,* and I do not understand this fear about red ink. There are many different colours of ink and they can all be used for writing. The red one was in the house with the paper and the pen. So it was used for writing the letter.'

'*I am Katiyu*! I hear you had all the things in the house for writing letters. I say you also have black ink. What is the reason why you used the red ink?'

The 'defendant' admitted that there had also been black ink at home, but denied that the red ink had been selected for any particular reason. His reply did not convince the 'plaintiff' however, and the point was pursued by several other questioners. But the 'defendant' did not budge, and it seemed that the debate might well end in a stalemate.

It struck me, however, that the general mood had now noticeably changed in favour of the young plaintiff. In the beginning his behaviour had received a good deal of critical comment, especially from older speakers taking the defendant's part. With one or two exceptions those playing 'plaintiff' had been young men, relatively little versed in the skill of *mumanjemanje*. In spite of their sometimes shrewd questioning they had seldom scored a telling point. Moreover, they were likely to be looked upon as youngsters naturally inclined to support one of their age mates. The defendant, though he himself had skirted the proper rules of procedure, was a senior headman who could better afford taking some liberties in this respect. Broadly speaking, until Nyakanyanga forced a discussion about the red ink the debate had essentially involved the hierarchical premises of traditional authority, values dear to all older people and (on this occasion) never seriously challenged by the younger speakers. Had the debate remained confined to these issues and had the letter, however severe its verbal contents, been written in black ink or pencil, the young teacher, handicapped by age as well as his status as a bachelor (and 'foreigner') and by the evidence of his impetuous behaviour, would probably have stood little chance of winning his case.

But the tide had turned visibly after a man of evident authority had with quiet determination removed the public's inhibition openly to discuss the one question which undoubtedly had occupied everyone's mind: Why *red* ink?

I noticed that the older speakers now playing 'Katiyu' not only outnumbered his young supporters (in fact, only one or two had since risen to ask a question), but that the number of those willing or able to play 'Mudzengerere' had rapidly dwindled.

Mumanjemanje was becoming a rather barren performance because several 'plaintiffs' failed to rouse a counterplayer. Many people kept looking at the defendant, who muttered to himself with his head bent down, and I saw both puzzled anxiety and pity in their faces.

It was the neatly dressed teacher who offered a possible way out to save the old headman's face. 'Perhaps Mudzengerere did not write the letter himself; perhaps he told someone to write about the boundary, and perhaps that other person had a grudge against Katiyu and put in a fearful redness (*cishava*); perhaps Mudzengerere never saw the letter [before it was sent off].'

I saw the old *vutonga*, Kaukonde, suddenly lift his head, looking at Mudzengerere with an expression of hopeful expectancy.

The defendant's eldest son answered.

'It is true, it was I who wrote the letter. But,' he added lamely, 'my father stood next to me telling me what to write.'

There was some sniggering among the younger ones. Kaukonde sighed and his head sank back to his knees. The sound of singing drifted up from the village below. The beer party was evidently in full swing. The people on the rocky site were getting restive and suggestions about 'giving the case to the judges' were heard. But the issue was as yet undecided, and the *munyai* refused to pass the word. The young plaintiff himself wanted to say something, but the *munyai* sharply told him that he had no right to speak yet.

Then Jojo, the 'Son of the Spirit' (who had kept silent since his opening query) went to the *munyai* for a whispered consultation. When he went back to his place he gave me a wink, and I knew that I could expect something out of the ordinary.

The *munyai* briefly consulted the *vutonga*, who nodded approvingly. Then he spoke: 'It is said that the *varungu* (whites) invented the custom of writing, for it was unknown to us before they came. There is a *murungu* present, listening to how we decide our cases. We ask our *murungu* to tell us whether it is a good or a bad thing to write with red ink.'

I was grateful that the manner in which I was involved at least did not make it necessary for me to 'identify' myself with either party, a position which (as Jojo knew well) I would on principle have refused to take. I decided to hedge, however, by saying that there were many occasions when the use of red ink was a harmless thing. Some of my teachers at school, for instance, had the habit of marking my written homework with red or green ink. Some of the young educated ones nodded approval, but one of them retorted: 'Was this not to warn you for having made mistakes?'

'Surely,' I said, 'but this was not a bad warning. It merely said, "Take care of this kind of mistake".'

I then told that I had a typewriter with a black-red ribbon, and, 'I use the red for words I especially want to remember.'

But had I ever written a whole letter in red ink?

I said I could not remember whether I had, as I usually wrote with black or blue ink.

So it was at least unusual for *varungu* to write letters in red ink?

I had to admit that it was not common, but flippantly added that the 'letters' of my bank manager sometimes showed red figures, as a warning that my money was finished.

Was this not dangerous, a threat that I would starve because he, the bank manager, 'refused to give more money for you to buy food, like an unjust father refusing food to his child?'

I tried to explain that the bank manager was not like my father; I was only allowed to use as much of my own money as I had given him to look after.

Now a middle-aged man stood up and asked if I had seen the 'poles with different lights that change colour' in the streets of Salisbury?

I said I knew them and that they were put there to show the people when they could cross the street.

What was the meaning of the light that showed like a bright red eye?

I said it meant 'Stop', you were not allowed to cross.

Was it not a warning of danger?

I agreed that it might certainly be dangerous to disobey the red light, but suggested that the red light, instead of threatening me, kindly warned of possible danger.

My opponent smiled triumphantly.

'Danger! You have all heard it. Even the *varungu* use red when they want to show, "Here is danger".' Nor did he believe that this was 'kindness', for he had seen 'some people being arrested by *mapurisa* for not watching the red.'

In the rumble of approval that rose from the floor, another man shot a question at me. What was the meaning of the red cloth tied to a bundle of long poles on the back of a motor-truck travelling along the road?

I said it was a warning to those travelling behind not to come too near, for the truck might suddenly swerve for something they could not see and the poles might hit them.

Could such a truck with a red cloth even *kill* a person?

I admitted that this had happened to some who had not watched out properly.

'*Cokwadi*, this is the truth!' he shouted, and then summarized: 'Red, meaning danger; danger which you cannot see; and it may even kill a person!'

This decided the issue, and even the co-judge, Cindenga, audibly remarked that Mudzengerere had done 'wrong by writing and sending the red letter'.

The people were now becoming really impatient to see the end of the matter. (One young joker suggested that the quickest way to reach a decision was to take a vote by raising hands, but he was booed.) Some were already leaving in the direction of the merry-making village.

The *munyai* called Katiyu and asked if he wanted to consult his elders before his case was 'given to the judges'.

The young plaintiff withdrew with his headman and a few friends. When they came back a few minutes later, the *munyai* announced, 'The case is now given to Careva.' The message was first conveyed to a younger brother of headman Cindenga, by him to Cindenga himself and by the latter to Kaukonde.

Kaukonde's son, Marikopo (who often acted as a functionary at Careva's court and who had sat with the 'Mountain Keeper' and the 'Son of the Spirit' during the present process), now stood up: 'I am the mouth of my father. Since we are in the territory of Cindenga, they will cut (*kugura*) the case together.'

The two old men had a whispered consultation. Then Kaukonde spoke. He began by saying that Katiyu had 'mentioned things about Mudzengerere, a *mambo*, which he should not have said'. There was a loud protest from the younger section of the audience, and he had to wait until he could continue. 'But Mudzengerere acted very wrongly in the matter of the letter. He should not have done this. For this reason Katiyu shall receive back the five shillings he put down in the *dare* (court), but Mudzengerere's money shall remain in the *dare*.' (The *munyai* promptly took five shillings from the old hat and handed the money to Katiyu.)

He turned to the plaintiff, asking him if he 'agreed', adding: 'You should now tell us if there are other things you want us to do.'

Katiyu, clapping respectfully, said that he was quite satisfied. He did 'not want Mudzengerere to pay me (compensation). I only wanted to know that I have done no wrong so that I may visit my friends again.'

Mudzengerere, addressed in turn, evidently did not agree. He kept muttering furiously about the young people's evident disrespect for their elders. He clearly felt humiliated by this defeat. In fact, he cut such a pathetic figure that someone suggested that Katiyu, having won his case and having stated that he did not want any compensation, might as yet try to 'convince Mudzengerere that he respected him' by offering the old headman a chicken 'which they could eat together as a sign that all is well again'.

It was an obviously sincere but futile effort at reconciliation. Katiyu was prepared to play his part. He offered one shilling, explaining: 'I have no chicken at home, but if the *mambo* will regard this as my chicken, I am willing to give it to him.'

But Mudzengerere refused the gesture, saying he would only be satisfied with the refund of his court fees (i.e., with a reversal of the judgment).

The sun was dipping low and most people were now gathering their belongings in order to leave. So Kaukonde announced: 'The matter is finished.'

There was some deferential clapping of hands, and all except a few hurried into the direction of the village below, where the sounds of laughter, drums and singing voices signified that the beer had been good and plentiful.

I took Kaukonde back with me, as he said he was tired and wanted to go home.

He was silent and looked a bit depressed.

I tried to buoy him up, saying there had been some clear speaking about a difficult matter, and that his judgment in my opinion had been right.

He did not reply, but after a while sighed deeply: 'Ah, these young ones!'

I asked him if Mudzengerere, since he had not 'agreed', would permit Katiyu to visit friends in his area.

The old man looked surprised.

'How could he refuse Katiyu? You have heard what the people said. No harm will come to him, for if he were to die all people will know it is because of Mudzengerere.'

II. ANALYSIS

In analysing this case we should keep in mind that there were some uncommon factors at play which influenced not only normal procedure, the venue and the composition of the adjudicators, but probably also the way in which the latter fulfilled their roles.

The venue

For a start, I doubt if, without the explicit instructions from the District Commissioner, the court of Careva would have been involved in this particular dispute. If not Mudzengerere but any of the other headmen of the 'House of Careva' had been one of the litigants, the old *vutonga* of Careva and his regular counsellors, operating at their customary venue, would have been the obvious tribunal. But Mudzengerere, for reasons I have mentioned earlier, was the one dignitary of Careva's lineage who could not enter Careva without incurring the wrath of the dominant Tribal Spirit. It was, therefore, the accepted practice for him to 'take his cases' instead to chief Mutoko, a practice with which Careva apparently concurred. The District Commissioner, though correctly assuming that the issue was one which a traditional tribunal might handle more satisfactorily than a European court, was not aware of these special circumstances. Both parties being resident within a tribal political unity known as Careva and 'represented' by an officially recognized functionary ('he who wears the emblem'), his instruction that the court of Careva should deal in first instance with the matter was logical from his point of view. The officials of Careva evidently were unwilling to flout an explicit order from the highest district authority, but had to find a different venue in order to solve their own particular problem. Cindenga's being the senior branch of the Careva lineage, his territory offered the most obvious compromise. Mudzengerere was free to come there and, though an acknowledged ward headman within the tribal power structure, could be expected to recognize the senior status of his 'elder brother'. We therefore see how, apart from a spiritual prohibition affecting the defendant, an extraneous factor – the District Commissioner's instruction – considerably influenced the usual procedure. That the change of venue was indeed considered a serious matter is proved by the early query formally raised by the 'Son of the Spirit': why here at Cindenga's and not at Careva? There is no doubt that he knew the answer. But the very fact that it was he, the well-known son of Careva's spirit-medium, who raised the point before the hearing had started, and the highly elaborate and most formally 'transmitted' public explanations which followed, show that this was not a minor technicality to be briefly clarified for the benefit of possibly uninformed and puzzled members of the public.[9]

I have suggested that this was a public declaration (demonstration) to remove any possible doubt that the change of venue might be interpreted as a slight to the authority of Careva, that is, to the *spiritual power* behind this authority. This interpretation is reinforced by the fact that this Spirit is also widely believed to have exceptional powers to provide rain. Not only the Spirit, but also the people, therefore had to be reassured.

A good deal more, however, was involved in this change of venue. The District Commissioner had instructed that the dispute be dealt with by the court of Careva. But we may well ask if it was, in fact, the *dare* of Careva

9. I doubt, moreover, if there were many people who were ignorant about Mudzengerere's particular difficulty as regards his access to Careva's 'own' domain.

which constituted the judicial authority at this *ad hoc* venue? There were two *vatongi* (judges) instead of one: the old *vutonga* of Careva, and Cidenga the 'owner of the area'; it was explicitly stated that these two would 'sit together', sharing the power of giving judgment. *Vutonga* Kaukonde was readily assumed to be the senior judge, but he nevertheless found it necessary, before he pronounced judgment, to stress again (his son speaking on his behalf) that he and Cindenga were 'cutting the case together'. To speak here of a recognition of the latter's 'territorial jurisdiction' would be wrong, for in this case Cindenga had no such powers, as neither the defendant nor the plaintiff resided in his area and the dispute, moreover, had occurred outside his boundaries. On the other hand, to involve Cindenga as co-judge was not a mere courtesy on Kaukonde's part, but a clear and *necessary* recognition of the fact that, though he was the 'supreme judge' in the political entity constituted by the House of Careva, he might, if acting solely, be infringing the territorial integrity and internal authority of one of its component units. Cindenga's presence as co-judge would forestall any apprehension that the court of Careva, through circumstances compelled to operate away from its home base, might ignore or usurp the authority of the 'owner of the *nzwimbo* (area)'.[10] One might even suggest that Kaukonde, the *vutonga* 'appointed by the Spirit' to act at the Careva cult centre itself, felt uncertain about his own authority now he had to operate off-base, and, for this reason too, felt he needed Cindenga's support. (He certainly seemed ill at ease, and his performance, especially when he gave judgment, lacked the quiet assurance he normally displayed.) But this is a matter of speculation, for I failed to discuss it with him.

There is other evidence to indicate that it actually was *not* the 'court of Careva' which adjudicated this case. Though some of its principal officials were in fact present, they were sitting, so to speak, on the sideline, some distance away from their *vutonga,* instead of closely flanking him as they normally did. Except for the *munyai,* who had done most of the preliminary work as a messenger and go-between and thus was the obvious person to act as principal 'channel of communication' between judges, parties and public, these Careva functionaries were unusually inactive and had intervened only once or twice when the process seemed to have reached an impasse – but this was something any determined member of the public could have done.

10. In this respect also note that Mudzengerere's corroboration of the *munyai*'s explanation for the choice of site was first addressed to the headman of the village which used it as threshing floor.

The most likely conclusion to be drawn from all these observations appears to be the following. It was a situation without precedent: Cindenga was the local judicial authority but had no jurisdiction in this particular case, while Kaukonde did have jurisdiction but could not adjudicate the matter at his normal *dare* and in the locality where his authority was beyond question. Though they were acknowledged judicial experts they did not, when the meeting convened, constitute a *recognized* judicial forum. The formal and lengthy explications as regards venue and Cindenga's co-adjudicatorship should, therefore, not be interpreted as an elaborate and largely superfluous piece of public information, but as a necessary means of establishing this *ad hoc* forum as a publicly recognized judicial authority competent to deal with the dispute. Only after this was accomplished (no objections were raised) could the actual process begin by requesting the litigants to deposit their 'judging-fees'.

Procedure

In spite of some unusual features the litigation itself clearly exhibited the three distinct phases which are characteristic of the Shona judicial process: the formal opening phase during which both parties (here, each with his 'principal witness') are given an uninterrupted hearing and have their accounts duly transmitted (that is, repeated) to the presiding adjudicating officer by the official intermediary; the more or less informal phase of public participation in the inquiry (here, largely by means of the method of *mumanjemanje*); the concluding formal phase when the case is 'given back' to official judicial functionaries for summary and judgment.

About the first phase I have little to add. That the *munyai*, 'messenger', also played the role as intermediary (inter-communicator) is not unusual. The latter function is undoubtedly the more important one in the judicial process, though the Budya do not normally give it a distinctive term. If another happens to have carried out the actual summons he is given a few shillings for his footwork (*tsoka*, 'feet'), in which case the intermediary gets a share of the court fees. Separate (token) payments like the Hera *gwiro* ('climbing') and *ruvundzo* ('asking') have here merged into one '*rutonga*' ('judging') to be deposited by both parties before the hearing can start. The term itself implies that the payment is visible evidence of the payer's willingness to submit to the adjudicating process or, rather, that he recognizes the jurisdiction of the tribunal without, however, necessarily having to accept its judgment as a final verdict if there is a higher court he can appeal to. But he does at any rate forfeit his *rutonga* if the judgment goes against him.

The fact that of each party only one 'principal witness' is heard (and not cross-examined) during the formal opening phase and that, as I have stated before, this one largely corroborates his party's testimony without revealing new evidence, makes us ask how other witnesses are introduced to provide further evidence, should this be required. The answer is that the names of likely witnesses are usually mentioned by both sides during the lengthy opening addresses and that these persons may be called upon to testify during the second, 'public', stage of the inquiry. In the *mumanjemanje* procedure this may be formulated like: '*I am* . . . and I ask that (name of witness) should tell me whether it it true that . . .'; or '*I am* . . . and I say this cannot be true because I heard X telling Y that he saw . . .' This sort of challenge usually produces the desired result,, in that the speaker rouses an opponent (or supporter) who can shed more light on the matter. In this way *mumanjemanje* participants do not merely act as cross-examiners but also as witnesses with regard to disputed facts. Strictly speaking, the role-identification in *mumanjemanje* would preclude a speaker from giving an eye-witness account of something the litigant himself could not possibly have seen, but the game is not always played quite so strictly and this kind of slip is often overlooked. Yet the really skilful actors may on such occasions refer to themselves in the third person. (For instance, Jojo: 'I am . . . and I say that Jojo saw [what happened] and he says that . . .')

In Budya procedure *mumanjemanje* normally is left largely to members of the public. There is nothing, however, to prevent a court official, except the presiding *mutongi*, from participating. In such an event, however, he should literally 'change places' and speak from among the public ranks, as a visible and unmistakable indication of his temporary change of role. In the case I have described, Mountain Keeper Nyakanyanga gave a demonstration of this when he made his intervention. (Also Mudzengerere's son and 'principal witness' left his father's side to conduct a *mumanjemanje*-style argument.)

Usually, however, court officials, including the presiding *mutongi*, retain their places because they are entitled to ask questions or give opinions without playing 'defendant' or 'plaintiff' in order to clear up any obscure point. 'Question-time' need not, therefore, be conducted entirely by way of *mumanjemanje*. If there are skilful and well-informed debators at hand *mumanjemanje* may run its own course without any intervention from the side of the officials until the *munyai* considers that the time has come to 'give the case back' to the adjudicators. But it is the duty of the court officials to supervise the debate and to ensure that sufficient 'clarity' is reached before they resume formal control. If the debate remains inconclusive, in that there does not emerge a clearly predominant public opinion as regards the main issues of the dispute, they take a hand in the matter by posing questions or expressing views themselves. If in spite of their efforts a stalemate seems likely because public opinion remains fairly equally divided (this, too, means 'no clarity'), question time may be temporarily suspended and the parties advised to withdraw, each with his immediate following, for a private consultation (*kusungana*, to tie together). Quite often this results in a formal announcement of a compromise proposal which, if it is not readily acceptable to the opposing party, becomes the subject of a resumed *mumanjemanje* performance. Should such an intermezzo yield no results, it will be the adjudicators who get into a huddle to decide upon one of three possible courses:

a. They can announce that the case has 'defeated' them (*kukunda*; or *kukurira*, to 'outgrow'), in which event both parties ought to get a refund of their deposited 'judging fees' and are expected either to come to a mutually negotiated settlement or (more likely) to go to a higher tribunal;
b. They may postpone the continuation of the hearing until a subsequent session. I have seen this happen when the issue seemed to hinge on the testimony of some absent witness, but also after a particularly heated debate when the adjudicators apparently hoped that a 'cooling-off period' might lay the storm of conflicting emotions. In such an event the fees 'remain in the *dare*', that is, retain their function when the hearing is resumed;
c. The adjudicators may, in spite of evident public controversy, decide 'to cut the case'.

In my experience the last course is under these circumstances seldom taken at the intermediate level of tribal jurisdiction (i.e., tribal ward), especially if the appropriate chief's court is fairly accessible. But I also found that even a conscientiously operating chief's court seemed reluctant to lay down a decision in the face of a clearly divided public opinion. One reason for this reluctance may be ascribed to the fact that any chief knew that not he but the District Commissioner was the highest local judicial authority to whom a troublesome matter could be referred.[11] Yet I doubt if this is the main reason, for I noted that it was likely to be the less capable, often younger

11. The Rhodesian structure of African jurisdiction was considerably changed by the *African Law and Tribal Courts Act of 1969*, which among other things strengthened the jurisdiction of recognized tribal courts, modified the powers of the District Commissioner and made provision for the institution of regional tribal appeal courts consisting of chiefs' panels.

and impatient, chiefs who were rather inclined to 'lay down the law' under such circumstances. But their peremptory behaviour did not enhance their public esteem and they seemed to have difficulty in exerting their authority generally, with the result (though I did not keep an exact tally) that there were many appeals from their decisions to district headquarters.

Though the court of Careva did not officially rank as a chief's court, its peculiar position and the ability of its functionaries gave it a measure of authority matched by but few chiefs' courts that I attended. Its assessors and the old *vutonga* were certainly not afraid to upbraid people when necessary. Yet I cannot recall any occasion when, *in their summary and judgment*, they either went against prevailing public opinion or pronounced judgment before an initially clearly divided public had veered towards a substantial measure of consensus.

It was sensitively proud of its high reputation and, in fact, people rarely appealed against its judgments.[12] Its main strength lay in the ability of its functionaries to listen well and observe sharply, to guide arguments subtly towards those facts and aspects (legal and social) that really mattered. During the vital stage of public debate they did not so much argue or 'state the rule', but rather posed the kind of question that would elicit the 'right' response from their audience – 'If a person has done all these things, would he not be right to expect . . .?': 'If a person says he made a serious proposal, but he failed to . . . would not the person listening to him think this was just idle talk?'

There is a subtle persuasiveness in this method, but it takes time and patience, especially in relation to the *mumanjemanje* procedure which invites opposition and argument. The members of the community are not merely permitted to voice an opinion; they are directly and sometimes provocatively involved. The element of 'stage-play' makes this involvement more attractive, not least because the actors may freely change sides and thereby avoid giving the impression that they are personally committed to one party or the other (something which might turn a dispute between two litigating parties into a cleavage between considerably larger factions of the community). At the same time their critical faculties are aroused, which may

12. During my ten months' stay in the area I knew of only one such case, in which the District Commissioner (wrongly, in my opinion) had reversed its judgment. At the next session the court of Careva opened with a public announcement stating that its own judgment had been right 'according to the laws as our people know them' and warning that 'those who seem to prefer whitemen's law should not come here to waste our time, but go straight to the District Commissioner, whose decision had made us like fools in the eyes of our children.'

both widen and deepen the enquiry until it becomes focused upon a few aspects which appear crucial in the public mind and upon which a large measure of consensus should be reached. This is the result at which the court officials aim and towards which they direct their interplay with public opinion. The reason is obvious for, having reached this aim, they can resume formal control of the proceedings and exert their judicial authority with the knowledge that they have the necessary public support.

The case is then 'given back' to them, and the manner in which they act changes. Usually at least one assessor now addresses the presiding judge, giving a systematic summary of the main aspects of the dispute. This time he no longer poses the kind of cautiously framed questions which, during the previous stage, were meant to elicit a clear public response; he *states* his findings, carefully, sometimes bluntly, stressing the 'right' point of view (thereby almost invariably reflecting the prevailing opinion which emerged from the *mumanjemanje* debate). This may, and sometimes does, include references to general principles of reasonable and lawful conduct applicable to the case. Quite often, however, such general references are omitted and he confines himself to the actual behaviour of the litigants, stating that X 'was wrong' in having acted thus or that Y 'did the right thing' when he acted as he did. In such a case the actions referred to are presumed to be self-evident illustrations of a violation of or adherence to the principle or 'rule' involved. In other words, although an assessor will tell you that when summing up a case he 'explains the law to show what was wrong', he actually does not necessarily refer explicitly to recognized abstract norms when he deals with the specific issues of the dispute he is summing up. One might suggest that there is no need for him to cast his summary within a normative frame of reference, for is he not addressing the judge, who ought to know the law? But then we misinterpret the dual nature of his task, for his words are undoubtedly also meant for public consumption. What he presents to the judge is a brief and coherent account of the most important facts, views and sentiments distilled from an often far from coherent inquiry. It has to be a balanced and unbiased account, striking a chord of approval among his critically listening audience. The people are not supposed to interrupt him, but they seldom fail to nod, shake their heads, grunt or in some other noticeable way show when they agree or disagree with him. If, as often happens, some points of law or fact have been sharply debated, he will undoubtedly present these in his summary together with other evidently relevant aspects. In this way his summary is both descriptive and interpretative. It is, in fact, a pretty clear precursor of the judgment itself, at least as far as questions of guilt or liability are concerned.

It is not uncommon, especially in complex cases, that a second assessor also addresses the presiding judge, reinforcing his colleague's findings or stressing points which in his opinion the latter should have mentioned.

The presiding *mutongi* has the last word, for he must 'cut' the case by giving the final verdict. This involves two aspects which are also distinctive in a Western law system. First, the question of guilt or liabililty (in Shona: *mhoswa*) must be settled. Then there is the question of a possible punishment ('sentence'), award or compensation (in Shona, *muripo*, 'payment', covers both 'fine' and 'compensation').

Considering all that has preceded the judgment, the outcome in respect of the guilt question is usually highly predictable, in the sense that it is unlikely to go against the party who has gained predominant public support in the course of the process. Yet even this part of the judgment involves a good deal more than stating that one party is right and the other wrong. He should at least tell them why he thinks so. This may sound (and probably often is) fairly easy because, if the judge has listened attentively and if his assistants have done their work properly, he should have a pretty good idea in whose favour the balance of justice should be tipped, and why. Many if not most cases, however, come before him after a fairly long history in which a party, feeling aggrieved, has repeatedly tried to find redress – by direct negotiation with the other party, by putting the matter before their village headman if both belong to the same village or before their headmen if they are from different villages within the same tribal ward. Moreover, daily life (and therefore, also, conflict) in a tribal community for the most part takes place among people that know each other well and entertain certain relationships with and attitudes towards one another. Most disputes must, therefore, be seen within their particular social context and be evaluated against a normative background of certain patterns of conduct which are considered appropriate and reasonable in the kind of relationship obtaining between the disputants.

The Shona, in common with most other tribal folk, believe in reasonableness and the principle of give-and-take in community life. They also have a fine sense of human dignity and sensitively react to anything that, in their own view, might result in a loss of face or self-esteem. Apart from this they are, on the whole, extroverts, inclined to talk things out rather than secretly harbour their grudges. Most 'matters' (*nyaya, ndava*) are therefore first discussed in the intimate circle of family elders on both sides or, with little formality except due courtesy, in the presence of the village headman or headmen concerned. The first aim is amicable mutual settlement (*kuenzanisa*, to arrange or straighten out together). But if those efforts are not successful, the sense of grievance and hurt pride may become more acute and the need for 'justice' more keenly felt. But justice can now only be obtained at a higher level, before a formal tribunal and in the presence of a much wider public. The emotional 'stakes' are now likely to be much higher, for both parties hate losing face publicly. In fact, the mere aim of obtaining a favourable public verdict in respect of the 'guilt' issue may now be more important than the prospect of gaining (or the fear of losing) material value. Court and public know this. They also know from experience that few quarrels reaching formal litigation can at his stage be confined any longer to a single wrongful act committed by only one of the parties. In other words, the dispute now before them is more like a chain linking a succession of actions and reactions in which, though one party may on balance be considered clearly more blameworthy than the other, neither is likely to have been entirely blameless. Therefore the judicial inquiry, especially during its public phase, is directed not only towards establishing the facts of the parties' right or wrong conduct, but at least as much towards finding the motivations for their actions. Fact-finding and motivation-finding are the indivisible twin components of this search for 'clarity', and in the final picture neither party is likely to emerge in the unblemished white of righteousness or the absolute black of unmitigated wrong. The picture is shaded, but more heavily on the one side than on the other.

A good judgment should present this kind of picture, with its shades of right and wrong, and of reasonable and unreasonable conduct, drawn with a firm hand. The Shona expect from their judges that they 'listen well', and the most damning opinion I have heard about a few of them was that 'They listen only to the plaintiff.'

A good judge should, however, also 'tell the people how to act rightly', and he is therefore expected to correct the wrongful aspects of a party's conduct by referring to accepted norms or to specific examples of right behaviour and to reprimand him or even threaten him should he persist in doing wrong.

If we now return to Kaukonde's judgment on the issue of right and wrong in the case under review we may well think that he did not fully measure up to what would normally have been expected of him. (I admit that I myself was rather surprised at the brevity of his judgment, though I knew him as a man of few words.) Yet, in his very brief verdict he did meet three important requirements:

a. He drew attention to and expressed his opinion about the two main incidents which had provoked this formal trial: the plaintiff's remarks at the agricultural demonstration meeting and the defendant's letter;

b. By stating that both parties had acted wrongly he carefully avoided giving a wholly one-sided judgment, thereby offering at least some solace to the party probably most sensitive to a loss of face;
c. By neatly distinguishing the plaintiff's (implicitly) 'wrong' conduct and the defendant's 'very wrong' conduct, he clearly tipped the balance of his judgment in favour of the former party and in conformity with the final trend of considered public opinion.

The *vutonga* neither gave nor tried to give any further explication. He may have felt, as I did myself, that under the circumstances there was no need for this and that, moreover, the people were eager to leave.

He sufficed with asking the parties the question normally asked at this stage of the verdict: 'Do you agree?' This question has a dual purpose. It is a means of verifying whether the parties are prepared to accept the first part of the verdict, that is, the decision as to right and wrong. If both agree, the court can with some confidence proceed towards the second issue on which, if necessary, it also has to pronounce a verdict, i.e., some 'sanction' in the form of punishment or award. In the present case the plaintiff (asked first) agreed, but the defendant did not. Normally such a disagreement places the court in a situation similar to the one I have described above; it must decide whether to proceed (and if so how?) or to admit 'defeat'. However, knowing not only that it had the backing of a clearly expressed public opinion, but probably also sensing that the plaintiff did not intend to press for damages (a matter which might well have provoked further disagreement), the court did not take the defendant's 'refusal' (*kuramba*) seriously. Considering the man's senior status his muttered protests were probably regarded more as an understandable expression of wounded pride than of an outraged sense of injustice. (In fact, he subsequently made no effort to appeal against the judgment, nor tried to resist the young plaintiff's access to his area.) The important point is that the court did not, after its decision as regards right and wrong, itself proceed to award a suitable form of compensation to the successful plaintiff, but first asked the latter what else he wanted the court to do for him. Here the rules of procedure clearly show that the questions of guilt and of award are separate issues requiring separate decisions. Moreover, as regards the second decision the court declined to express its own views but invited the successful party to make a specific proposal. It would be wrong to infer from the present case that the court was prompted to do so because the plaintiff had not, so far, given a clear indication of *whether* he intended to claim some form of compensation. For it is quite customary for a Shona court to act likewise also in cases in which an aggrieved party has from the outset clearly indicated that he expects some form of material recompense. In some types of misdeeds, like seduction and unlawful impregnation, there are locally more or less standard rates of compensation, and a plaintiff need not necessarily specify the amount when he presents his claim. In other cases the amount of compensation will largely depend on the nature of the injury or ascertained material value of the loss sustained. The plaintiff's *initial* plea, though giving a detailed account of his losses, usually refrains from turning this into a specified claim for recompense. ('So you see that I have suffered greatly.') His tale still lies in the disputed field of 'evidence'. It has, like all other testimony, a bearing on the verdict, but it usually does not (yet) constitute a claim for a *specific* award. It is, therefore, common to hear an aggrieved party end his tale with a much more general appeal: 'These are my words, what can I do? I ask the court to help me.'

And indeed, the issue is then still in doubt. The other party has yet to speak; other evidence will be forthcoming and weighed, some of it debunking the plaintiff's stated loss, or mitigating the circumstances under which he sustained injury, or making him at least partly responsible for the alleged offence or trespass. We may argue that, by prematurely specifying what amount he wishes the court to award him, the plaintiff unduly exposes himself to the risk of having to 'back down' later (and thereby to lose face) when a much smaller award is granted. For this part of the verdict, too, may be subject to public deliberation, of finding out what should, considering all circumstances, be a reasonable and bilaterally acceptable award. Therefore not only the court, but also both parties, should 'listen well'.

After the plaintiff has been given a favourable verdict on the 'guilt' question, however, he becomes *muridzi wemhoswa*, the 'owner of the case'. The term implies that he is now publicly invested with a certain power over his adversary and that the court is in principle prepared to support a claim for compensation. But the same tribunal (public, plus judicial functionaries) that has granted him this position after a painstaking and balanced inquiry is not likely to endorse exorbitant demands. It is prepared to support a reasonable recompense for personal injury or loss of property; it has little liking for a vengeful claim. I have seen many a *muridzi wemhoswa*, flushed with a sense of victory, losing all sympathy and being sternly berated because of his excessive demands. 'Having defeated [or outwitted] a person at the *dare* is no reason for trying to kill him [with an exorbitant claim] afterwards.'

In Katiyu's case there had been no question of material loss and, considering his insignificant social status (being both a 'foreigner' and an unmarried young man), the humiliation he suffered at the hands of the irate headman would not be taken too seriously by the older section of the public. Yet (I was later told) the demand for a goat or two on account of his having been 'threatened with death' would have received the support of the court. (Whether the defendant would have paid up was a matter on which my informants dared not speculate.) Acting with a wisdom beyond his years (if not actually prompted to do so by his advisers) he declared that he was satisfied to know that he had done no wrong and so would be able again to visit his friends; he did not want the old defendant to pay him.

It would have been normal practice for a Shona court publicly to repeat such a declaration. This would serve the dual purpose of lending authoritative affirmation to the plaintiff's own expressed intention not to seek any further compensation (an effective estoppel, should he later wish to change his mind) and of adopting his statement as the court's own decision. Kaukonde omitted to do this (possibly because the abortive reconciliation effort intervened) and merely ended the session by declaring that the matter was 'finished'. A stickler for rules of procedure might have faulted the old *vutonga* for this omission. I raised the point as a matter of curiosity with Mountain Keeper Nyakanyanga a few days later. His response is worth recording. 'It is true that the *vutonga* failed in not repeating Katiyu's words. But it does not matter, for surely no one was confused about the way the case was judged.' It sounded like a gentle rebuke, an appeal not to split hairs with regard to procedural technicalities when the cause of justice had been conscientiously and openly served in a manner fully understood by people of common sense. Some of our Western judicial officers might well take this to heart.

Conciliatory aims and formal acts of reconciliation

In a recent publication van Velsen charges the 'majority of writers' on African law (myself included) with overconcentrating on the conciliatory aspects of African courts and tending to 'ignore the judges' task of applying laws' (1969: 144). He concurs with Epstein's and Gluckman's views that 'although reconciliation is an important value, it is not an "ultimate, almost mystical, value" of African courts to which legal norms are sacrificed.'

He finds that, in the frequent comparisons between the characteristics of Western and African judicial process, there has been a tendency to stress the former's 'justice by decree' and the latter's 'justice by agreement of persuasion' aimed at maintaining social harmony, and to present these as 'mutually exclusive alternatives' without explicitly acknowledging that in Western courts (especially the lower ones), too, compromise and reconciliation are often deliberately sought; and that African courts (especially the higher ones?) are certainly not invariably so much preoccupied with reconciling parties and restoring social equilibrium as to prevent them, if necessary, from giving judgments and enforcing legal norms without the parties' concurrence.

I subscribe to these views, with some reservations. For I have indeed witnessed some tribal judicial processes in which a recognized right and clearly acknowledged legal rule was 'sacrificed' in favour of an amicable settlement with the concurrence of all present. The court in these cases openly admitted that the decision was against 'our laws as we know them' (and therefore should not be regarded as precedent), but under the circumstances was better than the almost certain prospect of serious trouble.

I also doubt whether I have been guilty of 'ignoring the judges' task of applying laws', though Shona judges, in common with many of their colleagues elsewhere in Africa, often do not *overtly* refer to formulated rules of law but prefer to render their arguments and judgments in more homely terms expressing approval of right and condemnation of wrong ways of social conduct. Nor do I think the statement which van Velsen (*ibid.*) quotes from an early (1950) paper of mine[13] that Shona chiefs 'would settle rather than decide, appease and reconcile rather than enforce' would warrant the implied assumption that I meant to present 'mutually exclusive alternatives'. Shona courts are faced with these choices, and those (especially the lower ones) that take their task seriously evidently prefer the former of these alternatives and often, as I have shown, take great pains and patience to achieve this aim. I believe this is largely due to the nature of the community in which they live (a prevalence of 'multiplex relationships' – Gluckman's term) and the fact that they are not professional judges but like other members very much involved in other community activities which depend on mutual goodwill and co-operation among participants. The people look to them to preserve or restore harmony (and are prepared to add their bit) and – in Nader's terms[14] – 'to make the balance' rather than to present the kind of 'zero-sum (win or lose)' judgment which, as I have explained above, is likely to leave one party (if not a part of public at large) with the grudge that the scales of justice did not sufficiently register the weight of his own grievance. The court's own authority therefore largely depends on its ability and patient efforts to make its judgments acceptable to parties and

13. Included in this volume; *cf.* p. 4 above.
14. Nader, 1969: 69ff.

public. My reference, in the paper quoted by van Velsen, to the summary disposal of cases ('concise interpretation of the relevant points of law and snappy judgments') by some Shona chiefs, which I called an 'innovation rather than renovation' of Shona tribal process, was aimed precisely at those (government-subsidized) chiefs who were inclined to pronounce judgment – including the amount fined or awarded as compensation – without first sounding out the parties or public opinion. They lacked the prized ability 'to listen well' and were not very highly regarded by the people. (Van Velsen doubted the validity of this observation, but he misinterpreted my statement as implying that in traditional procedure *no* legal interpretation takes place.)

Van Velsen states (p. 144) that 'in general, writers identify reconciliation with the court's decision' but fail to recognize that a court actually (usually or always?) makes more than one decision. He himself distinguishes two: first, 'as to relevant facts and the appropriate legal rules to be applied (this is the judgment or verdict)' and subsequently, 'as to the appropriate sanction for the judgment (this is the award or sentence)'. Without going into the question of whether in ordinary or technical English usage these terms do not often have at least partly overlapping connotations[16] and may, therefore, miss the sharp distinctions which he seeks to introduce, the essence of his remarks is clear and, I think, valid. From both cases described *in extenso* in this volume, it is clear that in Shona procedure, too, questions as to guilt and possible fine or compensation are treated as two distinct issues requiring separate decisions (though they may or may not be pronounced at the same time). Yet the concept of 'judgment' (*rutongo, mutongero*) – the verb construction *kutonga* (or *kugura*) *mhoswa*, to judge, decide or 'cut' lawsuits, is more common usage – includes the levying, if any, of a 'fine' or 'award' (both '*muripo*', payment). For instance, to the question, 'How was the case judged? (– *tongewa*, passive voice)', the answer is likely to be, 'He was made to pay (*ripidza*)' – a response which would not be uncommon also in Western society. The Shona response, however, implies that the parties *did* concur (grudgingly or not). If this had not been so, the answer normally was that the litigant(s) had 'refused' (*wakaramba*), and the court's decision – if it had pronounced any, for a lower court would hesitate to do so in the face of sustained disagreement – would normally not

15. 1969: 145.

16. *Cf.* Osborn, P. G. *A Concise Law Dictionary* (5th ed. 1964); Shorter Oxford *Dictionary* (3rd rev. ed. 1964). Even a seasoned lawyer and impeccable writer like Judge Cardozo on occasion used 'judgment' and 'sentence' as interchangeable concepts (e.g., 1921: 11).

be volunteered, being considered of little consequence because the matter was not 'finished' (*pedza*).

In short, reconciliation, in the sense of mutual agreement, concurrence, settlement (with or without *muripo*) is so readily subsumed under the idea of a 'satisfying' judgment (i.e., one that will be voluntarily adhered to) that, in Shona eyes, this does not constitute a special feature. It is something of common sense and social realism, and they see nothing mystical in it.

However, when they do refer to 'reconciliation' they mean something more specific: a distinct, unequivocal, overt, shared or reciprocal *act*, which dramatizes the end of the 'hatred' between two parties which had threatened social peace and unity and the resumption of their friendly relationship as a solvent of social poison. For this sort of act, common terms like *-bvumirana, -tenderana* (agreeing together) or *-enzanisa* (repair, settle, straighten out) are not explicit enough, and words based on (causative) verbs like – *farinanisa*, – *onanisa*, – *dzoredza*, are used to indicate its purpose of making estranged parties 'live well together', 'see each other' or 'return to each other' again. Depending upon the severity of the breach that has to be repaired or the importance attached to the relationship to be healed, such institutionalized acts of reconciliation may range from the simple offer *and* acceptance of a token payment (accompanied by appropriate statements of mutual goodwill) to taking snuff together or eating specially prepared food (preferably meat) together. In fact, the most common expression for reconciliation in this explicit sense is 'sharing ('cutting') meat together', *kucekana nyama.*

Such *acts* of reconciliation may take place whether or not *muripo* is part of the court's judgment. More importantly, they are *not* subsumed under the concept of *muripo,* a term which most clearly represents what van Velsen distinguishes as the court's (second) decision 'as to the appropriate sanction' (award or sentence). Nor need they always take place in court as part of the judicial process itself, for they are sometimes carried out at any suitable place and time after the court has formally 'ended the case'; and indeed it is not uncommon for this kind of reconciliation to be effected without prior recourse to formal litigation.

The distinction that I have emphasized between a court's conciliatory aims (which are not the monopoly of the African judicial process nor its invariable practice) and overt, institutionalized acts of reconciliation which may sometimes result from its efforts to satisfy litigants and preserve the peace, clearly raises a number of points which merit further consideration.

I mention only two. First, I much doubt if such acts of reconciliation, even where they do take place in the course of a (formal) judicial process, can be construed strictly as a legal sanction. Like the moral command, 'Love thy neighbour', they cannot be effectuated without the voluntary co-operation and exercise of free will of the parties concerned, for in Shona society they are presumed to express an inner conviction which cannot be imposed by others. Unlike the imposition of a punishment, or a restitution of a loss sustained or a compensation for an injury suffered, they cannot really be *enforced.* Considerable pressure may be exerted upon the parties by public and court alike to become thus reconciled, but if they refuse to co-operate they cannot be forced.

In the case of the Troublesome Father public pressure was more sustained and vociferous than in the case of the Irate Headman. In the former case the defendant yielded; in the latter case he did not. Yet it would be wrong to deduce from this that the Shona themselves believe that the public's pressure could constitute the overriding power of enforcement. In the former case, Swikepi the father (a most authoritarian character) had without much resistance obeyed headman Capanduka's order that he should leave the area because he knew that he could be forcibly expelled. Yet he strenuously resisted strong pressure before he finally agreed to a recognized act of reconciliation, because he knew that this was a kind of sanction which could not be enforced upon him against his will. When he did yield, his own volition (genuine, for he was visibly moved), and not public pressure, was the overriding force.

This takes me to the second point I wish to raise. As regards the conciliatory aims and efforts to achieve a 'settlement' and to persuade litigants to 'agree' to judgments, which so often (but certainly not always) characterize the operation of African and other courts, I likewise subscribe to Gluckman's statement that these are not 'an ultimate, almost mystical, value' in African judicial process. I suggest, however, that the specific *acts* of reconciliation which I have distinguished and which are widely accepted by the Shona as part of their formal and informal judicial process, are not devoid of an element of mystical consideration. In fact, I believe this may be one reason for the comparative paucity of formal cases in which they are actually performed.

In the remote Sabi area (Hera territory) I suggested to some elders that it should be a fairly easy matter for people to conceal their enmity and to pretend to be friends again by publicly sharing snuff or meat. They looked shocked and bluntly asserted that this was 'impossible' (*hazwibviri*), for a person would 'fear to be poisoned' by the other, and poison was like *kuroya* (sorcery). The inference is clear. Unless you yourself are genuinely convinced of the other's goodwill, you are not prepared to run the risk of becoming a victim of a cleverly disguised act of vengeance. On the other hand, if you do commit yourself to such an act after having been clearly estranged it is like a solemn public declaration of having forgiven the other and a promise again to give and accept friendship. The Irate Headman Mudzengerere evidently was not prepared to go that far, so he refused to accept teacher Katiyu's offer of a token 'chicken'. (Since it was actually offered as 'evidence', *cioneso,* of the young man's true respect for him, he evidently was not convinced of that either.)

The relationship in the earlier case between father and son continuing to live in the same neighbourhood was, in Gluckman's phrase (1955: 78) one 'which it is valuable to preserve'. Hence their overt reconciliation became 'one of the main aims' of the adjudicating body. The relationship between teacher and headman, living some distance apart in separate tribal wards, was of little consequence socially and the suggestion of their being reconciled was not seriously supported by either the public or the court officials.

Summarizing this section, I would say that these are two illustrations (both at an intermediate level of the Shona hierarchy of adjudication) of my general impression that conciliatory aims and efforts to 'make the balance' are more evident when the parties live close together and the restoration of relations between them would serve the peace in their neighbourhood. Hence conciliatory efforts were less conspicuous at the highest (chief's) level of tribal jurisdiction, removed from and therefore less sensitive to the scene of social reality. (At this level, too, there would be less 'play' for an intimately involved public audience.) Such efforts would be negligible in disputes involving comparative strangers unlikely to face each other again. Moreover, if the cause of dispute was serious enough to warrant a heavy punishment, such a case would much sooner be submitted to the highest tribal authority, if not to the District Commissioner's court. And, finally, I found less evidence of reconciliation (in both senses I have distinguished) in more 'advanced' tribal areas and communities than in more 'backward' ones and again less in courts operating in a 'modern' way (with furnished courtroom and scribe but little patience with public participation) than at the traditional *dare* with both functionaries and people squatting in lively discussion under a shady tree in summer, and on a sunny rock in wintertime.

Marriage, bridewealth and women in an African society*

Preface

This paper comprises a series of four lunch-hour lectures which the National Affairs Association in Salisbury invited me to give in the second half of 1951. They have later been repeated, in substantially the same form, in Bulawayo and elsewhere. They are based on my field research in Mashonaland under the auspices of the Rhodes-Livingstone Institute, the Central African research institute to which I was attached as a Beit Research Fellow.

The very fact that they are now being published by a scientific institution (and not by a layman's organization as originally planned) has accentuated a problem already keenly felt during the initial preparation of these lectures: how to turn a technical and often complicated subject into a popular account without sacrifying scientific accuracy and the need for factual verification. Each of these lectures had to be delivered in the short space of thirty-five minutes. This itself drastically limited the number of aspects which could be discussed under each heading, with the result that a good deal of what, from a scientific point of view, would have been imperative had to be left out, while the choice of aspects included inevitably became arbitrary.

A similar choice had to be made between, on the one hand, a generalized treatment which would give a lay audience the widest possible grasp of the principal issues involved and, on the other, a detailed, comparative analysis in a restricted field, which would show up the element of variety in custom and behaviour, but would also tend to obscure the importance of a broad frame of similarity. For example, I found it highly desirable that the audience should understand that an institution like bridewealth is not an isolated phenomenon, but that it is closely related to the basic principles of kinship and social organization and that it has a profound bearing on such aspects as family solidarity and the position of women in African society. By concentrating on one tribal group I could devote sufficient time to

* 1951/53 – see also *Postscript*, p. 86 f.

making this relationship clear and thereby stress the vital importance of an aspect so commonly overlooked by the general public. I could, moreover, do this in a generalized style, because the pattern of the various Shona tribes is fairly uniform. If, on the other hand, I had included other tribes in this exposition, for instance the Rhodesian Ndebele, I should have pointed out, first, that the Ndebele kinship pattern differs significantly from that of the Shona; secondly, how this affects the operation of the bridewealth system in Ndebele society and influences the position of women in a somewhat different manner; and thirdly, that, in spite of these differences my basic argument, that bridewealth fulfils an essential and honourable function and that it is closely related to other fundamental aspects of patrilineal African society, remains unaffected.

To avoid possible confusion and tedium, and to save time, I therefore stuck to one tribal group, but warned the public against the danger of sweeping generalizations.

When it came to editing these talks for publication the choice seemed to lie between two widely different aims: was this going to be a contribution to anthropology, meant to be read by a comparatively limited number of fellow scholars; or should it retain its initial character as a popularized but scientifically substantiated explanation of a number of vital aspects of African tribal life and low which are badly in need of a better and more tolerant understanding on the part of European fellow citizens?

The first alternative proved to involve far more than merely editing the text. In fact, it meant regrouping and largely rewriting major sections which had been cast in a form and composition which I should normally never have chosen for a scientific essay on these subjects. It was agreed that the publication of these lectures should continue to serve their original aim. I have therefore left them virtually as they were, except for altering a word or two or reshaping a sentence here and there and cutting out a phrase or two which proved to be of an oratorical rather than informative nature. A few footnotes have been added to justify or modify certain statements, or to include one or two references.

Finally, at several places I refer with little appreciation to certain provisions in the Southern Rhodesian *Native Marriages Act, 1950*. These passages were written in a crusading spirit shortly after I had made strenuous but abortive efforts to dissuade the administration from putting into operation measures which I considered confusing, unworkable and detrimental to the majority of rural African communities. I see no reason for omitting them now, for although the Act lost little time in proving itself a partial failure, it has still not been repealed or amended; and having the power of law, it still constitutes a potential danger to rural African society, which has tolerantly ignored some of its main provisions. I included some scathing criticism of this Act in my book, *Shona Customary Law*, published by the Oxford University Press last year. In these lectures I referred to two of its provisions which I particularly disliked. *Section 11* of the Act limits the legally recognized amount of bridewealth to the value of £ 20 and renders any excess paid irrecoverable in law. There is, however, no evidence as yet of any appreciable drop in the value of *lobolo* passed between parties since the Act came into operation in January 1951. *Sub-section (5) of Section 11*, moreover, denies chiefs and headmen jurisdiction in any action in which the payment or recovery of bridewealth is involved, forbids them to take cognizance of such matters and prescribes a fine or imprisonment for contraventions. In spite of this I know from my own experience that tribal authorities ignore this order, for the simple reason that it would seriously impair their traditional judicial functions still entrusted to them.

Bulawayo, S. R. J. F. H.
November, 1953

Postcript (1970)

'Marriage, Bridewealth and Cattle in an African Society' – the title was suggested by Dr. Clyde Mitchell, then Director of the Rhodes-Livingstone Institute – was scheduled to be published as Rhodes-Livingstone Papers No. 26 about 1954. The manuscript was actually ready for the press, and only a few diagrams remained to be drawn, when somehow I mislaid it (and its only spare copy) when moving house in Bulawayo. It remained lost for some fifteen years, until I rediscovered it in Leiden while rummaging in an old trunk filled with dusty files and field notes. This is therefore the first publication of these lectures, and I wish to thank the Institute for Social Research of the University of Zambia (successor to the Rhodes-Livingstone Institute) for its courtesy in releasing its publishing rights in favour of the Afrika-Studiecentrum – a fine gesture considering my default in this matter.

The passage of time has added a few more problems to the ones I outlined above. For one thing, I cannot judge to what extent rural attitudes have changed since I left the field in the early 1950s. Another thing is that some statutory provisions which I strongly criticized at the time have since been repealed or substantially changed. The statutory £ 20 'ceiling' imposed upon the legally recognized value of bridewealth was removed in 1962 at the request of the then newly created Chiefs' Council. The jurisdiction in matters of bridewealth ('consideration' in statutory parlance), taken away from tribal courts by the *Native Marriages Act 1950,* seems again to fall within their reach after the major changes brought about by the new *African Law and Tribal Courts Act (No. 24 of 1969).*

A change in official nomenclature occurred in 1962, when, in order to accommodate African dislike of the word 'Native', the *Revised Edition of the Laws Act (No. 34 of 1962)* prescribed 'African' wherever the former word appeared in statute law and other official publications (the *Native Marriages Act* becoming the *African Marriages Act,* and so on). In the same year, moreover, Native Commissioners became 'District Commissioners', while their reorganized and partly dismantled Native Department became 'Internal Affairs'.

My text of 1953 – here reproduced – contains the usages then in force. Readers should therefore keep these changes in mind, especially when reading the polemic passages, for these I have also retained. Some of them have lost their actuality and now sound like flogging a dead horse. Yet they did prove to have been fully justified at the time and even now may serve as a caution to those who too readily seek to induce changes in the social and mental disposition of a people by well-meant but ill-considered legislative action.

Leiden J. F. H.
July, 1970

I. THE SIGNIFICANCE OF THE LOBOLA SYSTEM

The information on which these talks are based applies primarily to the Shona, a group of kindred tribes which occupy most of the eastern half of Southern Rhodesia. I say this as a warning because tribal law and custom differ from one place to another, and one should therefore be careful with generalizations, especially with regard to factual details. On the other hand, in spite of differences (*e.g.,* in the pattern of kinship relations) there is a broad similarity in the concepts of bridewealth (*lobolo*) and marriage among most patrilineal tribes in central and southern Africa. However, by giving our undivided attention to one fairly uniform group of tribes we stand a better chance, with the limited time at our disposal, of understanding the vital importance of certain institutions in at least one African society; and this knowledge and understanding is useful when you later deal with similar institutions among other tribes.

Another warning: I shall be talking about African concepts and institutions in rural areas, where the traditional fabric of African society, though torn at places, is still largely intact. I shall not deal with the ten percent of the African population in the Colony living in urban and peri-urban areas. Here the traditional pattern of life has been so much broken up that a completely different approach to a study of marriage in its various aspects is needed.

In this first talk I want to discuss the *lobola*[1] system, one of the most fundamental of African institutions, because on it rests the whole process of family procreation and marriage along legal, orderly and structural lines. It is also an institution which has been most grievously underrated and misunderstood by the European public – legislators, administrators and missionaries not excluded.

In order to make you understand its deep significance and essential function in this African society, I must first make you familiar with the particular social setting in which this *lobola* institution has originated and from which it cannot be divorced. That is, I must explain to you a few principles and concepts of Shona kinship and affinity, because on these principles the structure and organization of society are based; without them this society would be unrecognizable and, in fact, cease to exist as an organized body.

Try to visualize an African tribal society as comprising innumerable lineages,[2] i.e., kinship groupings which are smaller than 'clans', but much bigger than our 'families'; which are patrilineal among the Shona, because their membership is based upon descent through the male line, from a common male ancestor. Moreover, and this is important, these lineages are exogamous, i.e., a man of one lineage can under no circumstances marry a woman belonging to the same lineage, no matter whether she is a close relative or only remotely related to him. Such a marriage would be considered incestuous, and in African society this is an even worse thing than in ours.

Think of the lineage as a pyramid (see Diagram I) with the founder-ancestor (for instance a great-grandfather or great-great-grandfather) on top.

1. I use the Zulu-Ndebele term *lobola,* instead of the Shona *rovora,* because it is the term under which the bridewealth system is most widely known in southern Africa. It should be noted that the verb is *ukulobola* (Shona, *kurovora*), to marry a woman in exchange for bridewealth; the noun is *ilobolo* (Shona, *rovoro*), bridewealth.

2. The use of the term lineage in this context is vague and from a scientific point of view unsatisfactory, especially when it is realized that, in its technical sense, it is too narrow with regard to the principles of exogamy, and too wide with regard to the kin-group normally concerned with marriage transactions. It has been used here merely to simplify the broad principles and to avoid practical complications.

Diagram 1

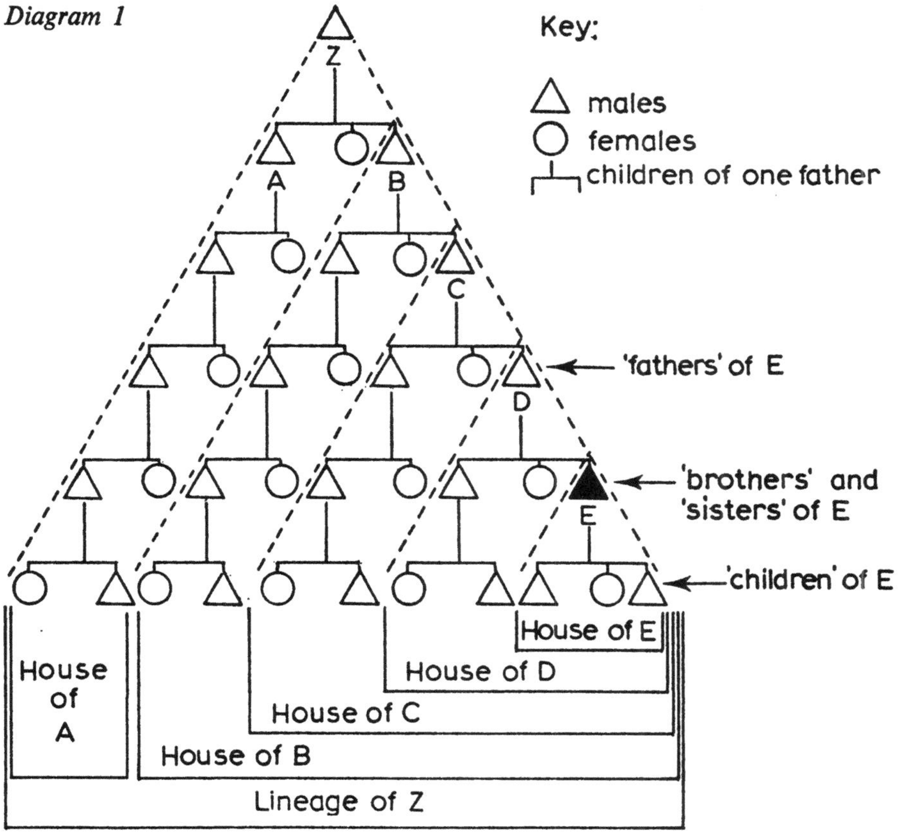

This man has a few sons who, likewise, form the tops of their own smaller pyramids or lineage sections (or so-called 'houses'), and their sons after them, and so on. Every smaller section, however, including the youngest ones consisting of fathers with their unmarried children, remains part of the total lineage structure. And so the lineage grows, through its smaller units, thus forming an expanding genealogical hierarchy in which every member, living or departed, has his place in the order of succession,[3] like an unbroken chain linking the generations of the present with the generations of the past.

These continuous links are important, because the living feel themselves dependent upon the mystical protection and help from their lineage ancestors, and the stronger and more numerous the links the better. Hence the

3. Although both males and females are members of their father's lineage, only males are ranked in a single order of succession.

urge and vital necessity – I would almost say, obsession – in African society of begetting children, so that every man should have his sons upon whom his name could be bestowed[4] and thus perpetuated.

You could therefore regard the lineage as an organic unity, a growing and reproducing entity. One indication of its unity is the kinship terminology applied between its members. Among his own immediate family a man recognizes, in his own generation, his brothers, younger and older, and his sisters. A generation higher are his father and father's sisters (his 'female fathers'); while in the generation below him are his children. He regards the wider lineage grouping as an extension of his own family, that is, the brothers of his father are his 'younger and older fathers', the sisters of the latter again his 'female fathers'; the children of his father's brothers are again his 'brothers and sisters'; and the children of his brothers are of course his 'children'. This is the principle of classificatory kinship, which extends as far as agnatic ties are recognized and this is very far indeed.

It is only natural that the prevailing unity between family units which have become remotely related through patrilineal descent is not very great in practice; but if such units have a grandfather, or even great-grandfather, in common, the sense of cohesion may still be strong. At any rate, as far as the principle of exogamy is concerned, this unity (and with it, the prohibition of intermarriage) applies throughout, even when social or political ties have lost their actual value. One example may suffice: in the Sabi Reserve a boy and a girl were found guilty of incest because they were regarded as 'brother' and 'sister'. When I traced the actual relationship between them, I found that they were fourteenth cousins.

I have emphasized the common unity in these kin-groups for a special reason, and that is that marriage in this African society is regarded in the first place as a lawful and orderly means of reproducing the paternal family of the husband (and in this manner, his wider kin-group) and only in the second place as an exclusive marital union between husband and wife. Marriage is contracted between the respective *families*, with the co-operation of the individual parties. The marital union between husband and wife is established as a new reproductive cell within a wider kinship organism; the children that are begotten by the new couple are undoubtedly *their* children, but the thing that really matters is that these children take their places in the order of succession of their much wider paternal kin-group.

Let us return to the principle of exogamy. Exogamy implies that a lineage,

4. The inheritance of a predecessor's *personal name*, as a part of the succession to his office and estate, is common among the Shona, but not generally found among other tribes.

although it comprises both male and female members, cannot reproduce itself through its *own* females. It needs the females of other lineages to bear its children. In other words, the lineage *itself* is an incomplete and unreproductive organism until it establishes ties of affinity with other lineages, whereby it receives wives for its men and, through these wives, a new generation of children. It is obvious that all lineages are in a similar plight; all must reproduce themselves but cannot do this alone; all need women of lineages other than their own to help them. The process of reproduction therefore means that the male members of a lineage raise children with wives from other lineages and that their sisters are married off to fulfil the same function for the paternal kin-groups of their husbands. Reproduction and marriage are therefore essentially – and in this society, inevitably – a question of *exchange of reproductive power*, a *reciprocal arrangement* which serves the vital needs of both parties contracting the marriage.[5]

The easiest and most simple procedure would seem to be for two families to *exchange daughters*, but unfortunately this admirable solution is in conflict with the basic laws of Shona kinship. To make this clear I must tell you a little more about this kinship system. You have seen how the members of a lineage all have their proper places as relatively junior or senior in relation to each other member in the genealogical hierarchy and how this is expressed in their social relations by an appropriate kinship term and attitude of respect and obedience towards all who are senior and therefore superior. I must now emphasize that a similar classification in rank obtains between relatives *by affinity*, that is, between people belonging to different but related lineages but excluding those that are each other's cognates (such as maternal cousins). The basic rule in Shona society is that, when two families establish ties of affinity between them, the representatives (that is, the *men*) of the family providing the wife are ranked higher than the representatives of the family receiving the wife. This superiority of the wife-providing family over the wife-receiving family is expressed, among other things, in the term 'father-in-law' (*tezwara*) by which *every male affine* of the wife-providing family is addressed by the members of the wife-receiving family. And on the basis of classificatory kinship this term, as well as its corresponding attitude of respect and subservience, is extended to the male members of the wider paternal kin-group to which the wife-providing family belongs. In-

5. This idea has been worked out on a comparative basis for patrilineal and matrilineal societies in Gluckman, M., 'Kinship & Marriage among the Lozi of Northern Rhodesia and the Zulu of Natal', in Radcliffe-Brown and Forde (Editors), *African Systems of Kinship and Marriage*, Oxford University Press for the International African Institute, London, 1950.

versely, all the males of the wife-receiving family[6] become 'sons-in-law'. For instance, when I marry a woman not only my wife's father becomes my *tezwara* or father-in-law, but also her brothers, half-brothers and classificatory brothers, as well as the sons of these brothers, and so on. Inversely, not only I, the husband of this woman, am called son-in-law (*mukuwasha*), but also my brothers, half-brothers and classificatory brothers, as well as my father and paternal uncles, and even my grandfather.

Diagram II

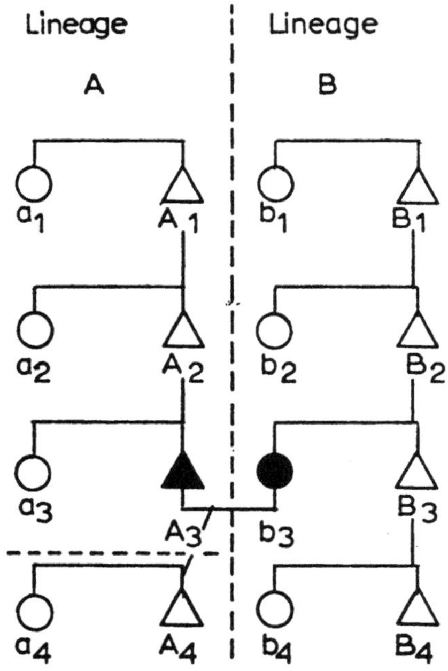

A_3 and b_3 are husband and wife: A_3 calls all the males (B) of his wife's lineage 'father' – and so do his father A_2 and grandfather A_1; the males of B lineage say 'son'(-in-law) to A_3 as well as to all other A males (except those of the 4th and lower generations of A, for they are B's cognates and called 'grandchildren').

Now you can easily see (Diagram II) that, after woman *b* has become the wife of man *A*, brother *B* cannot marry sister *a*, because *B* cannot, being a 'father-in-law' to family *A*, also become 'son-in-law' of *A*. As these kinship laws are basic in Shona society, a man cannot, in relation to the same people, simultaneously be a 'son' and a 'father' without causing confusion

6. That is, *affines only*; cognates, such as the children of these sons-in-law, become *vazukuru* ('grandchildren') in relation to the males of their mother's lineage. For a detailed analysis of this kinship system see my *Shona Customary Law* (Oxford University Press, 1952), Chapter I.

in the social order. Such marriages do occur occationally and under very special circumstances, but they make the everyday relationship between the families extremely difficult. In short, a direct exchange of women between two kin-groups is in conflict with orderly Shona kinship and social relations and does not, therefore, exist as a regular feature of marriage traffic. The exchange of reproductive power between the marrying kin-groups which, as we have seen, is both an essential and inevitable aspect of family reproduction therefore has had to be arranged in a different manner. And now I come to the crux of the *lobola* or bridewealth system. When family *A* approaches family *B* (see Diagram III) in order to marry a *b* woman who can bear children as the wife of an *A* man, family *B* cannot demand that an *a* woman be given in return; but family *B* can and does demand that family *A* give such compensation as will enable *B* to marry a woman of some other, *C*, family for the production of *B* children. In other words, the compensation which family *A* must give to family *B* must be the equivalent of the value of which *A* receives from *B*, which is the value of the capacity of one woman as a wife and bearer of children. This compensation is the *lobolo*, the equivalent in African society of the reproductive capacity of a normal woman. The marriage transaction between *A* and *B* now serves the vital needs of *both* families. *A* receives a wife from *B*, and *B* receives in return the means through which a wife can be obtained from another family. This is what the Shona call *kurovorana*,[7] a well-balanced, *reciprocal* arrangement for the production of legitimate children. This is the *lobola* system in a nutshell; this is the basis of about ninety-eight percent of all marriages[8] contracted among the rural Shona.

Diagram III

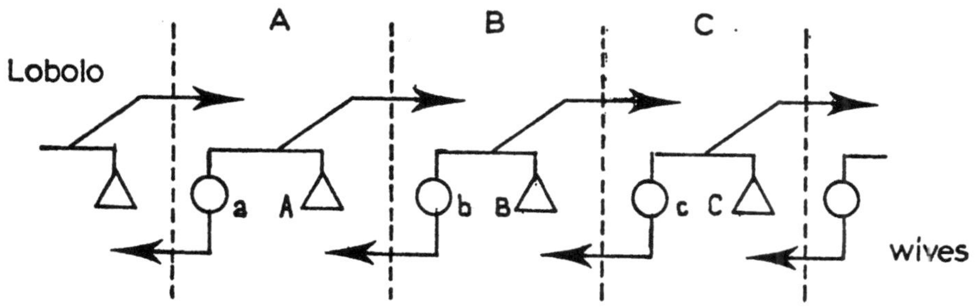

7. The suffix *-na* indicates reciprocity.

8. This figure is based on a survey of about 1,200 marriages in the Sabi and Wedza Reserves, supported by a sample test covering more than 10,000 marriages registered at the Native Commissioner's offices at The Range, Chibi and Mtoko.

Can this be regarded as 'buying a wife'? Is this a commercial contract of purchase and sale? Before I refute this unfortunately still current belief, let us first analyse the meaning of the *lobolo* compensation a bit further. The payment of bridewealth to family *B* enables family *A* to raise legitimate children with the woman family *B* has provided. Through the payment of *lobolo*, *A* is therefore entitled to regard all the issue of the womb of this woman as legitimate members of his family and lineage and to exercise paternal control over them. The importance of this point is best illustrated by a quick look at marriages in which no, or only an incomplete, *lobolo* has been handed over to the woman's family. There are a few types of these marriages, but they are rare, because they are an anomaly in Shona law. In only one of these types, the antiquated *uranda* marriage, was the question of *lobolo* definitely ruled out: in this case a bondsman used to get a wife in return for his lifetime services to his master. But in the *uranda* marriage the legal position of the children born of this union depended almost entirely on the whims and wishes of the father-in-law, the bondsman's master. The bondsman had no legal security in this matter but could expect, as an act of grace by his master, to be allowed to keep one or two of his children; the rest belonged to his father-in-law.

In another type of service-marriage, *ugarira*, the son-in-law would spend a long time in the service of his father-in-law, but could always win his independence by tendering *lobolo*. In theory the period of service would be taken into account as a part of the marriage compensation; in practice, however, this mixture of intangible and tangible values proved so difficult to calculate that in most cases the son-in-law gave a full *lobolo* in order to get full and indisputable control of all his children, regardless of the length of his service to his father-in-law. The same uncertainty regarding the position of children also arises in a *lobolo* marriage whenever the son-in-law fails to complete the payment of *lobolo* in the manner this had been agreed upon.

And so you see that the compensation for the reproductive capacity of a woman to her family by means of *lobolo* is the legal way in which a father can secure for himself and his kin-group full paternal rights to his offsping. And since this is the essential function of the *lobolo* transaction, those critics who still maintain that African wives are 'bought' therefore suggest in effect that in African society families reproduce themselves by a process of buying and selling children!

Let us turn to the actual *value* of the bridewealth and the sources from which it is normally derived. I want to stress that the value of *lobolo*, that is the value of a woman's reproductive capacity, was never low. During some times in the past, when for some reasons or other the people had no or hardly any cattle or other livestock, bridewealth could be paid in iron hoes, twelve to twenty in number, or in other material values, for instance a gun. You must keep in mind that hoes and other iron work were produced by a highly exclusive guild of craftsmen who were paid a relatively high price in grain or small stock and that the price of an old muzzle-loader, even in the days when cattle were still rather scarce, easily amounted to one or two head. Apart from that, other material values were practically non-existent, so that twenty hoes, modest as it may seem nowadays, represented a fortune to an African a hundred years ago.

When livestock, and especially cattle, became generally owned, bridewealth became almost invariably expressed in cattle. In the early 1900s when, according to government statistics, the number of African-held cattle was on an average less than two head per family unit, the current rate of *lobolo* for one wife was four head of cattle in central and southern Mashonaland, that is, more than double the material value of an average family estate.[9] Nowadays the standardized rate of *lobolo* for *normal* marriages in many parts of Mashonaland is ten to twelve head of cattle. This seems excessively high, until we realize that the number of African-held stock has increased in even greater proportion. In fact, the figures for 1948 show that the average family unit possessed about $5^{1}/_{2}$ head of cattle, while the *lobolo* rate was ten to twelve head. In other words, in comparison with the number of African held stock, the value of the *lobolo* has not risen, but actually decreased slightly.[10]

You may now argue that this comparison is false because I failed to take the enormous increase in the cash value of cattle into consideration. But the answer is that the cash value of cattle is hardly relevant in this respect, because, in connexion with marriage transactions, most Shona still think primarily in *numbers of cattle*. It is only when no or insufficient cattle are available for a particular transaction that they try to translate the value of a cattle *lobolo* in terms of cash; and even then I found that their evaluation does not nearly approach the current market value of cattle. This shows again that we should be careful before we start thinking of the *lobolo* transaction in terms of economics and commerce.

During the last twenty-five years or so, an additional feature has emerged

9. This is a rough calculation, in which 'family' was taken as a unit comprising husband, one wife and three unmarried children.

10. At that time the destocking scheme had been in operation for some years, but the resulting decrease in African stock had not yet shown a corresponding lowering of the current rate of *lobolo*. I have no up-to-date figures to ascertain whether such a trend has become noticeable in recent years.

in marriage transactions, a cash payment of some £5 – £15, which has become accepted as a part of the bridewealth.[11] This cash amount has undoubtedly increased the total value of the bridewealth; but on the other hand, there has also during this period been a vast improvement in the avenues of remunerative employment. In short, in spite of increased cash requirements and the increased number of cattle needed for bridewealth, it is reasonable to assume that, generally and comparatively speaking, it is no greater burden than in the past for a family to provide wives for its sons.

Even so, you may say, if we accept the fact that now, as in the past, the bridewealth for one wife already exceeds the material value of an average family estate, how is it possible for a family with more than one son to provide a wife for every son? For an answer I must lead you back to what I explained earlier: that the reproduction of the family means, in effect, the replacement of daughters by wives. Marriage traffic under such high rates of compensation obviously can only be sustained when the daughters are married off in order to provide marriage cattle for their brothers. And this is exactly what happens in the vast majority of cases. The principle is contained in what the Shona call the *cipanda* system. *Cipanda* means a forked stick, and the term expresses a situation in which a brother and a sister – the two prongs of the fork – are 'coupled' or 'linked' for the purpose of *lobolo*. This arrangement implies that the eldest brother in a family is 'linked' to his eldest sister, preferably his full sister, the next brother to the next sister and so on. A man will refer to his 'linked' sister as 'my *cipanda*', because he knows that he has a preferential right to the cattle that come in when this sister marries. This represents a man's basic share in his family's estate, and the *cipanda* system is therefore the basic principle underlying Shona estate law.[12]

It happens, of course, that there are more sons than daughters in a family, and in such cases the eldest son has a clear preference to the first available cattle; but he also incurs the obligation of helping to provide marriage cattle for his younger brothers, if necessary by giving them cattle derived from the marriage of his own daughters. And one should also keep in mind that 'family' in African society is a much wider concept than in ours and that,

11. The cash payment (*rutsambo*) should not be confused with the various cash and other small gifts (*zwipeto* or *zwiduku*) which are habitually handed to the bride's family during the marriage transaction, and which have nothing to do with the bridewealth as such (see p. 104 f.)

12. This is referred to as 'cattle-linking' among the Lovedu of N. E. Transvaal. See Krige, E. J. and J. D. *The Realm of the Rain Queen*. Oxford University Press for the International African Institute (London, 1943) Chap. IX.

if a man has no *cipanda* sister in his own family unit, he may fall back upon the other family units of his wider paternal kin-group. And the wider the kin-group, the greater the chances of finding a balanced number of boys and girls.[13]

Under this *cipanda* system, which is still very much in force today,[14] most young men are therefore assured that there will be marriage cattle available by the time they wish to marry, no matter how high the current *lobolo* rate. It is obvious that this system can work smoothly and without undue hardship only if there is some kind of local stabilization of *lobolo* rates, for it will help a father little if he receives four head of cattle for his daughter but has to provide twelve head to find a wife for his son. Fortunately – and contrary to the belief of many outsiders who think that an African father 'likes to sell his daughter to the highest bidder' – there is, except in urban and peri-urban areas, little speculation in marriage transactions. It is true that you often do find a good deal of 'bargaining' in marriage negotiations, but this is a part of the traditional attitude of 'antagonism' between the families-in-law[15] and is usually a spirited mock show. Normally, that is in the vast majority of cases, the parties stick to a standardized rate of *lobolo* which, in many Shona tribal areas, now amounts to about ten head of cattle. There are, also in the rural areas, undoubtedly marriages in which a much higher amount is demanded and paid, but if you investigate these you are likely to find that they almost invariably reveal some irregularity or unlawfulness – usually that the husband has courted his wife when she was the affianced bride or wedded wife of another man. In these cases there is, therefore, not only a question of bridewealth, but of additional damages for adultery or breach of contract which, for the sake of convenience, but erroneously, are registered as part of the so-called 'consideration' payable by

13. Whether a man may fall back upon the resources of other units within his paternal lineage as a matter of course largely depends on (*a*) the proximity of the relations between the two units and (*b*) their prevailing sense of common unity. In principle, community of *lobola* interests exists within the lineage section known as *cizwarwa*, the descendants of a common grandfather. Outside the *cizwarwa* assistance could still be given to a needy family, but the 'house' of the person so helped would then become specifically indebted to the 'house' that provided assistance and would therefore have to reciprocate in due time.

Nowadays the *cizwarwa* unity is fast breaking down, and it is not uncommon to find that even between two half-brothers help is given on a reciprocal instead of a communal basis.

14. In the Wedza Reserve I found (1948) that 85% of the married young men had married with *cipanda* cattle.

15. See p. 102-105 below.

the second husband. In areas where this sort of immorality is prevalent the marriage register may show a considerable percentage of marriages in which this consideration appears to be excessively high. But if you know the facts and local circumstances, and are therefore able to analyse these figures objectively, you will realize that it is both wrong and unfair to blame the bridewealth system as such for these excesses because they have little to do with *lobolo.*[16] The government, however, prefers to think along these lines, and that is why the latest *Native Marriages Act (1950)* arbitrarily lowers the legally recognized value of the bridewealth to £ 20, a figure so low that it bears no relation to the principles and reality of the *lobola* system.[17]

I have stressed the importance and the active function of the *cıpanda*

16. The cause of these abuses lies beyond the operation of the *lobola* system. It is a symptom of a crumbling tribal organization, in which tribal authorities fail to give guidance in such cases. The blame for this must in the first place lie with the Administration, which has underrated the vital importance and stabilizing influence of hereditary chieftainship and authority. In the Chibi area, for instance, some of the most important tribal offices were held by people other than the rightful heirs, and half a dozen other high vacancies were occupied by 'temporary' and relatively junior caretakers. None of these could inspire public confidence or exercise real authority. The decisions of these 'judges' in matters of divorce and claims for compensation often went completely haywire, the implicit understanding apparently being that every complainant should be satisfied to the extent of his, usually exorbitant, claims. There was little evidence of the element of public ridicule with which excessive demands are usually treated in communities governed by a stable tribal authority.

In theory Native Commissioners, with their powers of review and re-trial, could counteract the effect of slovenly tribal administration of justice, but the painful fact is that they are seldom in a position to do so. It takes time and careful study to analyse the social ailments of a particular society and to develop effective measures against these. Most Native Commissioners, however, are overburdened with paper work and economic development schemes. The result is that little time is left for the administration of justice or for a careful assessment of social problems generally. Moreover, their tenure of office in any one district is, on an average, so short that even those who do manage to diagnose the local situation have no chance to develop a suitable policy which could be continued under their successors.

It is this absense of continuity of policy, together with the inevitable ignorance of local circumstances, which tends to inhibit the best efforts of the rural administrative officers.

[For a recent analysis of the causes of failure on the part of district administration, see my *Chief, Council and Commissioner*, Van Gorcum, Assen, 1969, p. 30ff.] – J. F. H.

17. *Section 11* of this act does not make the £20 ceiling on *lobolo* transactions obligatory, but lays down that any amount in excess of this is void, and that, if a higher amount has been paid, not more than £20 is legally recoverable in the event of divorce. So far the result of this ambiguity has been that the *lobolo* rates have not dropped to any noticeable extent, but that the vital issue of return of *lobolo* in cases of divorce has become extremely confused.

('linking') system because it is too often overlooked by people who ought to know better. Even some Native Commissioners have made such sweeping statements as, 'These claims (for bridewealth) have grown to such proportions that it is quite impossible for the majority of sons-in-law to meet their obligation.' If you take the trouble to collect statistical material on this point you will find that the facts do not support such a strong general statement.[18]

Finally, let us see whether the traditionally high *lobolo* has any positive social advantages to offer, if only because it would seem unlikely that an African society, with its flexible laws and institutions, would for generations have tolerated and supported an institution if it had caused undue hardship to its members. Like any other society, African society seeks stability, and one of the most important spheres where stability is needed is in marriage and the pattern of relationships established by marriage. A high *lobolo* has proved to be one of the most powerful factors supporting marriage stability, because neither the wife's not the husband's family can afford to lose bridewealth received or paid without jeopardising their family estate. The husband and his family know that they cannot divorce the wife without good reasons, because the wife's family may then refuse to hand back the *lobolo;*

18. Of about 1,000 husbands questioned in the Wedza, Sabi and Chibi areas, less than ten percent still owed their fathers-in-law a portion of the bridewealth.

I have no figures for the urban and peri-urban areas, where the position may be different. H. Cripps, in a short article in NADA, 1947 (p. 41 ff.), gives a gloomy impression of the plight of present-day sons-in-law in an unnamed urban or peri-urban area in which the rise of *lobolo* has resulted in a corresponding degree of indebtedness. Unfortunately he does not reveal on how many cases his conclusions are based. He presents the *lobolo* as a personal obligation of the young husband, without reference to the 'linking' system or other help from his family, to which a man is normally entitled. Another interesting feature is that Cripps describes the *lobolo* as a purely cash transaction in which no cattle or other livestock are involved.

This article seems to corroborate my own findings that, if the *lobolo* becomes detached from the traditional subsistence economy (in which *family-owned* livestock play a major role) and becomes wrapped up in a cash economy (in which earnings are looked upon as individual property), husbands do indeed tend to become personally responsible for providing their own bridewealth. Since this economic transformation appears to be running parallel to a breaking-up of family solidarity, the *lobolo* tends to lose one of its essential characteristics as a common effort by the husband's paternal kin-group. It then becomes an anomaly and, because it is too deeply rooted in tradition to die easily, it is bound to cause hardship and confusion.

But this problem, however acute in certain areas, still only affects a small minority of the African population in the Colony. It needs careful study, and on no account should measures aimed at solving it be arbitrarily extended to the vast majority of communities in which the *lobolo* institution is still functioning well.

and without a refund of *lobolo* the husband may find it very difficult to marry another wife. Inversely, the wife and her family will take good care not to do anything which may give the husband a valid reason for seeking a divorce, because they are then liable to refund the bridewealth; and this they may find difficult to do, because in most cases these cattle have already been spent on the marriage of one of their own sons. In other words, the stakes are so high that both husband and wife and their respective families are forced to treat each other well and tolerantly and to strive for genuine friendship and co-operation. In practice there is, to be sure, quite often a convenient way out for the in-laws. If the wife finds a lover who is willing and able to marry her, it is actually he who foots the bill and provides the wife's family with the *lobolo* value which they must refund to the husband's family. Even so, you can imagine what the effect would be if the bridewealth were suddenly to be brought down to a level on which the risk of losing it is no longer considered a serious matter.

The traditionally high *lobolo* used to make it practically impossible for a young man to marry without the assistance of his family and, if necessary, of his wider kin-group. And although nowadays it has become fairly easy for a young man to earn his own money and contribute towards his own *lobolo*, he normally still needs the assistance of his family and the *cipanda* ('linking') system to collect his full bridewealth and to contract the marriage. This very state of dependency of a young man on his family forces him to submit to the authority of his father and other family elders, because they have the power to punish him by refusing to help him, and he cannot afford to stand alone. In short, the high *lobolo* value fosters a sense of family unity and common responsibility, obedience and respect for one's seniors. A reduction of the bridewealth to a value which comes within easy reach of the earning capacity of every able-bodied young man is therefore not likely to have a favourable effect on his attitude towards his elders and tends to result in a premature break-up of family unity.[19]

19. The effect can now already be observed in isolated instances. Normally, when a husband neglects or ill-treats his wife, his family are not slow in rebuking him, and since they have the power (based upon the grounds that *they* have contracted the marriage and provided the bridewealth) of denying him, if necessary, the use of his wife, their curbing influence is very considerable. As a contrast I have witnessed several cases in which a husband who had personally acquired his wife's *lobolo* was being accused of ill-treating her. Although his family (and especially his sister, see p. 117) did their best to reprimand him, their arguments lost most of their effectivenness when he turned to them, saying: 'When I married this wife of mine you did not help me with cattle or money. I myself had to work hard to earn everything. How can you now tell me how I should treat her?'

And last, but certainly not least, the traditionally high value of the bridewealth gives women a definite status in African society. I shall later discuss this point more fully,[20] but I must mention it here because it is an integral aspect of the bridewealth system and one which is usually ignored.

Summarizing I can state that in Shona society the bridewealth system has evolved as a logical and necessary corollary of the basic laws of kinship and exogamy on which this society is founded; that it represents the lawful and honourably way in which the vast majority of people marry and beget legitimate children – the essential and practically the only means through which paternal kin-groups can reproduce themselves and so fulfil the essential purpose of life as these people conceive it.

Having lived among the Shona for several years and in different areas with the specific task of investigating this and other institutions and to assess their real value in present day tribal life, I can say that, despite changing social conditions and some ill-advised and abortive efforts to discourage it, the *lobola* system still fulfils a necessary function and that it fulfils that function on the whole smoothly and admirably well.

II. SOME OTHER ASPECTS OF MARRIAGE

In the previous section I dealt almost entirely with the reproductive aspect of bridewealth marriages, an aspect which is focused upon the transfer of a wife to the husband's family and the compensation for her reproductive capacity in the form of *lobolo* or bridewealth to her family. Although this is undoubtedly the most fundamental aspect of the *lobolo* marriage transaction, there are other important aspects, some of which I want to discuss now.

In the first place, the transaction involves a *marriage*, an exclusive marital union of husband and wife, following the establishment of affinal relations between their families and wider kin-groups. This is important because, as in our own society, marriage and the formation of family units form the basis of organized society. It becomes even more important when we remember that in African society relationships established by marriage are not confined to the husband and wife and their immediate kin, but link up with a far more extensive fabric of kinship relations on which organized society so heavily depends. In this connexion I must remind you that in the pattern of kinship relations prevailing in Mashonaland the family of the wife are ranked superior to the family of the husband and that this situation is ex-

20. See p. 115 ff.

pressed in appropriate terms of reference and address ('fathers-in-law' as against 'children-in-law') and a corresponding attitude of deference, humility and sometimes subservience on the part of the husband and his family towards the wife's family.

In the process of establishing and maintaining a relationship-in-law we can therefore expect something of a tension between these two groups of people who, whatever their normal stations in society, are no equals as far as their relationship-through-marriage is concerned, but who must, somehow, overcome this tension in order to bring about a lasting state of mutual goodwill and co-operation.

There is also the distinction between the communal and individual aspects of marriage to which I referred before: this dual situation of a marriage, first, as the link between two *families* for the purpose of procreating their kin-groups; and second, as a marital union of husband and wife forming their own little family unit and estate as an integral part of the wider paternal kin-group and family estate of the husband's family.[21]

We should also consider the effect of marriage upon the personal status of the man and the woman.

All these are social rather than legal aspects, and we should not forget that the *lobolo* marriage, as a legal contract, is founded on the basic assumption that the two families will derive *equal benefit* from the transaction. This means that if one party has derived no, or hardly any, real benefit from the transaction, something has gone radically wrong with the marriage and this unequal situation should be put right, by legal action if necessary.

I mention these points, not because I want to make matters unnecessarily difficult for you, but to impress upon you the fact that contracting a marriage in African society is a serious and often complicated undertaking and that, *after* the marriage has been lawfully contracted, both parties (i.e., the husband and his family and the wife and her family) *continue* to have social as well as legal obligations towards each other which they must fulfil in order to avoid a break in their relationship. In short, do not think that a marriage comes into being merely by exchanging a woman and a number of cattle. A host of legal and other formalities are necessarily involved in the process.

Let me give you, by way of illustration, an abbreviated description of the

21. This distinction is common in Africa. Laura Bohannan has referred to the rights in a woman as a procreative unit as *jus genetricem* and the rights in a woman as a wife as *jus uxorem*. See Bohannan, L. 'Dahomean Marriage: A Revaluation', *Africa* XIX, (1949), p. 278. See also Barnes, J. A. *Marriage in a Changing Society*, Rhodes-Livingstone Paper No. 20, Oxford University Press (Cape Town, 1951), p. 113 ff.

procedure followed in regular proposal marriages among the Shona. I choose this type of procedure, not because it is the most common – in fact, in many areas the elopement marriage is far more common[22] – but because it reveals, more clearly than other procedures, most of the aspects which I mentioned.

There is, to begin with, the initial formal approach, whereby the boy's family ascertain from the girl's family whether the prospect of a relationship-in-law between the families is agreeable to them. Normally this step is taken after the boy has fallen in love with the girl and has privately obtained a love token from her. Keep in mind that, no matter how cordial the pre-existing social relations between the respective partens may have been, the establishment of ties of affinity between them will involve a new and totally different pattern or relationship. As far as the prospect of relations-in-law is concerned, the two families are therefore 'strangers', or in African parlance, 'they don't know each other yet'. Consequently, the first formal approach and subsequent negotiations must be conducted through an intermediary, a disinterested third party who establishes contact between the families and who acts as a go-between and principal witness right through the marriage preliminaries and, in important matters, sometimes even after the marriage has actually been concluded. His functions are indispensable in Shona marriage.

The initial marriage proposal, made through the intermediary, must be couched in a concrete form, that is, by way of a tangible gift or token in which the proposal is, so to speak, contained. This, too, is essential, because no parent would take such an important message as a marriage proposal seriously, if it were made merely by word of mouth. The *acceptance* (in a literal sense) of the proposal by the girl's family means that, in principle, the prospect of a marriage is agreeable to them and that further negotiations (especially with regard to the bridewealth) can now be arranged. The remarkable thing is that *from this moment onwards* the future relationship-by-marriage is *anticipated* and its peculiar kinship pattern comes into operation. You may, for the sake of convenience, speak of a state of formal 'betrothal', but the real situation is that of a legal state of affinity between the families in anticipation of the actual marriage. One aspect is that the family of the prospective groom recognize the superior position of the girl's family as the 'wife-providing family': these people are now treated as 'fathers' and addressed as such by their 'children', their prospective in-laws. This implies that at every stage of the subsequent negotiations the boy's family have to behave humbly and respectfully, while the girl's family assume an

22. Among the Hera of the Sabi Reserve, for instance, a survey of about 700 marriages showed that the elopement procedure was almost four times as common as the regular proposal procedure.

attitude of superiority which they express in a certain aloofness, as if they were reluctant and even unwilling to co-operate in the matter. The boy's family must now gradually wear down this formal attitude by tendering gifts and tokens and often by rendering small services to the girl's family. For instance, they have to persuade the girl's father to state the amount of bridewealth he wants by giving him a gift as a 'mouth-opener'. To make him feel kindly disposed they present him with an overcoat, blanket, shirt, hat or some other thing he fancies. They curry the favour of the girl's mother (a most 'fearful' person in this new relationship!) by sending her a length of cloth, or a goat, or some cash; and very often the boy and his younger brothers will cut firewood for her. When matters have progressed so far that a representative of the girl's family comes to inspect the cattle to be given as *lobolo*, he must be given a shilling or so 'to provide shade on a hot day': he is given another shilling to make him enter the village, a shilling to strike up a conversation, a shilling because he may have picked up a thorn on his way down, and so on. The boy's family must kill meat for him because he is an honoured guest, but before he deigns to taste it he must be given another petty gift, and so it goes on: a sixpence or shilling to provide the stone on which he can stand to view the cattle, another gift for pointing out the beasts he wants, yet another as 'whip' to drive the cattle home. At this stage it has usually become necessary for the husband's family to kill a goat to add the ritual element of blood to the transaction.

After this, the woman's family have sufficiently unbent to reciprocate some of the hospitality extended to them, and they may invite the groom's family to a party at their own village where, likewise, a goat may be killed for the festivity. This is not a 'wedding feast' in a strict sense, but an occasion on the eve of the marriage on which the two families partake of a common meal to give expression to their mutual feelings of satisfaction and friendship. Some time after this the bride may be escorted by one or two of her relatives to the village of her groom for the consummation of the marriage.[23]

And now a similar process of persuasion starts again, with every possible effort being made to win the favour of the bride and to make her feel at home. Upon her arrival she is given a rousing welcome, with everyone of her husband's village running out to meet her. But she refuses to enter the village until she is given a present. They want to see her face, but she keeps

23. The spectacular joint wedding feasts during which the bride is ceremonially transferred from her family to the family of her husband, such as are common among the south-eastern Nguni tribes, are virtually unknown among the Shona where, almost unobtrusively, the bride leaves her parental home escorted by a paternal aunt or one or two sisters (and often the intermediary).

herself covered, and only those who give her a trifling present are allowed to have a peep at her. Meat is killed in her honour, but she cannot start eating before she has been begged to do so with yet another present. In the course of the next few days she will have to assume certain household duties, but at every new situation and duty she shows this half-fearful reluctance, until she is presented with a petty gift. And so she is gradually inaugurated in her husband's home by his family, not as a mere incubator of children, a piece of acquired property, but as a respected member of a highly-respected family, a person with dignity, status and rights, who has agreed to become the wife of her husband and to bear children for his family.

The gifts I mentioned just now form part and parcel of the Shona marriage procedure. They are *not* bridewealth in the sense *lobolo* is, because they are not meant as a compensation for the reproductive capacity of the woman, in spite of the fact that, nowadays, their total cash value may amount to £10 or more. The importance of these gifts and tokens, and especially those handed to the girl's father, is that they add up to the legality of the marriage, because they are inseparable from the various formalities that have to be fulfilled. By this I do not mean that every single gift I have mentioned (and there are more) must necessarily have been handed over before the marriage can be considered valid. Some are so important (for instance, the initial proposal token and subsequent 'mouth-opener') that they are invariably given, but the variety of gifts and tokens is so great that probably in no marriage transaction is every known type given. The giving of these presents and tokens is rather the means by which marriage negotiations progress step by step, until full agreement is ultimately reached between the parties. They are therefore tangible evidence of the *manner in which* the families have established lawful marriage relations between them.

I referred to the communal and individual aspects of the marriage contract, and in the description of the marriage procedure I have given both these aspects are revealed. One more illustration may be given to show that this distinction is fully recognized in Shona law. In many tribes the actual consummation of the marriage does not take place until about a week after the bride has been formally handed over to the husband's family. During this week she will sleep in the hut of her mother-in-law. She is, so to speak, still the bride of the groom's *family*, and not yet of the groom himself. The conjugal union of husband and wife is not established until the husband's father or head of the family, who have married this woman and have given *lobolo* for her, sends her a token (nowadays often a two-shilling piece) with the message that she can now take her quarters in the sleeping hut of her husband. The term for this token, *rusunungunura,* is significant: it means to 'unbind'. That is, having thus far been the bride of the husband's family, these communal ties can now be slackened so that she may become the wife of an individual husband. In this manner, within the framework of the husband's family, a new marital union and a potential new family estate are formally created.

Do not think, however, that with this one act the new unit immediately acquires full independence, socially, legally or economically. Far from it. This is a gradual process of emancipation which may take years. In most Shona tribes the young couple cannot yet set up their own household. They do have their own garden plot and granary, but their food is, for the time being, still provided by the husband's mother and cooked in her hut. The young wife is treated very much as an unmarried daughter, supervised by the old woman. This period of apprenticeship may last from a few weeks among the Budya of the north-east to a year and longer among such tribes as the Hera, Rozwi and Govera of central and southern Mashonaland. In the latter areas a new wife is often not given her own kitchen or allowed to set up her own household until after she has borne her first child, the confinement of which normally takes place at her own parental home. When she comes back she feels that she is entitled to more privacy and independence. She is not supposed to state her demands outright and must therefore make known her feelings in another way. So she begins to pine, she laughs rarely and smiles wanly. She sings sad songs. In short, she looks most unhappy. When her mother-in-law notices this she has a talk with the husband's father, who then orders that a new kitchen be built. The whole village of the husband combines in this effort. The men do most of the building, the women contribute pots, plates and other household utensils. The young wife herself is not permitted to lend a hand; everything is prepared for her. When all is ready the mother-in-law and the women of the village throw a hens' party at which the new kitchen is formally initiated and handed over to the guest of honour, the young wife. A few days later she reciprocates with another party, this time proudly acting as hostess in her own domain. The culminating event takes place when the young housewife secures a nice piece of meat and prepares a tasty meal for her father-in-law. This is the formal gesture with which she announces to the head of her family-in-law that she now has her own kitchen and is therefore capable of taking full responsibility for her own household affairs. As far as everyday life is concerned, the young couple have now achieved their economic independence.

But in other respects emancipation is even slower and may, in fact, never by fully achieved, especially in legal and ritual matters. Unless the husband deliberately breaks away from his paternal family-group – and this very seldom happens because such a step is fraught with danger, especially in mystical ways – he and his family unit remain in the fold of his wider kin-group; and this means that he remains subject to the authority of his family elders. Of course he gains in stature as he grows older and wiser, and his family responsibilities increase as his own children grow up and marry. But unless he grows old enough to become the senior member of his family-group, he never achieves a fully independent status. For all practical and social purposes he may regard himself as having such status, and behave accordingly. But in really important matters, a law suit or the propitiation of his ancestral spirits in the event of death or illness, he will turn to the most senior member of his paternal kin-group for the necessary assistance. Only then does he feel assured of the effective support of his kinsmen.

About the position of married women I do not want to say more at this stage, because I shall devote the next section to this subject. Let us, instead, turn to some of the legal aspects involved in the marriage transaction. I have explained that the *lobolo* marriage is based on the broad premise that the husband's family marry a woman with normal child-bearing capacity in return for *lobolo*, the equivalent in this society of such a woman. It follows that the parties envisage that the benefits they derive from the transaction should approximately 'balance' each other. There are two aspects of this idea of balance which you must understand well. The first is that, for obvious reasons, such a balance cannot be achieved at the time the marriage is concluded, for it implies not only that the husband's family have fully met their *lobolo* obligation, but that the woman has fully spent her procreative capacity for the benefit of her husband's family. This means that, as far as the woman's family are concerned, their most important legal obligations *start*, rather than end, with the transfer of their daughter to the husband's family.

The second point is that however fundamental the idea of balance it is essentially vague and ill-defined. One should never attempt to express it in strictly arithmetical terms, as seems to be the tendency in our courts of law. It is true that, after a woman has spent her productive years with her husband, bearing him issue and serving him well, she is considered to have fully compensated the bridewealth given for her. But the strict interpretation that since a normal woman can be expected to bear five children, the value of each child should therefore be assessed at one-fifth of the bridewealth or two heads of cattle out of a total of ten head *lobolo,* has originated in our law courts and is foreign to traditional African law and thought. I shall come back to this point later;[24] for the present I want to stress that there is this

24. See the fourth section, *Dissolution of Customary Marriage.*

basic idea of balance, however vague, and to show what happens when this balance is seriously upset. I shall give you a few examples of such disturbances and the usual remedies offered by Shona law.

Assume that a husband, having paid full *lobolo,* finds that his wife fails to bear him children. Even if the woman has served him well in other respects, the basic object of the whole marriage transaction – that of reproducing kin-groups – is obviously not being achieved. Under Shona law this is interpreted as a failure of the *wife's family* to fulfil their most important obligation under the marriage contract. The husband therefore has the choice of two alternatives: he can either demand a dissolution of the marriage and a return of most of his *lobolo* cattle or he can demand that his family-in-law provide a second woman to raise issue on behalf of the barren wife. The first alternative should not be insisted upon when the wife's family are able and willing to provide a substitute, because a dissolution of the marriage, apart from the practical difficulty for the wife's family of refunding cattle which have usually already been spent or earmarked for their own marriage purposes, also means breaking off the affinal relations which had taken such efforts to build up. If, therefore, the wife's family are able to provide a substitute, they will normally do so, thus saving and further strengthening the relations between the two families to their mutual satisfaction. I must here emphasize that the first (barren) wife remains with her husband in that position and that the second woman is added to her 'house'. There is no question of a separate marriage in a legal sense; the second union merges with the first one, and no *lobolo as such* is given for the second woman to her family. But you will usually find that the husband's family, as a token of their appreciation, offer their family-in-law a few head of cattle.[25]

A similar procedure can be adopted when a wife dies prematurely, that is, at an early age and before she has fully spent her reproductive capacity. The fact that the woman may have left a few small children adds sentimental weight to the husband's appeal for a substitute wife. The father-in-law, however, may not be able to provide another wife right away. In that event he can still show his desire to help his bereaved son-in-law by offering him a

25. A marriage which remains childless on account of the impotency of the husband can be saved by a private arrangement between husband and wife, in which the husband allows the woman to have sexual intercourse with a third party approved by both. This so-called *kupindira* (to 'enter on behalf of someone') arrangement is secret and all parties are expected to behave with the utmost discretion. (See my *Shona Customary Law,* p. 218 ff., 273.)

few head of cattle as a 'breast for the children'. Do not think that with this gesture the father-in-law sends back some of the *lobolo* cattle. This interpretation is quite wrong because it would necessarily imply that the marriage relationship is thereby dissolved,[26] while on the contrary it has been greatly strengthened by this generosity. The idea behind this offer is that the wife's family, although they cannot, at the time, replace the deceased wife, want to make a substantial contribution towards solving their son-in-law's problem. These cattle are therefore *lent* to him, and he can, to a certain extent, make use of them as he thinks fit. He can use the milk for his youngsters, but he can also use the beasts to obtain another wife and step-mother in the meantime. If the wife's family at some later stage actually provide another daughter to take the place of the deceased one, such cattle with their offspring should be returned to them. But if they are unable to provide a substitute no cattle so advanced need be returned.

When a wife deserts her husband in favour of another man, the question of return of *lobolo* (or part of it) naturally also arises. (A woman past child-bearing age will rarely if ever attempt such a step.) In practically all such cases of divorce the husband's family therefore have a legal claim for a refund of at least a part of the bridewealth, for the simple reason that they have not had the full benefit of the woman as they are entitled to under the marriage contract. And this argument in support of a return of some cattle holds good even if the husband has been the guilty party.

I have so far mentioned a few instances in which the woman's family have, according to African law, failed to perform fully their legal obligations and in this manner disturbed the basic idea of balance implied in the marriage transaction. Obviously, this balance is also disturbed when the husband's family, after having received the wife and after she has raised a few children, fail to complete their *lobolo* deliveries. (Incidentally, full delivery of *lobolo* need not take place at the same time the wife is handed over to the husband's family; this may be done within a reasonable time after the conclusion of the marriage.) In such cases of default the wife's family can, if their repeated requests for cattle have failed, take the woman and children back, 'impounding them', so to speak, in the hope of forcing the husband to pay up. If this measure does not help, they may offer him an ultimatum: either to pay up immediately or to agree to a dissolution of the marriage, whereby the amount of bridewealth paid so far may, or may not, be considered sufficient to cover his paternal right to the children. If the husband is unable or unwilling to pay his debt the woman's family have the

26. See p. 122 ff.

right to marry her to another suitor and to accept bridewealth from him.

You will have noted that the death of a wife does not necessarily terminate the marriage relationship between the two families, because a substitute may be provided without additional bridewealth or another marriage contract. The death of the *husband* likewise does not terminate the marriage in a legal sense. It is true that the particular *marital union* of husband and wife is terminated. But you have seen that this is only one aspect of the marriage transaction; the basic principle is that the *family of the husband* married this woman and gave bridewealth for her so that she could be the wife of one of the sons and so bear children for this kin-group. For this reason, when the husband dies and the wife is still young enough to bear children, the husband's family are fully entitled to provide another of their relatives (preferably a full brother of the deceased husband) to be her husband and to raise children by her for their kin-group. This is their indisputable right and the woman's family will never interfere in this. If this appears to you a little hard on the widow, let me at once assure you that in practice there is comparatively little hardship because she has the right to choose another husband from among an often considerable number of her husband's relatives.[27] It may also be of interest to note that, unlike among some other southern African tribes, there is *no* question of 'raising up seed' *on behalf of the deceased husband*;[28] the second husband obtains the woman as a wife in his own right and raises his own children by her.

Only when the widow refuses to accept any of the eligible candidates her husband's family can offer to her does the question of a formal dissolution of the marriage arise, and with it, the inevitable claim for a refund of *lobolo* cattle. The matter is then comparable to a divorce resulting from the wife's infidelity, which gives the husband's family a legal ground for action. In other cases the marriage relationship continues, though with a different marital union, in accordance with the broad principles of Shona marriage as contracted between the two families.

Following my first talk the question of polygamy was raised from the audience, and I may make a few observations about this institution. Among many southern African tribes (for instance the south-eastern Nguni, of which

27. So long as the widow accepts one of the eligible members of her late husband's kin-group known as *cizwarwa* (see footnote 13, p. 97) she fulfils her family's obligation under the marriage contract; but the choice of any such relative other than one of the deceased's full brothers or half-brothers may result in a claim for cattle by the deceased's 'house' from the 'house' of the new husband.

28. For the Zulu, see, for instance, Gluckman, M., in *op. cit.*, p. 182 ff.; for the Tswana, Schapera, I., *Handbook of Tswana Law and Custom*, O.U.P., 1938, p. 164 f.

the Rhodesian Ndebele are an offshoot) a plural marriage results in a classification of the wives of one man, and their respective 'houses', into a definite *legal* order of rank. In this respect the Shona are different, that is, the children of the first wife have no special priority (for instance as regards succession to their father's position and name) over the children of subsequent wives. Each wife, with her so-called house (*imba*) is regarded as an independent and equal part of the plural family. Each wife has her own garden, granary, hut, *etcetera,* and runs her household independent of the other co-wives. But they share a common husband and are entitled to an equal share of his attention and help. Among themselves they may, and often do, make arrangements for mutual help in the cultivation of their fields and other duties, but each wife remains responsible for her own household and will prepare a plate of food for the husband's every meal. It is true that the first wife (in order of marriage) is generally regarded as senior. She is referred to as *vahosi* and her co-wives call her *mukoma* (elder sister). But her enhanced status is not legally defined. It is more in the manner in which we give our eldest daughter certain responsibilities regarding her younger sisters, using her as the person to whom we give orders applicable to all, letting her divide and distribute gifts and allowances meant for all. The first wife has no more rights than the others and is not entitled to a bigger share of what the husband dishes out. Owing to this individual independence and responsibility and their equal rights, the relations between co-wives are, on the whole, good, and I have so far heard only a few Christian wives condemning polygamy as such. There are, of course, cases of bickering and hostility among co-wives, and the principal cause of these appears to be that the husband has shown a clear preference for one of his wives and then neglects the others, especially in marital love. Such situations are a most fertile breeding ground for accusations of witchcraft, resulting in misery. But they are comparatively rare, because the average polygamist is aware of his duties and will do his best to guard against undue favoritism, if only because he hates domestic upheavals.

In a recent novel[29] by an American woman the main thesis seemed to be that polygamy should be condemned *per se,* because no man would be able physically to gratify several wives. In the case she skilfully describes, that of King Solomoni of the Zulus, this argument cuts ice, because Solomoni had scores of wives. But this is a very rare exception: the percentage of men having even three or four wives is extremely small.[30] The case against polygamy suffers from a good many prejudices which are not always sup-

29. Reyher, R. H. *Zulu Woman,* Columbia University Press, 1947.
30. Less than one per cent in a sample of 600 marriages in the Wedza Reserve.

ported by facts. At any rate, it is a minority problem which loses its proportions every year,[31] not so much on account of improved Christian morality, but as the result of increased economic pressure which wives bring to bear upon their husbands. Plurality of wives nowadays tends to be a greater burden economically than it is an asset socially.

The narrow space of a thirty-minute talk does not permit more than a cursory glance over some aspects of this wide and fascinating subject. Yet this should be enough to show you that some of the issues involved are radically different from those of marriages in our Western society. But I hope I have also made it clear that, in spite of these differences, the institution of African marriage is, in its own way and social setting, as inviolate and as anxiously protected by law and ritual as our own marriages are.

III. THE POSITION OF WOMEN

In the first section, on the significance of the *lobolo* (bridewealth) system, I showed that this type of marriage, instead of a degrading mercenary transaction, is the honourable and legal way in which families contract marriages and raise legitimate children in conformity with the fundamental laws of kinship and social organization in African society. From the second section, and especially from the description of one of the Shona marriage procedures, you will have gathered that the cautious and courteous manner in which the bride is received by her husband's family is inconsistent with another still common fallacy, namely that she is acquired as a piece of property, a person without rights or dignity. Closely allied to these misconceptions is another belief which still persists in many circles: that women in African society have no rights to property. This view was expressed in print by a senior official of the Native Department as late as 1948.[32] These three fallacies may be regarded as the unholy trinity on which the majority of the European public, here as well as abroad, have based a false and dangerous conception of the position of women in African society.

I therefore want to give you a brief outline of the actual position occupied

31. According to figures in the *Annual Report of the Chief Native Commissioner*, 1950, less than eight per cent of African husbands were polygynists, as against about thirty-two per cent in 1900. For some more figures on the declining incidence of polygyny see Phillips, A. A. (Ed.) *Survey of African Marriage and Family Life*, O.U.P. for International African Institute, 1953, Chap. I ('Extent of Polygyny').

32. Morkel, E. R., 'Native Administration and some Customs and Beliefs', *NADA* No. 26 (1949), pp. 40-42.

by women in Shona society, and I shall do this by picking up and further developing certain basic principles which I discussed in my previous talks. I follow this method because I want you to understand that the position of women – as so many other aspects of tribal life – is part and parcel of a wider and consistent scheme of things, and that, although different from ours, this scheme is nevertheless logical and, in its own way, adequate and equitable. In evaluating African customs and institutions one should not ask whether such institutions, taken at their face value and divorced from their natural setting, would conform to *our* ideas of propriety and morality, but whether, seen as a natural part of the totality of African life and thought, they serve a useful purpose fairly and equitably.

Let me, by way of introduction, state that we are dealing with a society in which public functions are in the hands of a few people. Traditional tribal government itself does not yet reveal that measure of differentiation in various 'departments' as we know it: Legislation, Administration of Justice, Police, Welfare, Economic Affairs, *et cetera*, are merely aspects of one indivisible task of 'government' and are therefore to a very great extent controlled by – or rather, supervised or guided by – the same set of office bearers. Tribal government in rural Mashonaland is in principle not very much more, or more complicated, than keeping harmony between, and looking after the interests of, members of a large family group. The traditional functions of a chief or headman are to a large extent a reflection, on a big scale, of the functions of the head of a family. It is a part-time, rather casual, task, which keeps the office bearers busy for perhaps a few hours a week and then usually only when the occasion (for instance, a lawsuit) arises. Tribal government and public representation have not yet outgrown the characteristics of domestic arbitration and family representation. Public offices in tribal life are mostly filled by people in hereditary capacity,[33] which

33. Not mentioned here are certain functions and offices created by the Administration, some of which are fulfilled by appointed or elected office bearers. Perhaps the most important of the latter are the members of the local African Councils, established in a number of tribal areas as a (not yet very successful) experiment in local self-government in a non-traditional field of interest (especially economic development).

People like departmental messengers, African agricultural demonstrators, African teachers, etc., working in tribal areas obviously belong to an entirely different category, because they represent an essentially European sphere of administrative activity.

Statute law (esp. the *Native Affairs Act – Chapter 72*, and the *Native Law and Courts Act, 1937*) has also placed certain duties upon the shoulders of chiefs and headmen, mainly to assist departmental African administration. Although under statute law *any* African can be recognized as a chief or headman, the Administration has, as a working basis, on the whole accepted hereditary tribal authority to fulfil these duties. The immeans that the office bearers – chiefs, headmen, principal councillors – occupy such offices because they happen to be the senior members of the families that have traditionally been associated with such particular functions in tribal life. These people are called upon to perform such public duties for the very reason that they are the heads of their particular families. And since in this patriarchal society only men, and not women, are the traditional heads of families, it is, except in very rare circumstances, inevitable that only men occupy public offices.[34]

Moreover, all important matters, whether a marriage, the taking up of fresh arable land, or a lawsuit, involve not only the individual parties concerned but also – and I am inclined to say, rather – their respective *families.* This means that any affair of any magnitude automatically becomes a matter of family representation, that is, the parties are represented by their responsible family heads, and again, these heads are never women. But before you think that this is an unfair restriction of the legal status of women, let me tell you that nine out of ten married men are in a similar position of so-called 'perpetual minority' because, unless they happen to be the most senior member of their family group they, too, remain more or less under the guardianship of their family head.

If you ask an African why you do not normally meet with women in public capacity, he may give you one short but all-inclusive answer: 'Because they are women.' In this sober statement of fact the question of merit or feminine capabilities does not even enter. It merely explains all there is to explain: that this sort of function lies outside the sphere of feminine activity. But it also implies that, if you want to find out about the importance of

---

position of these duties has, to some extent, introduced an element of regularity in the manner in which public functions are being discharged. For instance, most chiefs and headmen now have one or two fixed court days per week on which they deal with any matter which may come up for discussion or decision. But in spite of the fact that the government now pays them an annual salary in recognition of their responsibilities, very few of these tribal authorities look upon their functions as a full-time occupation. [For a full treatise on the position of the Rhodesian tribal chieftain, see Holleman, J. F., *Chief, Council and Commissioner*, 1969.]

34. There is one important function often fulfilled by women in Shona society, that of *swikiro* or spiritual medium of some ancestral spirit. If the medium represents *Mhondoro,* the spirit of one of the ancient chiefs, her influence in tribal affairs may be very considerable. A good example is Careva, the medium of the *Mhondoro* of the Budya tribes in northeastern Mashonaland, who has a decisive voice in matters of chieftainship and the admission of settlers in the tribal domain. (See Holleman, J. F., *Accommodating the Spirit among some North-Eastern Shona Tribes.* Rhodes-Livingstone Paper 22. Oxford University Press, Cape Town, 1953; also p. 48 above.)

women, you will have to explore those aspects of African life in which women figure naturally and prominently. And these lie, obviously, in the sphere of domestic activities and the rearing of children. I am aware of a tendency among our own ambitious womenfolk to look upon these functions with condescension, but I must remind you that in rural African society the greatest ambition of most men and women still is to be the parents of a large brood of children; that there is little more admirable than a woman who has not only raised a half-dozen strong children, but who also has a good name as a cook and brewer of beer. These issues are, among the peoples I studied, still most important in life. It is on these achievements that social esteem, public prestige and even political authority are largely based.

You will remember that I explained how the establishment of marriage relations and the procreation of children are part and parcel of a wide kinship structure and organization in which every member is placed in a position of relative superiority or subordination to every other member. In this system – the hub of tribal organization – the *men* of a family that has provided a wife to another family are ranked as 'father' (that is, socially superior) to the men of the family that has received the wife; and these 'fathers' are, in turn, 'children' (that is, socially subordinate) to the men of the families from which *they* have received wives. We may now ask: if this crucial social process is expressed in a system in which the *men* are placed in a particular position of superiority or subordination, and if full credit is given to the women for the part they play in this process of procreation, may we not expect that the position of women, too, is legally expressed in terms which do not merely convey the idea that they are cooks and bearers of children? In other words, what is the position of women in this important kinship structure, and how is this revealed in everyday life?

First a warning: I have found that many people, when speaking of women generally, are inclined to think of them mainly as so many wives of husbands. But the wife-husband relationship is not the only one in which a woman finds herself in normal social life. She is also, among others, a mother of children, a sister of brothers and a sister-in-law, and – very important in African life – the mother-in-law of her daughters' husbands. I mention this beforehand because the pattern of behaviour in each of these relationships is fundamentally different from the others, and you cannot possibly form a balanced opinion of the position of women in African society without giving careful consideration to these various aspects.

I have earlier explained that among the Shona the system of family procreation is based on the premise that every woman marries for a dual purpose: to reproduce the paternal kin-group of her husband by bearing children to him and to provide the means (that is, the *lobolo* or bridewealth) through which her own family can marry a wife for her brother and so help reproduce her *own* paternal kin-group. This is her natural function, and the vital importance of this is formally recognized and clearly defined in the kinship structure. It is not only expressed by the use of appropriate kinship terms, but is also revealed in the position of authority which a woman can rightly assume under certain circumstances.

Diagram IV

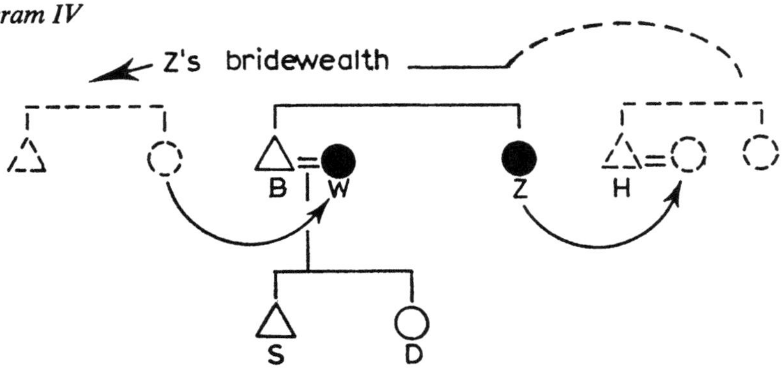

B married W with bridewealth received for sister Z when she married H:
W calls Z VAMWENE ('owner');
Z calls W MUROVORA ('woman of my bridewealth');
Z is called VATETE ('honorary father') by B's children S and D, and she is SAMUKADZI ('keeper of the woman') and 'executrix' of brother B's estate when he dies.

To the wife of her brother a woman is *vamwene* ('owner') because she is assumed to have provided, through her own marriage, the cattle through which this woman has been married to her brother (see Diagram IV). This places her in a position of authority over her brother's wife, as well as over the other female relatives of this woman's family. To her brother's children a woman is *vatete* or *samukadzi*. The first term can be freely translated as 'female father' (*va-* is actually the honorific plural prefix); the second is similar to *vamwene*, and means the 'keeper of the wife'. Both terms again indicate a position of authority, this time as regards members of the woman's *own paternal kin-group*.

What is the practical significance of these terms? It implies, in the first place, the acknowledgement that the family unit and estate established by a man owes its existence to the sister who provided the necessary cattle for his marriage. This places the sister in a position of authority in some vital matters concerning this family unit. She becomes the obvious arbitrator in disputes between husband and wife, and the children of this marriage will look to this aunt for help and advice. It is to her husband's sister that a woman will usually turn first when she is ill-treated by her husband, because it is this sister who, perhaps more than any other person, is in a position to bring pressure to bear upon her brother. It is also this woman who, after the death of her brother, is in charge of the proceedings by which his estate is distributed.[35] She is, legally, the 'executrix' – *samukadzi* – of her brother's estate. Among some Shona tribes[36] further tangible recognition of her function is shown because she is entitled to receive one head of cattle from her brother's estate. Do not think that this position is a sinecure. She can, and often does, wield great power in these important family matters.

Shona society therefore does not merely pay lip service to the part played by their women. It recognizes their biological function as one of the vital forces of its organized existence and expresses this recognition in a clear-cut, legally defined position of authority in the affairs of her own paternal family.

But Shona society does not stop here. The legal privileges I have described above are due to a woman in her capacity as a sister, sister-in-law and paternal aunt, that is, primarily in connexion with her own paternal kin-group. We should also consider her position as a wife, as a mother and, later, as a mother-in-law, that is, her position in what is primarily the sphere of her husband's family. It should be emphasized that she has entered this family as a stranger and that to a very great extent she remains a stranger because she never becomes part of her husband's family as her own children do. She remains an indivisible part of her *own* kin-group and retains her own clan names. When she becomes ill, her husband must notify her family so that her ancestral spirits may be propitiated. In some tribes (for instance, the Hera of the Sabi Reserve) her husband may not even but her waiststring after her death in order to set her spirit free: this must be done by a blood-member of her own kin-group. Upon her marriage legal responsibility for her actions is not even fully taken over by her husband. The husband merely becomes her guardian in all matters concerning normal social intercourse and the ordinary transactions and petty disputes which this may involve. But in serious offices, homicide, witchcraft, even adultery, her own family cannot deny responsibility. A Shona proverb says of a married woman: 'her husband gets hold of her legs, but her head remains with its owners', which, freely translated, means that the husband may marry her and use her as a wife, but can never wholly possess her.

35. For a full description of these proceedings and of the exact function of the sister (and sister's son) in matters of succession and inheritance, see my *Shona Customary Law*, p. 235 ff.

36. For instance the Mari and Govera of the Chibi Reserve.

Since a woman does not become part of her husband's family she has little ground for exercising rights in the domestic affairs of her husband's family. Legally speaking she cannot even exercise rights over her own children; but this certainly does not mean that she cannot, through other, informal ways, bring pressure to bear in all domestic matters. Whatever *rights* she has *as a wife* are based on her marriage contract, which binds both parties and their families to certain obligations, and one of these obligations is that the husband should maintain her properly and treat her well. If he does not do so, if he abuses his marital powers or neglects her, she can complain to his family, and if they fail to bring him to reason she can appeal to her own family, who have their legal remedies to apply pressure on the husband and his family. And, finally, she can always, with the help of her family, lay a complaint against her husband in a tribal court of law.

But through being a wife, she also becomes the mother of children and ultimately the mother-in-law of her daughter's husbands. And now an entirely new kind of respect is due to her, which manifests itself in certain privileges. We now leave the relatively safe and predictable ground of law and logic and enter into a sphere in which the connexion between cause and effect is unknown, or at least vague and unpredictable because of the operations of certain mystical forces which lie beyond the control of living men. Though these forces operate in a mysterious way, their practical effects in life are observable and real enough for an African to believe in them and so to do everything possible to avoid their antagonism. So it is believed that the power of procreation of a woman is not centred in her alone, but is in some way part of a wider procreative power which is seated in, and handed down along, the line of her *maternal* ancestresses, of whom her mother, mother's mother and mother's mother's mother are the principal representatives. As one Shona man explained: 'When these spirits stop speaking together, her house stops bearing children; when they speak together, she will bear children.' The husband who marries her knows this and takes great care to win the favour of her mother, as this woman is the direct link with this mysterious female ancestral body. There is, in fact, no person among all relatives whom a man fears and respects so much as his wife's mother. During his betrothal he will work in her garden, cut firewood for her, help build or repair her hut. Later he will give her presents, some as an informal, others as a formal tribute. Among the central Shona the most important *formal* tribute given to a mother-in-law is the *ngombe youmai* or 'motherhood beast', always a cow or heifer. It may be given when the *lobolo* cattle are handed over, or it may be given later. The important fact about it is that it does *not* form part of the *lobolo* – which is the bridewealth paid to the wife's *paternal* family – but belongs to the wife's mother as the representative of this *matrilineal* body which exercises such a power over birth and even death.

The practical significance of the motherhood beast, too, cannot be overrated. The animal is dedicated by the wife's mother to the spirits of her own mother and mother's mother and if possible is kept alive by her so that it may multiply. Whenever there is a question of some spiritual anger or disapproval, one of the animals of this stock is sacrificed to the angry spirit in order to avoid death and disaster. Consequently, there are not a few women in these areas who possess a sizeable herd of cattle in their own right, or rather as representatives of a matrilineal kin-group. The husband of such a woman has no right whatever regarding this estate.[37] On the contrary, he is scared of this property because he fears the mystical consequences of any mishandling or misappropriation. This estate will, therefore, after the woman's death be handed over to her own blood-relatives, who will look after it, likewise keeping the animals so that they may be available for the propitiation of her spirit and the spirits of her matri-line. Her *own* children and her full-brothers may benefit from this estate, for instance in matters of bridewealth. But her husband's children by another wife and her half-brothers (that is, those not borne by her own mother) cannot be considered: the spiritual right-holders would never allow this.

You may find other, similar tributes payable by a son-in-law to his mother-in-law. For instance, after the young wife has conceived for the first time it is customary to present two goats[38] to her parents, a male and a female. The male goat is given to the father and is killed and medicinally treated to 'protect the backs of the parents', who have been mystically threatened by this first pregnancy of the daughter. The female goat is given to the woman's mother and, like the motherhood beast, is kept if possible for ritual purposes.

Not everywhere in Mashonaland does one find that this maternal estate has assumed such great proportions as it has among the central tribes. Along the perimeter it exists only in rudimentary form. But everywhere it is potentially there, because the *mystical basis for its existence* is everywhere evident.[39]

37. For more details regarding this 'matri-estate', see my *Shona Customary Law*, Chapter VIII.

38. The two *masungiro* goats in connexion with the *kusungira* (binding, strengthening) ritual.

39. Among the Budya of northeastern Mashonaland the first instance of a 'motherhood cow' being given occurred in 1950, and there is every likelihood of this becoming a widespread fashion.

Among the Mari and Govera in the Chibi area, gifts of cloth or cash (five to ten

Apart from all this, a woman has the right to acquire property by her own manual efforts, for instance, by cultivating a surplus crop, by raising fowls and small stock, by making and selling pots. Provided that she does not neglect her duties as a wife, mother and producer of food for her household, she has a clear and indisputable right to the proceeds of any such additional efforts. In the same manner, all that she may earn as a skillful midwife or herbalist is her own and does not form part of her husband's estate.

I have so far confined myself to such aspects of a woman's position in Shona society as are part of the basic social structure. What I have given you are merely the rules according to which the game of life has to be played. As such they are important, not only because they show you the logical relations of one aspect to another in the total scheme, but also because they provide a substantial and rational basis for a discussion of a subject which has, from its very nature, many intangible, irrational, emotional and unpredictable aspects; because the game of life, like any other game, only becomes a reality when it is actually being played, and in the playing the personalities and characters of the players become major factors. I have not gone into these imponderable aspects because it is difficult to describe them accurately in general terms. But I may give you a few examples. Although there is no fixed division of labour in connexion with food production, and husband and wife are considered jointly responsible for the cultivation of their fields, the women seem to bear the brunt of hard labour. On the other hand, I know many husbands who work as hard as their wives do. At home the husband likes to behave like a lord, waiting to be served while his wife is slaving to get her housework done and to feed the family. I discussed this unequal situation with both men and women, but when I suggested that husbands should give their wives a hand in this domestic drudgery it was usually the women who opposed this idea most vigorously. They felt that this was *their* domain and proudly asserted that they alone were capable of performing these manifold tasks efficiently.

I do not deny that women in African society have a hard task to fulfil and that they are not always treated very civilly. But this again very largely depends on the particular relations between men and women. A man will generally treat his *wife* indifferently and curtly in public (although he is *by law* expected to lavish affection upon her in the privacy of their sleeping

---

shillings) are given to mothers-in-law, and a maternal estate, when available, is more likely to have developed from the *usamukadzi* beast, a woman's share of her brother's estate in recognition of her services as an executrix.

quarters); he will treat his '*sisters*' with more respect, his '*mothers*' usually with a great deal of respect and his 'mothers-in-law' with the utmost deference and courtesy. And as the result of the principle of kinship classification every man has many sisters, mothers and mothers-in-law. Consequently, the public courtesy which a woman cannot expect from her own husband is shown to her by all who are her so-called brothers, children and children-in-law.

I repeat that, publicly and legally, a woman is definitely subordinate to her husband, and he has the right to discipline her when she fails in her domestic duties, even to the extent of giving her a moderate hiding (though excessive and unreasonable beatings are actionable under customary law). This may shock you because it is not in accordance with the ideas of chivalry upon which civilized man is professed to act. But even in this respect other people may hold different sentiments. For instance, an old, wise and happily married African woman once confided to me in all seriousness: 'A woman who is never beaten by her husband, even when she deserves it, will think that her husband does not love her any longer.' Turn this over in your mind, and you will probably find a good deal of elementary logic and psychology in these words. And do not think of her as a meek, beaten old woman, typical of countless others who have learned to expect and silently suffer physical violence. She was certainly typical of her kind, but she was not meek and subdued at all. She had dignity and a good deal of fighting spirit. She could and did, in her own good time and in her own feminine ways, call the tune in her domestic environment; and her husband, too, would know when to listen to her imperious voice. I do not think there are many husbands who do not have a healthy respect for their wives once their feminine tempers are roused and their sharp tongues start slinging invective.

It is difficult to generalize upon these personal aspects of domestic life and authority, but I think that one broad generalization is justified. Women practically everywhere, and including our Western society, probably have a comparatively harder and more thankless task in life than men. This is not because they are inferior but because the Creator made them *women* and assigned to them the often dreary task of bearing and rearing the young and tending their homes, while the men were left free to attend to the more spectacular, public side of social life. In our society the hard struggle for female emancipation has been fought under the banner of 'equality' for men and women. This was because the pre-existing *inequality* was largely interpreted as a difference between male *superiority* and female *inferiority*. Shona society assumes, however, that this is not so much a matter of inequality as of *difference* between the sexes. And if we had, as Shona society has, accepted this biological reality and given women legal rights and authority accordingly, the fight for female emancipation, with its often ignoble incidents, might never have occurred.

I do not pretend that African society is paradise and that there is nothing wrong with the present lot of its women. Undoubtedly a great deal can be done to make life more comfortable for them. But we should be careful not to introduce 'improvements' which might wreck the social order. I have shown how the position of women in Shona society is determined by the natural functions of their sex, and how their strong legal and social status rests on the principles of the bridewealth marriage. Yet you commonly hear people talking of 'doing away with this debasing *lobola* business'. The latest *Native Marriages Act* does not yet 'do away with' *lobolo,* but the £ 20 legal ceiling[40] and other restrictions are a long step in that direction. The draftsmen of the Act unquestionable meant well. They wanted to curb certain abuses which they erroneously believed were due to the *lobolo system;*[41] they probably also meant to improve the lot of African women and of African society in general by trying to steer away from *lobolo* and other such 'uncivilized' practices. But these lofty ideals do not disguise the fact that they were guided by a common and dangerous misconception. They assumed, as most of us are only too apt to assume, that what is good for us must necessarily be good for others.

IV. THE DISSOLUTION OF CUSTOMARY MARRIAGE

Probably the best introduction to the principles underlying the dissolution of the bridewealth marriage is a recapitulation of the principles on which such a marriage is contracted. It is the agreement between two families that the one shall provide a wife with normal child-bearing capacity to the other who, in return, shall give such compensation (*lobolo*) as is the equivalent in African society of such a woman.

In this definition two basic aspects stand out very clearly:

1. that the marriage contract is legally a matter between the two families as the responsible parties;
2. that the performances of the two parties (families) should ultimately be approximately balanced, that is, the transaction will be satisfactorily completed when the woman has fully spent her capacity as a wife and

40. *Section 11* of the Act. [But also see p. 87 above – J. F. H.]
41. *Cf.* footnote 16, p. 98.

bearer of children for the benefit of her husband's family and the husband's family have fully discharged their obligations in connexion with the payment of bridewealth.

Note that I say 'ultimately' balanced, because in practice it hardly ever happens that the performance of the two parties run concurrently. Usually the husband's family have completed their *lobolo* obligation long before the wife has finished bearing children; and sometimes the wife has borne two or more children before the husband had delivered any cattle. But as long as good faith prevails this temporary lack of balance does not matter, because the parties have no reason to doubt that, ultimately, basic equality will be achieved. Marriages are, after all, meant to last a lifetime.

On the other hand, it is easy to understand that whenever marriages are broken up, it almost invariably happens at a stage when this ultimate aim of balance has not yet been achieved, with the result that some kind of settlement must be made.

The *dissolution* of the Shona bridewealth marriage is, to a great extent, a reversal of the process by which it was contracted. The basic idea is that the husband's family return the wife with all or a portion of her reproductive capacity unspent and that the wife's family return as much of the *lobolo* as would approximately balance the value of the returning wife. Or, to put it differently (but perhaps not so accurately), the husband's family should keep whatever children the woman has borne to them, and the wife's family are entitled to keep as much of the *lobolo* as would approximately compensate for these children.

Let us analyse this process in more detail. First of all, there is *no question of a unilateral action. Both families* participate in the divorce action: the husband's family by returning the wife (if she has not already deserted her husband) and the wife's family by returning *lobolo* cattle. Only when these two actions have been completed is the marriage dissolved. The belief, so often expressed in many circles, that an African husband can dissolve his marriage merely by sending his wife home with a rejection token is utter nonsense. Even if he could do so (and he cannot, without the assistance of his family-in-law) he would never be so foolish because he would in this manner forfeit his rightful claim to a return of cattle. I shall come back to this point later.

Another, most important point is that, unlike the situation in our law, a Shona marriage is not dissolved by an Order of Court. In fact, *no court,* whether tribal or European, has under Shona law the power to dissolve a marriage. You can understand this if you realize that it is the *concrete action of undoing the marriage,* that is, the actual physical return of wife and cattle, instead of an abstract order or decree, that dissolves the marriage. Even if a court would order such a divorce, the marriage would not be considered legally dissolved until the woman had left her husband, and the husband had received back such *lobolo* cattle as are due to him; and for the performance of these tasks only the two families, and not the court, can be held responsible. I am stressing this point because misunderstanding of it has caused the greatest confusion in our courts of law and has finally crystallized in exactly the wrong interpretation in the latest *Native Marriages Act,* a point to which I shall return later.

I repeat that the dissolution of the *lobolo* marriage is based upon the bilateral agreement by the responsible families that the marriage shall be dissolved by a liquidation of the principal 'assets' involved in the marriage, that is, in practice, by a settlement regarding wife, children and cattle. This agreement may be explicit and amicable, or it may be inferred from the way a party grudgingly submits to what he considers a hard but inevitable turn of events. Mere agreement, however, is not sufficient (just as mere agreement to marry does not yet constitute a marriage): it is necessary that the parties act upon this agreement and *actually effect a settlement* before a marriage can be considered dissolved. In other words, while in our law the question of divorce and the division of properties are two different legal issues, the dissolution of marriage and the distribution of the principal assets are, under Shona law, merely two aspects of one and the same thing: the legal liquidation of the marriage.

We can now ask for *what reasons* such a dissolution can be sought by either party, or, in other words, what are the recognized grounds for a divorce under Shona law. You will find that the position is entirely different from that under our own law system, in which a divorce can only be granted if a spouse can prove to the satisfaction of the Court that there exist one or two of a very limited number of recognized grounds for divorce (for instance, adultery or malicious desertion). The Shona view the problem from a realistic and practical angle. To them the only questions that really matter are these: is a continuation of the marriage under the circumstances *reasonably practicable or not;* and if not, *on which terms* should the marriage be liquidated.

Put like this, any conceivable reason which makes the continuation of the marriage impracticable may in principle lead to a divorce. At first glance this may give the erroneous impression that a divorce may be obtained for any trivial reason, while, on the contrary, it is comparatively difficult to obtain a divorce under Shona law; and low divorce rates[42] prove this. There are two main reasons for this: firstly, it takes *two* parties to bring about a divorce; secondly, a dissolution is inseparable from a return of *lobolo* cattle to the husband's family, and such cattle may not be readily available. This means that, while the husband may think that he has a good reason for divorcing his wife, his father-in-law may disagree on this point and refuse to hand back any cattle, without which no marriage can be dissolved. And even if the father-in-law agrees in principle that the marriage should be dissolved, he may have no cattle available, with the result that the marriage remains in force until such time as he is able to find cattle. And apart from this, there is the sharp realization that it has taken an enormous effort by both families to build up a good relationship-in-law. The interests involved are larger than a mere disagreement between husband and wife or the value of a few head of cattle. Moreover, the decision regarding a divorce does not rest with individual spouses, who may be young, emotional and impetuous, but with the heads of their respective families, elderly people who know about the ups and downs of married life and who are able to view the problem from a far wider and less passionate angle. And because they are able to weigh the issue in all its aspects – not only the advisability, but also the practical possibility of a divorce – they are not apt to make rash decisions.

For these reasons you will find that even if a wife commits an act of adultery this will seldom the first time lead to a dissolution of the marriage, provided that she behaves in the future. As a matter of fact, the habitual failure of a woman properly to cook her husband's food is often considered far more serious than an occasional lack of marital fidelity. A good many husbands have assured me that 'you can always forgive your wife when she has slept with another man; but if she cannot cook well by the time she gets married, she is useless, because this means that she will never learn.'

A lazy, disobedient or quarrelsome wife may sometimes be returned to her parents for a period of correction and sent back again when she is supposed to have learned to behave better. But if there is no sign of improvement, and her behaviour is a constant source of social disturbance, the husband's family will seek a divorce.

A Shona husband need not be maritally faithful, so long as he does not neglect his wife's sexual needs and tells her about is extra-marital love affairs. His failure to keep her informed mystically threatens the well-being of his wife and children; and the death of a child, believed to be due to his un-

---

42. In the southern Sabi Reserve: one-half per cent; northern Sabi Reserve (immediate environment of Buhera and major D. R. Mission: two per cent; in the more sophisticated communities of the Wedza Reserve: four per cent. All these figures include cases in which widows refused to be inherited by their late husband's relatives.

confessed adultery, is sufficient reason for his wife to leave him 'because my husband is killing my children.' This is tantamount to an accusation of witchcraft and, like any other accusation of witchcraft by either spouse, is serious enough to cause a dissolution of the marriage.

But a woman's most common complaint is probably either that her husband neglects her or his children or that he maltreats her. She may first complain to his sister or mother about this, but if the husband's family fail to bring about an improvement she may seek refuge with her own family, provided that she can produce concrete proof of his neglect or misbehaviour, such as her tattered clothes or bruises on her body.

The reasons mentioned above are mainly matters of personal incompatibility which, if they are serious or persistent enough, may lead to a divorce. Then there are the reasons based upon the non-fulfilment of the basic obligations under the *lobola* marriage contract which I discussed in some detail in the second section: that is, the failure of the husband's family to deliver *lobolo* as promised or the failure of the wife's family to provide a substitute or a seed-raiser or other suitable remedy when the wife dies prematurely or fails to bear children. These reasons weigh heavily because they go to the root of the marriage transaction. And then, finally, the reason which leaves very little scope for argument or hope of saving a marriage: when the woman deserts her husband in favour of a lover and refuses to return.

You now have a rough idea of the various reasons which may lead to a dissolution of the marriage. Let us now consider the *procedure.* Keep in mind that the dissolution of a marriage can only be brought about by the actual settlement regarding the wife, the children she may have borne to her husband, and the *lobolo.* It is obvious that a wife will not, in the event of a divorce, stay with her husband; it is also established practice that, whenever the *lobolo* or a substantial part of it has been paid, the children born so far will be retained by the husband's family. The practical result is that the only issue upon which everything ultimately depends is the return of *lobolo.* Of these cattle the wife's family are presumed to be the possessors, but in practice they seldom are: they have usually used the beasts (quite legitimately) for their own marriage purposes. The procedure therefore becomes a battle of wits between the husband's family who want their cattle back and the wife's family who want to avoid the calamity of having to refund these cattle from their own, usually inadequate, stock. The issue is largely dominated by two concepts: firstly, *mhoswa,* that is, the matter of guilt; secondly, *kuramba,* literally, 'to refuse', that is, the question of which party is to be regarded as the one who does not want to continue the marriage. 'Guilt' in this sense is any act or omission which may give the other party a reason for seeking a divorce. The failure of the wife to bear her husband children therefore renders her family 'guilty' as much as a reckless abuse of marital power by the husband would render his family 'guilty'.

In the beginning the matter of guilt may loom large, because it is the element which sets the ball rolling. But because it is often a very vague and difficult thing – both parties may not be blameless – the question of *kuramba* or 'refusal' very soon dominates the field. This needs an explanation. The basic idea is that divorce with its disruptive effects is a bad thing and that, whenever possible, serious efforts should be made to save a marriage. The parties should therefore be reconciled rather than divorced. Public sentiment (and therefore also any tribal court's sentiment) being like this, each party consequently will, in its own interests, aim at a reconciliation, or at least pretend to do so, thereby manoeuvering the *other* party into the unfavourable position of the 'refusing party', that is, the party that does not want a reconciliation. And in these tactics the question of guilt (*mhoswa*) may often fade into the background. A few examples may illustrate this.

A wife repeatedly commits adultery and the husband wants a divorce. He takes her back to his family-in-law and tells them: 'The blanket you gave me is too big; it overpowers me. I want my cattle back.' The father-in-law says: 'I agree with you that my daughter is guilty of bad behaviour, but undoubtedly she still loves you. She should therefore kill a fowl and prepare this nicely for you, as a sign that she repents.'

If the husband accepts this offer and takes his wife back, he can, with the assistance of his father-in-law, institute a claim for compensation for adultery against his wife's lover. If he rejects the offer, he forfeits his claim against the lover, *and* he places himself in the unfavourable position of the 'refusing party'. Because he rejects what appears to be a reasonable attempt to save the marriage, he cannot mobilize the support of a tribal court in forcing his father-in-law to refund cattle immediately. The court will tell him: 'Why do you want your cattle back when your wife promises to behave better and to go back to you? If you want your cattle you will have to wait until the woman has found another husband who is willing to give cattle for her.'

Here is another example. A husband ill-treats his wife and she runs away to her parents. She can show the bruises on her body, which clearly prove the husband guilty. If he wants a divorce at this stage he cannot expect his father-in-law to find cattle immediately for the liquidation of the marriage. Yet he wants his cattle, or his wife. He therefore goes to his in-laws, pleads guilty, and offers to give his wife something as a compensation for his bad behaviour, so that she might come back to him. If the offer seems reasonable the father-in-law may prevail upon his daughter to accept reconciliation and go back to her husband. Buf if she, or her family, reject the offer, they become the refusing party and liable to refund the necessary cattle at the earliest possible date.

A third example. A woman no longer loves her husband. If she runs away she places her family in the unfavourable position of the refusing party. So instead she tries to provoke her husband into *sending* her away. She may dish up his food in a broken vessel, or deny him conjugal privileges, or neglect her household duties. In his rage the husband may now send her away with a rejection token (a shilling or a basket with her cooking stones). In this manner *he* becomes the refusing party, thereby stengthening the hand of his father-in-law who can 'prove' that his daughter has not left her husband on her own account.

A final example. A husband is tired of his wife, but does not want to drive her away with a rejection token because he cannot then claim immediate return of his *lobolo* cattle. So he tries to provoke her desertion. He may frighten her by making her believe that she is being bewitched (for instance, by cutting some of her green crops or by placing ashes or blood on her doorstep). Or he may deny her sexual gratification in the hope of driving her into the arms of a paramour. If she falls into the trap and deserts him, her family become the refusing party and have to return *lobolo* immediately. But if she has steady nerves, she may manage to stay with her husband until, in his desire to see the last of her, he sends her home with a rejection token. Then he himself becomes the refusing party, and he will have to wait until it suits the father-in-law to return the cattle.

Within this limited space I cannot, unfortunately, go deeper into this aspect, but these few illustration may at least have given you an idea of the strategy and tactics of Shona divorce proceedings. The whole matter becomes considerably easier for both parties if the woman has a lover who is willing and able to pay the necessary cattle for her (plus some additional compensation). If this happens the wife's family loyally take the side of the husband and help him to sue the lover, while they themselves run no risk of losing any cattle at all. The lover foots the whole bill.

What is the function of a tribal court in these matters? I have stated that under Shona law the court has no power to dissolve a marriage; but the court may, and often does, fulfil two important functions. Firstly, if the parties cannot agree upon the question of *whether* a dissolution is reasonable under the circumstances the matter may be referred to a court, and both parties are then given an opportunity of explaining in (very great) detail their view of the matter. As in all other cases of formal litigation, the matter is thrashed out in public, with the assistance of everyone who thinks that he can contribute towards a solution of the problem. The court is then in a position to recommend ways of reconciliation, and if such a course is clearly impracticable, may *advise* the parties to dissolve the marriage. Secondly, if the parties are in principle agreed to dissolve the marriage, but cannot reach an agreement as to the *terms* on which the dissolution is to be effected, the court can, after having learnt all about the circumstances of the case, decide what number of cattle should be returned to the husband. But it is up to the wife's family (or the guilty lover) to provide the cattle and so actually and legally dissolve the marriage.

And this brings us to *the terms upon which lobolo* marriages are dissolved. In principle there should be a balance between the benefits retained by the husband and the benefits retained by the wife's family. The basic idea therefore is that there should be a balance, either between the number of cattle retained by the father-in-law and the children retained by the husband or (and this seems the more practical view) between the number of cattle returned to the husband's family and the remaining reproductive value of the woman. If this were the only consideration the issue might be decided on a roughly proportionate basis. But inevitably a host of other complicating factors are involved. I may mention a few: the matter of guilt, lack of good faith, the previous relations between the families which may determine an amicable or a hostile attitude towards the problem, a possible element of fear of future retribution, the fear of being bewitched by an aggrieved party at some future time. All these factors influence the final settlement in one way or another and may produce the most surprising results when the marriage is ultimately liquidated, especially when the matter is kept between the parties and not brought before a formal tribunal. And again, the whole idea of 'balance' may be completely lost when there is a guilty third party involved who is able to marry the woman and pay the necessary compensation. In such cases you will usually find that the husband recovers practically all of his *lobolo* (and sometimes even more) in spite of the fact that he also retains all the children the woman has borne to him.

Our courts of law have tried hard to bring some uniformity to these divorce settlements, but with little success.. For one thing, their approach to such problems is different from African law. In African law the courts seek a *solution* that will satisfy both parties; our courts impose a *decision* which satisfies the legal mind of the judge. Our courts are inclined to determine the amount of returnable bridewealth according to arithmetical formulae, cold calculations based on numbers of cattle and children and years of service rendered by the woman to her husband. Add to, or subtract from, this so much for the element of guilt, and out comes the answer, accurate to the nearest pound or shilling.[43] The African also keeps these things in mind but does not try to compute such values arithmetically, because there are so many factors involved which vary in every case and which probably never come to light in the all-too-hurried proceedings of a European court.

The result is that our courts' record in connexion with marriage law in general and the dissolution of marriage in particular is not a very happy one, at least not from the African point of view. It should have been recognized long ago that the proper authorities to deal with these matters are the tribal authorities, who have the time, the patience and the natural bent to explore the innumerable issues and side issues which invariably come to light in these highly explosive and emotional cases. Unfortunately our Legislature holds different views upon this subject and is determined that tribal courts shall have as little as possible to do with these cases.[44] And this leads us to the last point: the dissolution of customary marriages under statute law.

Let us first consider the position before January, 1951, the date when the new *Native Marriages Act* came into force. Before this date the position was

43. The case of *Kuzowomunhu v Eneleta & George*, 1949 N.A.C. 199, is a good example of this. The facts were briefly as follows. A husband had paid, *inter alia,* £15 and six head of cattle as *lobolo* and had been married to his wife for seven years, when she deserted him. Three children had been born, one surviving.

The Native Commissioner, granting a divorce, made the following deductions from the *lobolo:* £7.10/ - for seven years' services by the wife; one head of cattle for each of the children, whether alive or dead.

The husband appealed against this judgment, claiming that the deductions were too severe. The Native Appeal Court, upholding his appeal in part, changed the deduction for the wife's services to £2, in view of the fact that she had deserted her husband.

I put this case to the tribal court at Careva, Mtoko Reserve, to invite discussion. They looked slightly puzzled at first, then amused. But what provoked undisguised merriment was the unsolicited remark by a junior member of the public (who had scribbled some calculations on a slip of paper) that, according to 'the big Chief in Salisbury', the services of a wife were worth £1.1.4½ a year if she was faithful, and less than six shillings a year when she was not!

44. *Sub-section 5 of Section II* of the *Native Marriages Act, 1950,* lays down that 'a chief or headman shall... have no jurisdiction in or cognizance of any action or suit in relation to payment or recovery of marriage consideration.' And, before this date, *Section 6(2)(a)* of the *Native Law and Courts Act* (Chapter 73) laid down that a Native court should have no jurisdiction in an action or suit in which the dissolution of a marriage was sought.

The first-mentioned provision has proved to be unenforceable and is therefore largely being ignored by tribal authorities (p. 86); the second provision has always been irrelevant from a customary law point of view.

rather confused. *Section 3(1)* of the *Native Law and Courts Act* says that 'in the determination of any civil case between natives by any court of law the decision *shall be in accordance with native law and custom.*' There is a provision in *Section 2* of the same act which says that such law and custom should not be repugnant to the accepted ideas of natural justice and morality. But since there was nothing unjust or immoral about a divorce under African law, the dissolution of all African marriages (except Christian or civil marriages) should therefore have been governed by African law. This act further lays down (*Section 6(2)*) that tribal courts are not competent to grant divorces. This last provision is wholly irrelevant, because we have seen that under Shona law *no* court has such powers. The confusion arose because our courts were ignorant of the nature of a divorce under customary law. They could not get rid of the idea that, as with our own marriages, African marriages could be dissolved only by an order or decree of a court of competent jurisdiction. For this reason they assumed that the Native Commissioners' Courts (which had been given rather sweeping judicial powers under *Section 14* of the *Native Affairs Act*) had the power to dissolve African marriages.

The Native Appeal Court now went a step further. Ignorant of the principles customary divorce laws, this court not only assumed that Native Commissioners could dissolve customary marriages, but even went so far as to declare[45] that only such 'dissolutions' as were based upon a formal order or decree were legally valid. This conclusion is unwarranted and, in fact, in conflict with the superior authority of the *Native Law and Courts Act,* which explicitly recognizes *customary* law in these matters.

We must therefore come to the remarkable legal conclusion that whenever European courts assumed this (non-existing) power and divorced Africans by order or decree (as they have done in hundreds of cases), they acted *unlawfully!*

The whole position has, however, changed since January 1, 1951, with the operation of the new *Native Marriages Act. Section 17* of this act says clearly that 'no marriage... shall be dissolved except by Order of a Court of competent jurisdiction.' Parliament has the power to make and break laws, and there is no doubt that with this explicit provision the customary law principles with regard to the functions of a tribal or any other court have been overruled, and that, according to law, the dissolution of an African customary marriage can now only be *legally valid* upon the order of a

45. One of its most recent decisions can be found in *Moses v Mawaro*, 1949, N.A.C. 195, in which the President deliberately ignores customary law on this point.

competent (that is, European) court. This does not mean, of course, that under the new law such matters as the return of bridewealth will no longer be considered. Our courts will continue to decide upon the fate of *lobolo* cattle and other bridewealth in the same way as they have done so in the past: as an 'incident' of the dissolution of marriage.

In the very narrow space afforded me I have tried to sketch the basic principles of a large and vital chapter of Shona law and custom. These are not the dusty and curiously-shaped bones of a dead skeleton, but the co-ordinated body of a living force which controls the lives of a few million Africans in the Colony today. I have especially tried to make it clear that, although different from our system, this legal system is, for the peoples whose minds and habits have shaped and developed it for many generations, a logical, adequate, fair, efficient and adaptive system; that is, insofar as we have not unduly interfered with it by imposing ill-advised 'improvements'.

The administration of Africans is a difficult, complicated and often thankless task. It is in the hands of a department whose officials are keen and whose integrity and desire to do the right thing can never be doubted. They have achieved many things of which they can rightly be proud; they have also, in good faith, made a number of bad mistakes. One of the worst of these is the *Native Marriages Act, 1950*, to which I have referred with little appreciation several times before. If this act is enforced as the Administration meant it to be enforced (and this, fortunately, in practice appears to prove a doubtful proposition) it will weaken the fabric of organized African life in a manner never contemplated by the Administration.

Perhaps the main reason why I agreed to give these lectures was the desire to help create an atmosphere of better public understanding of the vital issues involved and so hasten the day when a better marriage Act will be substituted for the ill-advised piece of legislative patchwork now in force.

Cash, cattle or women: a conflict of concepts in a dual economy*

Before we are one hour older, if I have done nothing more, I hope at least to have persuaded you that the apparently fanciful title of my talk is scientifically justified and that in posing the choice between cash, cattle or women, I have given the briefest summary of the vital conflict of conceptual values which our underdeveloped African rural communities are facing in the course of present-day economic development.

I realize that in this talk I shall drift from the field of southern African anthropology – with which I am supposed to be familiar – into the field of economy – of which by training I am expected to be blissfully ignorant. While I shall therefore tread warily and diffidently, my passage may also be eased by the hopeful expectation that we may discover a fringe area of interest, a no-man's land of enquiry which neither you nor my discipline has yet successfully occupied and where, with a little goodwill on both sides, a joint excursion might yield fruitful results with regard to a better understanding of some of the problems of socio-economic change in our Southern African communities.

Speaking as a social anthropologist to economists, and knowing only too well the dangers of getting our wires crossed when we start using the more refined intra-disciplinary definitions in our inter-disciplinary communications, I would ask you to agree to my using two terms in a broadly understandable, though perhaps not strictly technical sense:

1. 'Economic(s)' and 'economy', in the sense of relating to the production and distribution of wealth;
2. 'Wealth', in the sense of a value concept implying material well-being, but not excluding social well-being. (Here bearing in mind that man may choose to pursue wealth either for his immediate or his future well-being).

If you accept these expressions as working formulae for the sake of our mutual understanding we can talk, without fear of terminological contradiction, about wealth as an economic as well as a social concept, both in

* Paper read to the Economic Society, Durban, October 1962. I am grateful to Miss Joan Knox who gave me some much-needed economic guidance.

Western societies with an exchange and money economy and in tribal societies with a so-called subsistence economy; and it will be possible for us to discuss, on a comparative basis, the *pursuit* of wealth as an economic process with social implications. And we shall have little trouble in recognizing the existence in both kinds of society of an urge to *accumulate* wealth, although the nature of wealth may be substantially different in one society from what it is in the other.

Having thus agreed to compare the accumulation of wealth in both types of society, I would pose as a first question: *How is wealth being accumulated?* Since I need in this gathering not waste my time by outlining how wealth is being pursued in societies with a Western economy, I can proceed to traditional tribal society. Since we are here accustomed to thinking in terms of subsistence economies, we might as well first observe how wealth is *not* likely to be accumulated in tribal society: namely by agricultural (crop) production, which was, and very largely still is, geared to meet bare subsistence needs, that is the food consumption requirements of each family or such other social unit engaged in crop production. Some qualification is necessary. Although the absence of a developed marketing system and the lack of suitable storage facilities made it unrealistic to expect traditional farming production to aim at more than subsistence requirements, and because for this reason the accumulation of wealth had no place in the normal process and aims of traditional crop production, small surpluses *were* in fact occasionally produced. Indeed, among some hard-working folk such surpluses were probably fairly regularly produced and disposed of in a variety of ways, for instance either by eating more than strictly necessary or by being extra lavish with hospitality and beer at the producer's home. Although in both ways a sense of material and social well-being was induced, and although in principle the imbibers of a host's beer were as often as not expected to render some manual service (thrashing, tilling, weeding) in return, it is doubtful if you would consider this an 'economic' return for the surplus produced. Yet a Zulu, for instance, would find little difficulty in regarding overeating or freely imbibing nourishing beer as an acquisition of personal wealth: *umuntu ocebile,* a 'fat' man, being synonymous with a 'wealthy' or 'prosperous' man.

There is, however, a third way of getting rid of excess quantities: by exchanging these for other consumer goods (pots, utensils) and, preferably, small (and rarely, large) livestock. I repeat, however, that since such transactions are of an *ad hoc* nature and not a regular feature of traditional crop production we may, by and large, exclude tribal crop husbandry as a field of economic enterprise associated with the accumulation of wealth among common folk.

For reasons which will become clear I shall leave animal husbandry until later and first deal with one or two other activities. Even in traditional society there was a measure of industrial specialization, and the stereotyped picture of tribal families all being perfectly capable of, and used to, fulfilling the whole range of their own consumption requirements – utensils, clothing, housing, furnishings, etc. – needs some modification. There always were people with special skills in some fields and little or no skill in others. These recognized potters (women), wood-, skin- or iron workers (men) and so on, though primarily farmers like all others, were part-time producers of marketable goods. Their production was definitely aimed at an output exceeding their own domestic requirements and at a deliberate and profitable disposal of the surplus production. If you add to these people other specialists – such as diviners, herbalists, midwives– who were and are paid for their services, you must conclude that, even in a society with a so-called subsistence economy, there exist scattered but fairly numerous instances of economic enterprise in which not the satisfaction of bare subsistence needs, but profit-making and the accumulation of wealth through exchange transactions are the primary (or at least an important) aim. However modest their scale, the *incidence* of these activities was regular enough for the development of some locally recognized standard values, for instance, the exchange value of a clay pot being its contents in grain; among the Shona, the contents of one *hozi* (storage compartment) as the equivalent of a head of cattle; iron spear heads, hoes, etc., having recognized values in terms of small or large stock.

In these private 'home industries' therefore, as well as among the few types of professions, one recognizes the kind of economic activity that could without difficulty also be found in societies with an exchange economy; and although they were often haphazardly conducted, there is no doubt that one can in these cases even speak of production for a 'market'. (With regard to the highly specialized iron industry among some Shona tribes, for instance, even a fairly well developed and widespread inter-tribal exchange system existed.) In short, co-existing with an agricultural production geared to subsistence needs, there were in tribal society recognized other means of production by which some individuals could and did accumulate wealth in terms compatible with those found in a Western exchange economy.

Let us now ask the next question: *Why do people want to accumulate wealth?* There are probably a host of reasons, but I shall confine myself to a few major ones which are comparable in both types of society:

(a) Purely or mainly for the sake of amassing a fortune, that is, accumulation for the sake of accumulating and of satisfying the sheer sense of possession. Here the classical stereotype of the miser regularly counting his growing pile of money for the joy of dipping his hands into his wealth is to some extent parallelled by the owner of a flock of sheep in the Buhera Reserve in Southern Rhodesia who refused my offer of four times the market value when I wanted to buy one of his multitude. Although he barely had a shirt to cover his back, he refused to sell because he 'much preferred to keep counting all his animals and enjoyed merely looking at them'.

(b) The second reason why people accumulate wealth may be for the *enhancement of one's social status and prestige* and, going one step further, in order to *gain political power.* I do not want to go into psychological aspects, except for noting what we have all observed: that the display of material wealth, the ability to entertain, and in other ways disseminate the knowledge that one is wealthy, can be and often is a powerful contributory factor towards gaining social status and prestige; and provided the means are large enough and ambitions are led into the right channels, wealth can also play an important role in the manipulation and acquisition of political power.

The same can be said of traditional Bantu society, with the qualifications that the odds are likely to be stacked more heavily against the *parvenu.* This is so, partly because the range of material needs is much more limited and the accumulation of material possessions (excepting livestock) becomes rather meaningless after consumption needs are adequately satisfied; perhaps even more important, however, because there is a tendency in tribal society for *wealth to be associated with rank in the genealogical and hereditarily conditioned political hierarchy.*

It may be desirable to elaborate a little on this. The concept of personal property did exist in traditional Bantu society, but was very largely limited to articles of personal use – clothing, adornments, weapons, utensils. With regard to commodities of wider utility, even if individually acquired – such as food grown, forest produce collected, monies earned by personal labour – the individual's right of 'ownership' was (and still often is) almost invariably modified by an inherent 'communal' quality. This means that, if necessary, such property could be called upon to serve a wider community of interests (the family unit of the primary owner, or even a wider group of kinsmen, say a lineage segment of some three generations deep). In other words, with regard to the latter kind of property, although the individual who acquired it would undoubtedly have a preferential right to the fruits of his own labour, a communal 'right of avail' (I am diffident about using the term 'ownership' in this connexion) would obtain, which entitled this wider group of kinsmen to look upon this property as forming part of a common family 'estate', of which the group could avail itself for the benefit of its more needy members. In this concept the family estate (which thus involved all but the most 'physically' personal property) was *part and parcel of the structure of these kinship groupings themselves*, and the management of the family estate was therefore vested in the hands of family elders, those that were genealogically senior. A junior member, who by luck or hard work had succeeded in amassing a fair amount of property of a not strictly 'personal' utility value would not be permitted to exercise an unrestricted right of ownership over such property without consultation with his family elders; and might, in the interest of his wider family group, even have to forfeit some of these assets in favour of a more needy (or senior) near relative. Refusal to recognize the legitimacy of these wider claims would be tantamount to insubordination, and might well lead to his estrangement from his kin-group. Without its ritual, legal and social protection, to which he and his immediate dependants would normally have been entitled, life itself would be rendered insecure, and he would think twice before risking such consequences.

Do not think this is all past history, an anthropologist's reconstruction of the social fossils of a buried age. A good deal of this is still very much alive today in virtually every rural African society, though exposure to Western economy does steadily weaken this communal fabric.

This hierarchical family control over individually acquired property, while not completely discouraging all individual efforts to accumulate property (the person concerned did, after all, retain a preferential claim to these assets, and a rough tally of how much other relatives 'borrowed' from him was kept), had at least a depressing effect upon the amount of fun the individual worker hoped to derive from the fruits of his efforts, and this itself is probably one important reason for the odd lack of African response to the type of incentive to which *white* workers normally do respond.

Then there is the political factor. Since the management of worthwhile property (i.e., wealth) was the prerogative of the genealogically senior, and since the genealogically most senior were likely to be also the political leaders in a society organized very largely upon kinship structure, wealth was also an attribute of the politically powerful and therefore associated with the relative few in hereditary positions of tribal authority. (On the other hand, these leaders were expected to be generous and extend hospitality on a large scale.) The rank and file of the community would accept material egalitarianism not only as a social norm but as a matter of political prudence. While modest departures from this norm would be tolerated (as long as one was prepared to share), a spectacular increase in wealth of someone not well up in the political hierarchy was almost bound to arouse envy and suspicion, and even today would be tantamount to inviting an accusation of witchcraft. We struck quite a few examples of this during our recent research in Swaziland.

One reason for the well-known Zulu institution of *ukusisa* and its counterparts among other tribes – that is the distribution in usufruct by an owner of a large herd of cattle among widely dispersed relatives or friends – was undoubtedly the fear of disclosing the full extent of one's amassed fortune, and to avoid creating a climate of envy and jealousy in which witchcraft actions and other forms of retaliation so readily flourish. (At the same time, of course, in this veiled manner, wealth nonetheless constituted a useful instrument to exert influence and command allegiance among the recipients of the distributed stock.)

In talking of amassed wealth in African tribal society, I spoke in terms of livestock. Having previously said that the range of other material needs was strictly limited, this should not surprise you. Indeed, livestock and especially cattle may, even within the context of tribal economy, be regarded as 'real capital' (in the Western economic sense), being 'produced means of production'.

Have we now reached the point of summing up, can we now come to the conclusion that in the production and reproduction of livestock in an otherwise subsistence economy, we have found the nearest equivalent of a Western concept of capital formation, production and economic growth? In other words, does the investment in and reproduction of livestock (cattle) present an end in itself, the most meaningful and ultimate aim of the pursuit of wealth in traditional Bantu society?

Before we draw this conclusion, let us examine the economic role of livestock, and especially cattle, a bit more closely. Among people like the Zulu and other southern Bantu the use made of cattle was fairly extensive: milk formed a fairly regular part of the family diet; skins of dead animals were used for shields, straps and clothing (calf skins mainly); horns had some use as containers; dung was used variously as manure, fuel or floor polish. After the introduction of the plough, cattle became useful as draught animals. Slaughtering, however, was an irregular event – among commoners even a rare event – more often than not induced by ritual exigency, the propitiation of ancestral spirits or some other ceremonial event of considerable importance, which reduced the use of cattle as a meat supply for regular domestic consumption. While the killing and cutting up of a beast for (food) *exchange* purposes was normally not common, cattle did form a source of security in time of food scarcity.

Turning to the Shona tribes across the Limpopo, cattle and other livestock, while apparently prized as possessions and objects of capital investment, were (are) very little used as a milk supply, and, as far as I could judge, few beasts were killed without some pressure having been exerted by the spirit world. The introduction of the plough made cattle very popular as draught animals but also vastly increased the proportion of oxen in the cattle population which, so I was told by some people, did adversely affect the rate of natural increase. (In some areas bulls were so scarce that when a certain ritual prescribed the sacrifice of a bull, an ox might have to be killed together with a rooster, in order to render the total offering unmistakably 'masculine'.)

Only during the past forty years or so, when cash needs have increased and stock sales have begun to fulfil a necessary function, has a new dimension been added to the economic value of cattle. On the whole, however, speaking of traditional Bantu society, and thinking of the domestic use made of livestock, I am inclined to think (though I may be biased by my Shona experience) that the 'economic' role (in the Western sense) of cattle has been much overrated.

The primary use of livestock (cattle especially) and their main 'productive' or 'capital' value, however, lay in quite a different field of human enterprise, that of *the exchange of women in marriage and the procreation of the family*. This is, as I understand it, not a field which economists have so far been prepared to accept as part of their province. It is one of my aims to persuade you that it is, for the simple reason that I cannot see how you could study the process of economic growth in underdeveloped communities without taking cognizance of what, according to the patterns of conceptual thought in these communities, does form the very core of the traditional concept of property, wealth and the pursuit of wealth – at least, among cattle-keeping tribes.

To understand the dynamics of this conceptual frame you will have to think in terms of two basic and closely interrelated ideas:

(*a*) that indigenous communities like those of the patrilineal Bantu of southern Africa comprise large numbers of different agnatic kinship groupings (call these 'lineages') each of which is conceived as an expanding unity of kinsmen, departed, living and as yet unborn. That is, the spirits of the dead ancestors, the living members and the unborn progeny all form interdependent parts of a separately identifiable and growing kinship organism;

(*b*) these lineages are exogamous. Although both males and females are members of such lineages, a lineage cannot reproduce itself through the mating of its own males and females; even if the actual relationship is pretty remote, such unions would still be regarded as incestuous. In lineages with a patrilineal line of descent (i.e., in most southern African Bantu tribes) this means that the needs of procreation, this driving biological and mystical urge to reproduce one's own blood and lineal kin-group, can be satisfied only with the help of females obtained from other lineages. Since every lineage is in a similar plight, some inter-lineage exchange arrangement had to be evolved, through which the process of reproduction of agnatic kin-groups could take place in a regular and legitimate fashion. The systems that operate depend on the particular kinship structure of the societies concerned, and various types are possible.

The simplest solution (but a rather rare one) is for two lineages to exchange women as wives, for instance in a direct exchange of husbands' sisters (*Diagram V*) or by involving females of successive or alternate generations (one of the 'cousin marriage', *Diagram VI*). But even among tribes in which such marriages are regarded as preferential, the actual incidence of these bilateral exchanges is rather low. By far the most common is a system in which progressively more lineages become involved. If you turn to *Diagram VII*, the principle becomes very clear. Lineage or family A gets a wife from B, B from C, C from D, etc. In all these separate transactions, however, the wife-receiving group (e.g. A) *gives a compensation* to the wife-providing group (B), and this compensation enables the latter group (B) to obtain in turn a wife from a third (C) group for the satisfaction of its own needs, and so on. The marriage transaction therefore fulfils the vital needs of *both* contracting groups, and what is exchanged between them are *equivalent reproductive values*: A obtains from B a woman of normal child-bearing capacity who will reproduce A's family and lineage; B obtains from A the means (usually a locally more or less standardized number of cattle) of obtaining from a third family a woman who will render the same reproductive servives to his own (B) family and lineage. This is the so-called *lobola* or *bohadi* system in a nutshell; among the Shona tribes, for instance, this system accounts for ± 98% of all rural marriages (pagan as well as Christian), and any other marriage (except the feudal 'service' marriage[1]) is here in conflict with the fundamental ideas of agnatic procreation, if not with the principle of 'incest'.

I do not want to go into matters of customary law and ethics tonight, except to emphasize that under no circumstances is there a question of 'buying wives' (a shocking supposition): not the woman's person (which re-

1. Instead of paying *lobolo* a man would obtain a wife in return for a lifetime's service to his in-laws. Although in theory he obtained paternal rights to (at least some of) his children, in practice the position was often so obscure that he would ultimately tender a few head of cattle in order to establish an indisputable claim to his offspring.

Diagram V

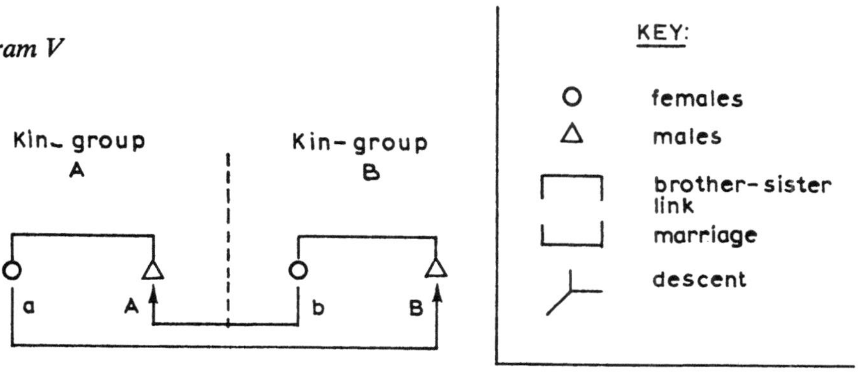

Diagram VI

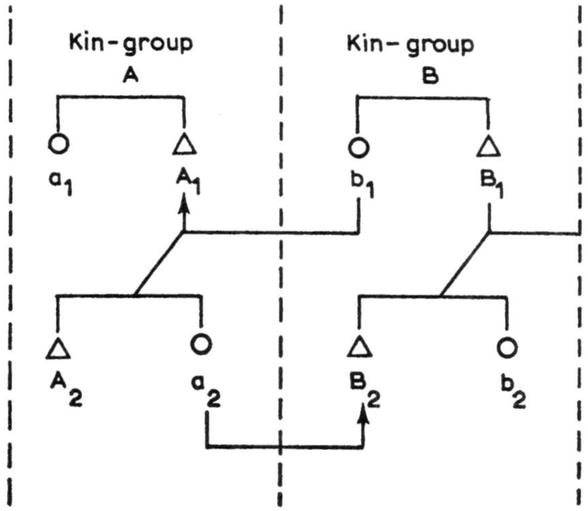

Diagram VII

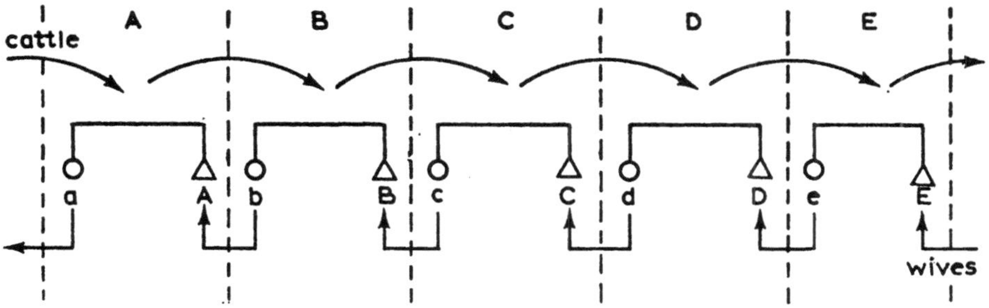

mains identified with her own kin-group) but her reproductive services are obtained, and the transaction is essentially one of an exchange of reproductive capacity.

What is of importance in this context are the socio-economic implications. First of all there is here a question of 'evaluation' and often even of a 'standard value' for normal transactions which can be measured in economically significant terms. Although there will be some strenous 'bargaining' (much of it stereotyped custom) during the preliminary negotiations, *lobolo* values are pretty well standardized: among the Shona in the 1940s and 50s, for instance, ten to twelve head of cattle for a wife with a full reproductive history ahead of her. Among many tribes with a strongly developed hierarchical political structure and without a collateral system of succession (as have the Shona), the *lobolo* value may be graded according to the political status of the bride's father; say ten head for the daughters of commoners, fifteen or twenty for a headman's daughter, much higher still for a chief's daughter. But even these values are more or less standardized (with or without the help of legislation, as in Natal). The main point is that even the lower standard *lobolo* rates represent values which are considerably higher than the average family's cattle holding. Among the Shona, for instance, the average cattle estate was five and a half head during the late 'forties, that is only half the *lobolo* value of a single young bride; in the early 1900s, with less than two heads of cattle per family, the *lobolo* value was four or five beasts, again more than twice the average cattle estate.

Does this mean perputual bankruptcy of Bantu families for the sake of family reproduction? Of course not, for families do not only have sons who require *lobolo* to marry wives, but also daughters who bring in *lobolo* by marrying husbands in other families. In many tribes this relationship is specifically recognized in a system of 'linking' particular brothers and sisters for the purpose of securing a young man's *lobolo* (e.g., the *cipanda* institution of the Shona). And since, for the purposes of marriage and family reproduction, the kinship units were fairly large and the number of boys and girls within these wider groupings more or less equal, marriage traffic with other similar units could be sustained by balancing incoming and outgoing *lobolo* (if necessary, with a period of 'credit' thrown in) even with high standard rates of *lobolo*.

One implication of this system is immediately apparent: whatever the economic functions of livestock in the more conventional Western sense, these functions are eclipsed by the role of cattle in the process of marriage and the reproduction of lineal kin-groups.

A perhaps less evident but inescapable part of the same concept, however, is another implication of immense importance: because of the interchangeable values of marriageable brides and *lobolo* cattle, not only livestock but also *wives and marriageable daughters* (or rather, the reproductive capacity of these) *from part of the family estate* and are in fact the most valued elements of 'property' and 'wealth' in these traditional Bantu societies.

Again I must warn you against jumping to the facile conclusion that therefore women – wives and daughters – are regarded as 'chattel' to be disposed of by a male-controlled society, for even a cursory study of customary law relating to the position of women will refute this fallacy. The key to an understanding of their position in the family estate lies in a wider and more fundamental concept of wealth, which has become virtually lost in our materialistic society. What the Shona call *pfumo* and the Zulu *umfuyo* can be interpreted as something between 'property' and 'wealth'; it has the connotation of 'asset' in a productive sense, also of potential well-being, strength, richness, and a promise of prosperity in a more-than-material sense. The Shona term *nhaka* (a deceased persons's estate) and the Zulu term *impahla* (property), besides referring to personal belongings, have this in common that they include, together with cattle and other livestock, the *lobolo* value of unmarried daughters. *Nhaka,* moreover, very definitely includes widows – or, more correctly, their unspent procreative capacity. These are the primary 'assets' included for distribution in a deceased person's estate.

(I should here add that land – a primary 'asset' or 'property' in western society – was *not* as such included in the concepts of *nhaka* or *impahla.* While land was (is) utilized in individually recognized and legally protected allotments, it could not as such be 'owned' or 'appropriated' in these tribal societies. Even nowadays, in spite of the growing scarcity of land and the enhanced value attached to individually occupied holdings, the reluctance to accept land as 'property' is still widespread.)

In these tribal societies, then, wealth is primarily conceived of as a productive and *organic* concept. So strong and self-evident is this organic quality that it has even been ascribed to the money economy concept of *interest* derived from capital investment: e.g., the common Zulu term for interest is *inzalo*[2], that is, live offspring.

In short, wealth (and for that matter 'capital') in traditional Bantu society represents primarily the *actual or potential capacity of the family or lineal kin-group to reproduce itself.* In a society with a strictly limited range

2. Matters of Zulu terminology were discussed with Dr. D. McK. Malcolm whose guidance is hereby gratefully acknowledged.

of material wants, the only really meaningful pursuit of wealth is that which aims at the multiplication of one's progeny. For herein lies the strengthening of one's primary resources in times of need and the provision of material, social and even spiritual security and well-being: blood-kin to grow and gather food for sustenance, the expanding family as a corporate social unity for the mutual protection of its members and the broadening ranks of descendants who will minister to the vital needs and whims of the ancestral spirit world. At the same time it is also the way to social prestige and, ultimately, political status and power.

Having outlined these fundamental concepts, I want to put it again to you: if the science of economics is concerned with the production and distribution of wealth, if the formation of capital is an economically meaningful object of the accumulation of wealth and if real capital represents the produced means of production and reproduction; and if, within the context of traditional indigenous society, the only really meaningful form of capital is that which can be utilized for the reproduction of one's own blood, family and lineal kin-group (if on all these points we agree), then the whole indigenous conceptual complex of 'productive property' and the pursuit of 'wealth' aimed at the perpetuation of lineal kin-groups must, I should say, logically fall within the field of economics as much as it should demand the attention of social anthropologists.

To deny this heritage of an underdeveloped past a place in the study of economic theory, if not practice, seems to me an unwarranted restriction of your discipline. I would go further and maintain that *unless* you take due cognizance of these fundamental principles of primitive economy, the structure of your theoretical framework is incomplete. Moreover, the application of your science to such problems as the stimulation and development of the economy of the indigenous communities of Africa will be badly handicapped and often be (as indeed it has only too often been) disruptive rather than constructive. For your ideas and aspirations about 'economic growth' (so fashionable nowadays) are esoteric growths on African soil. Your frame of mind and the conceptual tools of your profession are the products of an advanced stage in the socio-economic evolution of man, shaped at a time when, among the vanguard of human society, wealth had already lost most of its organic character and was no longer rooted in the pulsating flow of human life and procreation itself.

Today, economists direct their attention to underdeveloped areas, where among the great majority of tribal communities these concepts are still meaningful, even though, after the imposition of cash taxation, the lure of factory-produced consumer goods and other requirements of a dynamic and demanding new world, the value concepts of a Western money economy have gained a firm and rapidly expanding foothold. It is, in fact, the *co-existence* of both the Western 'materialistic' and the traditional 'organic' concepts of wealth in present-day African society which presents one of the most fascinating (and difficult) aspects of the study of socio-economic development.

The two concepts, though very different, are not always or necessarily in conflict with one another, for each has in African society to some extent its own sphere of operation, distinct from or complementary to the other. In brief outline, the situation is as follows:

On the one hand cash needs have become an integral and growing part of African rural life, *primarily* for the payment of taxes and for satisfying the demand for a progressively widening range of factory-produced consumer goods and other values of the western world (e.g,. education). Because, almost generally in southern and central Africa, the traditional resources of rural communities can at most meet only a very minor part[3] of the cash requirements, rural families have come to rely heavily on the earnings of their migrant workers, and these wage earnings have become an established and essential part of the economic basis of rural family life.

On the other hand, in the *traditional* sector of rural economy, there is an agricultural subsistence production, plus the pursuit and accumulation of wealth in the organic sense I have sketched. This sector caters *primarily* to the vital needs of the rhythm of life, death and procreation of corporate kin-groups.

Theoretically one may be tempted to regard this as a *double* economic structure, consisting of two separate sectors, each with its own system of values, its own set of needs and its own resources and recognized avenues to fulfil these needs, that is, as self-sufficient and mutually independent spheres of socio-economic activity.

In practice, of course, the two sectors are not entirely separate, and the values of both interpenetrate, so that we are in fact dealing not with a double structure, but with a *dual* economic system within a single socio-economic structure.

One of the most significant (and to agronomists, disturbing) penetrations is the increasing use of wage money for the purchase (not production) of food in the rural subsistence sector. (In Keiskammahoek District, for in-

3. Among the Swazi some 80 % of all cash income of *rural* families was found to be derived from wage labour outside the sphere of rural economic activity. Report Swaziland Survey, 1960 [published as *Experiment in Swaziland* – ed. J. F. Holleman, O.U.P. Cape Town, 1964, Chap. 8]

stance, even after a 'good' harvest, families have to buy food for nine months of the year.)[4] This development is due to a combination of factors which tend to inhibit adequate crop production. Shortage and diminishing fertility of arable land, as well as climatic hazards, are undoubtedly major factors in many areas, but certainly not everywhere. In Swaziland, for instance, there is no general shortage of African-held arable land and (except in the Lowveld) conditions are reasonably favourable to crop production. Yet, less than half the rural families produced (in 1960) enough staple food for their bare subsistence needs, relying mainly on wage earnings to make up the deficit.[5] A more fundamental factor is the change in African attitudes towards the role of land, which as a primary source of subsistence is yielding its place to a more rewarding migrant labour market. At the same time the value of land tenure tends to become assessed in terms of social and residential security rather than economic productivity.[6]

Other examples of interpenetration are legion: the introduction of cash payments in customary marriage transactions, in tribal litigation, in fees paid to witchdoctors and midwives, in payments made for occasional labour engaged in subsistence crop production – and so on.

From the other side, however, traditional values such as the continued insistence on *lobolo*, the social and political ramifications of material wealth, institutional kinship obligations, tribal associations, the pressure from mystical forces (ancestral spirits, witchcraft and sorcery) exert their influence upon African participation in the wage economy sector. In one way or another these factors influence the timing, duration, place, rhythm and even nature of migratory employment, as well as the pattern and volume of cash expenditure and investment.

The result is an often baffling interplay of different standards of evaluation with regard to one and the same commodity, depending on the particular context in which the evalution takes place. During the late 'forties and early 'fifties the cash equivalent of a full-grown head of cattle for marriage (*lobolo*) purposes was £5 among the central and eastern Shona tribes; and the same cash value applied in other 'traditional' contexts, such as in legal actions concerning the payment of fines or compensations. A person might settle such debts by handing over cattle (and not money) at this rate but, mindful of its market value in the 'commercial', non-traditional context,

4. Reported by Professor M. Wilson at the Social Sciences Research Conference, Durban, July 1962. See also *Tomlinson Report, Summary*, 1955, p. 86, 99-100.

5. Report of the Swaziland Survey, 1960, Chapters VII (Daniel) and VIII (Hughes).

6. *Report of the Mangwende Commission of Inquiry*, Salisbury, 1961, p. 29 ff. [also in J. F. Holleman, *Chief, Council and Commissioner*, 1969, p. 62 ff.]

refuse to sell an identical beast to a butcher or at a stock sale for £12 or £15. Question him about this discrepancy, and the chances are that he remains oddly unconcerned. To his mind there is no price conflict, because in either case he has been logically guided by the accepted standard of evaluation applicable within the particular context of the transaction; and since he has no difficulty in distinguishing the two, his mind can jump from one conceptual compartment into the other without becoming confused. Another example: A has run out of food and borrows half a bag of maize from B to feed his family. Another man C borrows half a bag of maize from A which he sows, after which he reaps and sells the resulting crop. Creditor B will be entitled to the return of only half a bag of maize from debtor A who consumed the loan to sustain life; but he may claim one bag from C who multiplied and commercialized what he borrowed.[7]

In these cases the functional contexts which determine the basis of evaluation are easily distinguished and no conflict arises. It is not always so, and instead of finding the organic and materialistic concepts of wealth juxtaposed in peaceful co-existence, they may in other situations present sharply opposed forces in a bitter tug-of-war.

Elsewhere[8] I described in some detail the changing role of the *lobolo* in modern African life and the effect of this change upon the structure and cohesion of the family. It is, briefly, that as the result of expanding cash wants, the cash load (in respect of *lobolo* and other marriage payments) payable by groom-and-family to bride-and-family has become an ever increasing burden which requires longer periods of wage employment to discharge. A very considerable part of this burden now falls upon the shoulders of the groom himself, instead of, as in the past, upon a common family estate. One result is that, while the median age of *white* bridegrooms upon first marriage has *dropped* during the twenty-year period since 1937 the median age of *African* grooms has *risen*. Nearly half of the white men in South Africa marry under the age of 25; just over half of the African men (those whose marriages are registered) marry *over* the age of 30, a difference in median age of more than five years. Of the protracted period of bachelorhood a considerable portion is spent in wage employment in an environment which daily displays the attractions and temptations of material

7. The claim may not always succeed in a tribal court. Much depends on the success of C's venture, the relationship between creditor and debtor and the circumstances under which the transaction took place.

8. 'Bantu Marriage at the Cross-Roads', Proceedings of the 8th Annual Conference of the Institute of Administrators of Non-European Affairs, 1959. [Included in the present volume.]

wealth and comfort. At the same time not only the urge of the blood has to be satisfied (leading to a large amount of promiscuity) but, inevitably, there is a mounting sense of obligation that a man should do his primary duty by marrying and starting to reproduce his own lineal kin-group in a legitimate fashion. Here every man's soul becomes a battlefield of two rivalling forces, two valid but different concepts, both giving meaning and purpose to the pursuit and accumulation of wealth and therefore persistently clamouring for recognition and priority in the hard struggle to make ends meet. In contemporary African society this is the razor's edge between the old and the new. Personal and group aspirations, obligations and loyalties, as well as material, social and spiritual needs, converge here. Much more is at stake than a personal search for suitable compromises between the conflicting values of a new and complex world. The legal basis of marriage and legitimate offspring, the respective responsibilities of husband and wife, of parent and child, the nature and strength of their wider kinship affiliations and obligations, in short, the very structure and coherence of corporate kin-groupings, are being affected in the groping search for new norms.

In this process of adjustment to rapid change, odd things can happen. Clyde Mitchell[9] reports from the Copperbelt that among *matri*lineal Northern Rhodesian tribes, traditionally without a *lobolo* institution and with an instable marriage situation, substantial increases in marriage payments are made by the groom's family in the hope that they will produce greater marital stability and (probably) enhanced paternal rights. Among our *patri*lineal southern Bantu, with a *lobola* system traditionally contributing to stable marital ties and a very strong paternal position with regard to children, the delayed start of formal marriage in urban environments encourages a growing crop of premarital and *maternally* affiliated children. Moreover, the not uncommon contribution by wage-earning *brides* to their own *lobolo* (in order to 'help their boy friends') facilitates lawful matrimony *as well as subsequent desertion* – which, again, tends to strengthen the maternal rather than the paternal ties with the children.

I have reached the stage when I should either lead you deeper into the as yet largely unexplored undercurrents of socio-economic behaviour in our transitional African society or call a halt in the hope that I have not yet begun to confuse you.

I have in this paper touched upon some aspects of this curious admixture of concepts which determine the socio-economic behaviour of our African

9. 'Aspects of African Marriage on the Copperbelt', *Rhodes-Livingstone Journal*, Sept. 1957.

population (in particular, rural communities in southern and central Africa) as the result of the confluence of two widely disparate cultures. It was meant to be an excursion in the field of a dualistic economy, and I have taken some pains to show that the phenomena I discussed are not confined to two separated spheres of human activity, but belong to *interlocking sectors* (one tradition-oriented, the other Western-oriented) of a *single socio-economic structure*. In this dualistic approach I have deliberately avoided giving undue emphasis to such commonly recognized 'dichotomies' as exchange versus subsistence economy or urban (industrial) versus rural (agricultural) economy. For I believe that, however attractive superficially, these divisions will prove to be artificial (and therefore deceptive) upon deeper analysis.

Indeed, after half a century and more of ceaseless labour migration, much of it a circulating movement and not a one-way current, it would be strange if town and country, exchange and subsistence, industry and peasantry, were not to some extent mixed up in both these sectors. If so, surely it would be more realistic, certainly from the economist's angle, first to accept that the erstwhile separate sectors have grown into an indivisible whole and then to examine the nature and extent of their interdependence and, in particular, the interplay of basic concepts, old and new, indigenous and Western, which motivate socio-economic behaviour in this transitional society. For it is in the sphere of conceptual thinking, in the uneasy co-existence of old and new, that we find the more fundamental dichotomy which cross-cuts all other divisions. In the field of African economy probably the most significant expression of this dichotomy concerns the meaning and function of wealth, represented in the juxtaposition (and opposition) of what I called the (Western-derived) 'materialistic' and (tradition-derived) 'organic' concepts of wealth. The clearest symbol of the former is money; of the latter, women, genetrix, or if you wish, cattle, for their exchange is the generating principle in the organic chain linking exogamous kinship units for the purpose of family procreation – and this represents in *any* organized human society the genesis of all social and economic growth.

African marriage at the cross-roads*

I. CUSTOMARY MARRIAGE

Probably the most dominant characteristic of customary Bantu marriage (and one in which it contrasts most significantly with Western-Christian marriage) is that the marital union between husband and wife is but part of a wider relationship-in-law, or affinition agreement, between their respective kin-groups.

In Western society this wider affinal relationship also obtains, but in tribal society this affinition is the primary, causative, and not the secondary, resultant, element of the marriage between the individual spouses. In other words, in our society we may say that two families are each other's in-laws *on account of* the marriage of their son and daughter; in African tribal society it is rather the other way round: the affinition agreement between the kin-groups (the formal agreement that they shall be linked by marriage) not only precedes – or is assumed to have preceded – the conjugal union of the individual couple concerned, but has a social and legal existence which in some respects is independent of the marriage itself.

[The remainder of this section has not been reproduced here in order to avoid undue repetition. It contained substantially the same views regarding the characteristics of customary marriages and bridewealth in Southern African patrilineal tribal society as I outlined in 'Marriage, Bridewealth and Women'. – J. F. H.]

II. STATUTORY RECOGNITION OF CUSTOMARY BANTU MARRIAGE

Generally speaking the status of all Bantu customary law in South Africa is that of a subsidiary law. Primarily the common law of the country applies

* Paper presented to the eighth Annual Conference of the Institute of Administrators of Non-European Affairs at Kroonstad (S.A.), September 1960. Published in *Race Relations Journal* XXVII (1960) No. 4, XXVIII (1961) Nos. 1 & 2.

to the indigenous as well as the white and other population groups, unless the legislature specially provides otherwise. Such special provisions exist and are broadly speaking of two kinds: (a) those that create new laws especially applicable to the indigenous population, and which therefore replace or modify the common law; (b) those that give partial or full recognition to certain sections of Bantu law, which likewise then take precedence over the common law. In the second category, however, a distinction must be made between those provisions which recognized Bantu law *per se* (sometimes in rather vague terms, such as in the important *Section 11(1)* of the *Native Administration Act* of 1927) and those that are ostensibly based on Bantu law but are in fact statutory creations to a greater or less extent divorced from the living sources of Bantu law. Examples of the latter are the *Natal Code of Native Law of 1932* (which aims at incorporating large slices of Zulu law) and the *Bantu Authorities Act* of 1951 which, in spite of its name, has little to do with traditional Bantu law. For this latter category the term 'Native law', in contra-distinction to Bantu law (or specifically: Zulu, Tswana, Xhosa, Venda or Shona law) is used here.

From the above classifications are excluded those sections of Bantu law which neither have become unlawful as the result of a specific enactment of the legislature, nor are specifically recognized as valid law. They include innumerable facets of indigenous law of which state and legislature are unaware, in the sense that they have received no statutory attention, but are nevertheless operative in indigenous society. These Bantu law fragments are in the odd position that, as far as the law of the land is concerned, they are therefore neither lawful nor unlawful, (i.e., they are 'not unlawful') and continue to exist without being enforceable in an official (Government) court of law.

The basic position in Southern Rhodesia is similar to that in South Africa. With regard to the recognition of Bantu civil law in more general terms, there is a potentially significant variation in the wording of *Section 3(1)* of the Southern Rhodesian *Native Law and Courts Act* (Chapter 73) which lays down that customary law 'shall' be applied in circumstances similar to those referred to in the South African statute. On the face of it this gives the Rhodesian courts no choice but to apply Bantu law in cases where the South African courts still have a measure of discretion. In practice, however, this has not rendered the application of genuine Bantu law either more imperative or more secure. For this depends on the courts' knowledge and understanding of local Bantu law, a qualification which is (as it is in South Africa) only too often sadly lacking.

When we now turn to the recognition of South African Bantu marriage law in particular, it may be said that the broad common premises which I have sketched here apply, but that differences in detail obtain between the four provinces, a heritage of the different legislatures and policies of pre-Union days, which the Union legislation (especially the *Native Administration Act* of 1927) has not fully wiped out.

I must stress the distinction between customary Bantu marriages on the one hand and civil or Christian marriages on the other. Although both categories are directly or indirectly governed by special Native legislation, the relative status and legal position of the two types of marriage are obviously widely different.

First, relating to the recognition of customary Bantu marriages, which are our main concern today, a brief summary of the situation before Union [1910] is necessary, because it has strongly influenced the phrasing and contents of South African legislation.

The position in the Cape Colony before the annexation of the Transkei was relatively simple: no recognition of Bantu marriages. The *lobolo*[2] transaction was not recognized when it was made in consideration of a Bantu marriage, but the courts could take cognizance of it in civil marriages as a contract *per se*, the argument being that in this sense it was not morally incompatible with marriage. The *Native Succession Act* (18/1864), applicable only to registered Cape Colony citizens, regulated the material consequences of customary marriages without recognizing these marriages as such.

The subsequent annexation of the Transkei brought about a change of policy as far as these territories were concerned. The Transkeian courts were given discretion to apply customary law in cases involving all-African parties, and Proclamation 140/1885 explicitly recognized both the Bantu marriage contract and its dissolution under Bantu law. This means that in the Transkei even polygynous Bantu marriages were fully recognized as valid marriages, until the *Native Administration Act* of 1927 modified this recognition.

In Natal, the *Codes of Native Law* of 1878 likewise did not hesitate to recognize customary marital unions as valid marriages, but proceeded to regulate a number of aspects (essential requirements for validity, rates of *lobolo*, etc.), thereby providing a Native-law frame for this Bantu-law institution.

2. [The Xhosa term is *ikhazi*. Throughout this paper, however, I used *lobolo* (Zulu), being perhaps the term most widely known to a white audience. Among the other indigenous terms, *bogadi* or *bohali* (Sotho-Tswana), *thakha* (Venda), *rovoro* (Shona) and *mabeka* (Swazi) may be mentioned. In South African case law and jurisprudence the English usage is 'dowry' and in Afrikaans 'bruidsprys', both terms of doubtful merit.] – J. F. H.

Entirely different was the pre-Union situation in the Transvaal, where the statutory language of the Zuid-Afrikaanse Republiek was bluntly negative. *Section 24 of Act 3* of 1876 stated: 'Tot bevordering der zedelijkheid wordt het aankopen van vrouwen of veelwijverij onder de kleurlingen [this includes Bantu] in deze Republiek door de wetten des Lands niet erkend' – for the promotion of public morality the buying of women or polygamy among the Coloureds will not be recognized by the laws of this Republic. Nine years later a new law (No. 4 of 1895) took its place, in order to 'provide for the better government and better administration of justice among the Native population of the Republic'. The policy declaration in *Section 2* generally pledges the preservation of the 'laws, habits and customs hitherto observed among the Natives', provided these had not 'appeared to be inconsistent with the general principles of civilization recognized in the civilized world'. *Section 5*, moreover, directs the courts to decide civil matters between Natives in terms of the provision of the present Act, 'and not otherwise', and in accordance with indigenous law, past and present, provided this did not cause obvious injustice and did not conflict with the accepted principles of natural justice ('natuurlijke billijkheid'). If this may sound to us a liberal reaction to the negative conservatism of the 1876 Legislator, not so to the Supreme Court justices of the Transvaal. In a series of decisions they declared that the 1885 legislation could not possibly have reversed the principles laid down in 1876, and that Bantu marriage, on account of its polygynous character, was inconsistent with the general priciples of civilization in the civilized world. The result was that all Bantu marriages were considered void, all children born of them illegitimate and therefore under guardianship of their mothers, who in turn were not considered to be under the tutelage of their Bantu husbands. *Lobolo* was unlawful and unenforceable in any court of law. The confusion with regard to Bantu marriage in the Transvaal was therefore complete.

Faced with these widely divergent policies the *Native Administration Act* of 1927 set out to effect a compromise. The result is an indirect and partial recognition of Bantu marriage as a second-rate marital union. No longer a 'marriage' as hitherto in Natal and Transkei, it is now a '*customary union*', which is defined in *Section 35* (as amended) of this Act as 'the association of a man and a woman in a conjugal relationship according to Native law and custom, where neither the man nor the woman is a party to a subsisting marriage'. Also in Natal the Bantu marriages under the Natal Code were suitably turned into customary unions. In the wording 'a man and a woman', recognition of the possibly polygynous character of the customary union is not excluded.

Read in conjunction with *Section 22*, which regulates the possibility of a subsequent 'marriage' (i.e., civil or Christian) of the male partner of this conjugal relationship, the attitude of the Union Legislator with regard to the legal status of Bantu marriage is clear. In any conflict between a civil (or Christian) marriage and a Bantu marriage ('customary union') – the latter evaporates. What happens to it is a matter of conjecture: its dissolution, not being specifically regulated, is merely presumed to take place when the subsequent marriage is contracted, and *Section 22* is only concerned with its material consequences. Where this clash of marital loyalties does not arise, however, *Section 11(1)* grants the courts the power to apply Bantu marriage law with the usual safeguards relating to public policy and natural justice; and it explicitly sanctions *lobolo* and similar institutions.

Neither the *Native Administration Act* nor any other legislation provides a specific code of nation-wide Native marriage law. It provides no more than an implicit and limited recognition-in-principle of customary marriage. Within these limitations, the specific application of the law relating to customary marriages differs from province to province, depending on whether provincial statutory provisions with regard to various aspects of marriage law do or do not exist. If such provisions exist (as in the Cape and Natal), they, and not the Bantu law, must be applied; where no such statutory provisions exist (as in Transvaal and Orange Free State) local Bantu law applies in terms of *Section 11* of the *Native Administration Act* and therefore becomes largely a matter of interpretation by the courts. The paradox now sometimes results (e.g., in relation to the dissolution of Bantu marriages) that in the Transkei and especially Natal, where traditionally a more sympathetic and understanding attitude towards Bantu institutions prevailed than in Transvaal and the O.F.S., well-intended statutory provisions replace and in effect ignore current Bantu law, while in the Transvaal and O.F.S. *Section 11(1)* of the *Native Administration Act* makes it possible for the courts to apply genuine Bantu law with the flexibility it requires.

In Southern Rhodesia the position is in a sense similar to Natal. There is the broad recognition of customary law in *Section 3(1)* of the *Native Law and Courts Act*, but statutory provisions, first in the *Native Marriage Laws* of 1917 and 1929 and finally in the *Native Marriages Act* of 1950, have replaced local Bantu marriage law on several important points to which I shall return in due course.

So much for the recognition of Bantu marriage law in general terms.

With regard to the recognition of the various specific issues of Bantu marriage law, I shall have to limit myself to only a few.

The *polygynous* character of Bantu marriage is recognized: in Natal specifically (Natal *Code* of 1932, *Section 57(2)*), in the rest of South Africa tacitly (*Section 11(1)* and *Section 35*); in Southern Rhodesia specific recognition is contained in *Section 4(1)* of the *Native Law and Courts Act*.

If we now come to recognition of the broad customary concept of the Bantu *marriage agreement*, then we find that neither in the legislation nor in the decisions of the South African (and Rhodesian) courts is there any clear distinction between either the marital and reproductive aspects of the Bantu marriage contract or between the individual conjugal union of the spouses and the wider, more fundamental and more enduring, affinition agreement of their respective families. The Natal *Code* of 1932 (*Section 57(1)*) emphasizes the individual aspect of the Bantu marriage as 'a civil contract entered into by and between the intending partners subject to the essential requirements of this Code, (enduring) until the death of the first dying, unless earlier dissolved by a competent court', and therefore ignores the existence of the wider affinal foundation of the relationship. The fact that it is 'essential' for the validity of the Bantu marriage in Natal to have the consent of the bride's father or guardian (or of the Native Commissioner if such consent is unreasonably withheld) and of the father or kraalhead of the groom whenever necessary does not imply a recognition of the principle of contracting kin-groups. It simply means that legal assistance is required by parties who are considered to be minors under the law.

The Transkei legislation is silent on the distinctions we have mentioned, and only safeguards the bride from marrying against her will, a protection also provided by *Section 57(1)(c)* of the Natal *Code*, by the Southern Rhodesian *Marriage Act* (*Section 7(1) (b)*) (both spouses) and by implication by *Section 11(1)* of the South African *Native Administration Act*, under which a forced marriage would be in conflict with the principles of public policy and natural justice. The courts have given recognition to the wider-than-individual contractual basis of Bantu marriage in a varying degree, but the full implications are not yet generally understood.

The issue crops up again with the *dissolution* of the Bantu marriage, and it is remarkable that, when viewing the marriage so to say in retrospect, the Native Appeal Courts lately appear to have obtained a much clearer understanding on this aspect. Largely on the basis of previous decisions in the Cape Colony, the Native Appeal Court for Natal and Transvaal, as late as 1944,[3] still upheld the old individualistic view that a 'Bantu marriage could be dissolved by the consent of the spouses themselves, and even unilaterally by the husband alone. A year later (1945), however, a sharp

3. [*Speelman v. Speelman*, 1944 N.A.C. (N & T) 53.] – J. F. H.

change of opinion occurred and the same Court bluntly stated that 'nothing is further from true Native Law' [than this individualistic concept]. 'The marriage . . . is a matter between the families . . . So also the dissolution is a matter between the contracting parties, i.e. the families . . .'.[4] About the same time the Cape and O.F.S. Native Appeal Courts saw the light and adopted the wider contractual basis of marriage as a true reflection of Bantu law.

In Natal, however, the individual point of view, firmly entrenched in the statutory provisions of the Natal *Code* (*Section 57(1)*), still prevails.

In Southern Rhodesia the statutory position is ambivalent. The reference in *Section 7* of the *Native Marriages Act* of 1950 to the bride's guardian and the 'intended husband' infers an individual basis of the marriage contract. The joint reference, however, to the common Bantu marriage and the succession marriage ('where a man takes to wife the widow or widows of a deceased relative') in *Section 3(1)* of the Act implies tacit recognition of a from of levirate, which is clearly based on the wider affinition agreement.

Again, the confusion in the Rhodesian Native Appeal Court with regard to the dissolution of customary marriages (customary law dissolution between families being recognized in some cases, not in others) would indicate that the distinction between the conjugal and affinal aspects of Bantu marriage has, at least until very recently, constituted an unsolved puzzle to the Rhodesian Legislator and Judiciary.

Only in Natal (and Southern Rhodesia) have the legislators prescribed special requirements for the *validity* of the Bantu marriage. In the rest of the Union prescriptions of local Bantu law are recognized with the usual safeguards under *Section 11(1)* of the *Native Administration Act.*

The Natal *Code* (*Section 59(1)*) prescribes three essential requirements:

1. consent of the bride's father or guardian (unless she is exempted);
2. consent of the father or kraalhead of the groom if he is under 21 and not yet married;
3. the bride's public declaration of free will and consent made before the official marriage witness at the time of her wedding.

Failure or omission of any of these requirements renders the Bantu marriage void.

Failure to *register* the marriage (a non-essential prescription of *Section 65)* does not invalidate it.

The Southern Rhodesian Legislator has over the years tinkered a good deal with its Bantu marriages. It has from the beginning protected especially the bride from being forced into an unwanted marriage and in view of the

4. [*Mashapo & Mashapo v Sisane,* 1945 N.A.C. (N & T) 57.] – J. F. H.

prevalence of so-called child-betrothal (*kuzwarira*), especially among the eastern (Shona) tribes it has taken a serious view of this practice.

Section 2 of the *Native Marriage Ordinance* of 1917, however, introduced the drastic innovation of the registration of the marriage as one of the essentials required for its validity. Since countless tribal folk did not bother to register their marriages, the 1917 Legislator can boast of the doubtful distinction of having fathered thousands of illegitimate children, the produce of so many invalid parental unions (the old Transvaal Legislator shares this distinction, but for other reasons – see above). This anomalous position was rectified in 1929, when failure to register merely became a punishable omission without actually invalidating the marriage.

In 1950 the Rhodesian Legislator tried again, this time with a new slant: Bantu marriages had to be formally 'solemnized' (*Section 3, Act 23* of 1950) by recognized religious or civil marriage officers in order to be valid (this solemnization automatically involves the proper registration). Mindful of the 1917 blunder, *subsection (3)* at least safeguards the legal position of children born of any unsolemnized customary marriage. What, apart from producing readily available documentary proof of a Bantu marriage, the Legislator hoped to achieve with this measure, is as obscure as the language in which these provisions are couched. The hope was expressed at the time that solemnization by State-recognized marriage officers would enhance the status of Bantu marriage. Even if this were to be made a solemn event in each case, it is doubtful whether the ceremony would have contributed much. And as practice since 1951 has borne out, solemnization, for all its lofty ideals, has only too often turned out to be a perfunctionary administrative chore, and about as solemn as the issuing of a driver's licence.

The definition of customary union in *Section 57(1)* of the Natal *Code* might at first raise the presumption that Bantu marriage in Natal may be contracted by fulfilling only the three 'essentials' laid down in *Section 59(1)*, to the exclusion of the requirements of Bantu (Zulu) law itself. But there is the definition of customary union in *Section 35* of the *Native Administration Act*, applicable to the whole country, which includes the phrase 'according to Native law and custom'. This means that, also in Natal, Bantu marriage law still enters into the picture; but the marriage, having been entered into according to Bantu law, still lacks legal validity unless it also meets the requirements of the *Code*.

A similar situation exists in Southern Rhodesia.

In all other areas under discussion, the requirements of local Bantu law must determine the validity of the customary marriage, a position accepted in principle by our courts.

This means also, however, that in social situations in which there is a partial or almost complete breakdown of the traditional social structure (as for instance in urban and peri-urban areas) the courts may be faced with the problem that the traditional requirements of the Bantu marriage contract (if it can still be regarded as such), and especially its ceremonial aspects, may sometimes have been reduced to bare essentials.

What, now, are the essentials of Bantu law which the South African courts in terms of *Section 11(1)* of the *Native Administration Act*, and the Southern Rhodesian courts in terms of *Section 3(1)* of the *Native Law and Courts Act* of 1937, recognize?

There is first of all the consent of the parties with which we have previously dealt. Whitfield (1948: 85) and Seymour (1953: 72) consider two more requirements to be 'essential':

a. the payment and acceptance of *lobolo* (Whitfield goes so far as to say, lobolo *cattle*);
b. transfer of the woman.

I submit that this, although it may reflect the most prevalent practice in the great majority of South African Bantu marriages, is an inaccurate, dogmatic and untidy statement of the principles of Bantu marriage law. For we have seen that (*a*) some customary marriages in which *lobolo* is explicitly excluded (e.g., the so-called service marriage) can be perfectly valid; (*b*) in some valid Bantu marriages *lobolo* (as distinct from other gifts in connexion with the marriage) is not given until some time after the consummation of the marriage, and such postponement has even become institutionalized among some tribes (e.g., Swazi and some Shona tribes); (*c*) in some cases there can be a perfectly valid Bantu marriage without the bride having been transferred to the husband's family (Sotho and some Shona tribes).

What has been lacking here is the ability to see the wood for its trees or, rather, to distinguish between cause and consequence. This has resulted in the failure to recognize that the grounds for the validity of the marriage are to be found in the essential affinition agreement between the contracting kin-groups and not merely in the successful establishment of the marital union, which is but one of its objects. It is essential to distinguish between the validity of the marriage contract and its completion in terms of the affinition agreement. The state of completeness has in the practice of Bantu law nothing to do with its initial validity. For, as I explained earlier, the parties know that by their affinition agreements they are in good faith committed to a long-term contractual relationship which involves the implementation of mutual obligations over a period of time. Of the major obligations, the passage of the wife and *lobolo* may (but need not) take place at an early stage and at approximately the same time. But at least one major obligation, the bearing of children, can be fulfilled only in course of time.

The veteran Whitfield comes close to understanding the 'stage by stage' realization of objects of the affinition agreement but, like others, he assumes that the completion of the marriage contract takes place 'upon the passing of cattle and the transfer of the woman' (p. 83-5). It is as wrong to base the validity of Bantu marriage upon the transfer of cattle as it is illogical to base the completion of the *lobolo* marriage contract upon the transfer of the woman. Both events are merely steps towards the ultimate fulfilment of the contract and an affirmation of a legal validity which was accepted from the time the parties concluded the affinition agreement.

Civil and Christian marriages

Only the most general outline can be given here. With one partial exception both civil and Christian marriages were before Union, and have been after Union, possible for the indigenous population of the Union, although there are some statutory differences in detail between the provinces. The possibility for such marriages has, however, been created by special legislation (i.e., 'Native law') which leaves the regulation of the various aspects of such marriages (essential requirements, celebration, relations between husband and wife, their property rights, status and property rights of children, dissolution of marriage) either to the common law or Bantu law, or to special Native law provisions.

Subject to these basic premises the general rule is again as outlined before, that the European common law applies to these Native marriages, except and insofar as certain aspects have been specifically excluded from the common law and provided for in special regulations or placed under the operation of Bantu law.

The situation in Southern Rhodesia is based on similar premises.

Natal provides an exception in that a *civil* marriage can only be contracted if both man and woman are exempted from the operation of the Natal *Code*. For such couples, only a marriage under the (European) *Marriage Ordinance* of 1846 (as amended) is possible with the full legal implications which a European marriage entails. In all other cases only a Christian or Bantu marriage is open to them.

In spite of its supposedly Western character, the field of the Christian marriage in Natal and of both civil and Christian marriages in the other provinces (and in Southern Rhodesia) is therefore governed by a composite (and rather complicated) law system. A few examples may suffice. The common law age of legal majority renders parents' consent unnecessary in a Native (i.e., Christian and civil) marriage in Southern Rhodesia and in all South African provinces, except Natal (Christian marriage) where the bride's guardian's consent is still required. *Section 11* of the Natal *Law 46/1887*, moreover, makes the remarkable provision that in a Native Christian marriage the personal status and property rights of the spouses will remain subject to Zulu law (i.e., in practice, Natal *Code*).

With regard to the status of children and the family estate, *Section 22* of the South African *Native Administration Act* supersedes the common law and substitutes new provisions which, apart from a near absolute 'no community of property' rule, to some extent take into consideration the tribal background of the spouses and the possible existence of a previously contracted (monogamous or polygynous) Bantu marriage. *Sections 13* and *14* of the Southern Rhodesian *Native Marriages Act* go a bit further and specifically retain customary law on these points.

The subsistence of an essentially monogamous civil or Christian marriage renders the conclusion of any other marriage (including Bantu marriage) void; in Natal such a step is moreover punished as *bigamy* (*Section 13* of the law of 1887).

The reverse, the conclusion (with a new partner) of a civil or Christian marriage during the subsistence of a valid Bantu marriage is, however, fully sanctioned and open to both husband and wife, who are thereby under statute law in effect given the power to disband their valid Bantu marriage by individual and unilateral action.

In no statute is the incidence of *lobolo* considered inconsistent with a civil or Christian marriage, and its common appearance side by side with these marriage transactions is therefore permitted. Since it does not, howver, form part of these marriage contracts, its Bantu-law sanctions fall away; default of *lobolo* performance is no ground for divorce, nor is its counterpart, failure of the wife to bear issue; nor, legally, does *lobolo* determine the status of the children. In cases of divorce the courts do take cognizance of the *lobolo* transaction as a separate entity, in that they may order a refund of (part of) the *lobolo* paid where the woman has borne insufficient or no issue to the husband. In other words, the Bantu principle of proportionate 'performance' in this respect may then be applied.

Christian and civil marriages can be dissolved only by a decree of a court of competent jurisdiction (in South Africa, the special Native Divorce Courts; in Southern Rhodesia, the Native Commissioner's Courts), and common law principles are applicable.

III. URBAN MARRIAGE

The very absence of the customary lineage structure in present-day urban African society renders it unsuitable for the continuation of the traditional concept of Bantu marriage as a transaction between two kin-groups for the purpose of family procreation. This basic difference in the social structure alone (quite apart from economic and other environmental differences) is sufficient to lift urban Bantu marriage from its wider affinal setting and to set it adrift as an individualized institution without anchorage in Bantu law. With it goes the traditional function of *lobolo*, the very essence of which is rooted in the traditional inter-lineage structure.

Yet a considerable proportion of African marriages in the urban area are referred to as 'customary unions' (that is, Bantu marriages) and in virtually all of these, and in other forms of urban marriage, *lobolo* appears to have been paid.

Two conclusions now seem inevitable: either such marriages were contracted in the rural area, where a still extant (though narrowing) traditional kinship structure implies that they are indeed Bantu *lobolo* marriages; or they were contracted in the urban environment itself, in which case the marriage cannot be a customary law marriage as we know it, and the *lobolo* cannot be the traditional institution known to Bantu law.

The first conclusion obviously refers to the still numerous couples who contracted a Bantu marriage in their rural homes before coming to live in town and the relatively small number who meet in town but go to their rural homes to have their marriage arranged for them by their respective kin-groups. These marriages are, legally at least, straightforward, although they may be subject to the same social problems as are other forms of urban marriage.

The second conclusion, however, immediately raises two vital questions. First: if these so-called urban customary unions are not proper Bantu marriages, what are they? And second: if they are not marriages under customary Bantu law, how can the courts legally apply Bantu law to them in terms of *Section 11(1)* of the *Native Administration Act*, as they have been and are doing?

Any attempt to give a clear-cut answer to the first question leads us straight into the near-chaos which the urban marriage pattern presents. Theoretically we are presented with three legally recognized varieties: the 'customary union' (including genuine Bantu marriage), marriage according to Christian rites and civil marriage. A fourth category, the so-called illicit union, covers all conjugal relations of varying stability which fall under no official classification and therefore find no recognition under the law of the land.

As the first three forms of marriage are legally recognized (though not in equal measure), each is by itself sufficiently valid, that is, safeguarded by the law of the land. It is therefore noteworthy that urban studies reveal that only the minority of urban marriages falls under one *or* another of these three varieties. The majority are a variable compound in which elements of two or even all three recognized forms are combined in one marriage: for instance, Christian marriage combined with civil rites and Native customary union; customary union confirmed by Christian rites; or Christian rites combined with civil rites. (Miss Junod supplies striking figures on this point.)

It is this apparently felt need to pile several individually recognized and legally self-sufficient forms of marriage onto the foundations of a single marital union, which casts grave doubt upon the real protection which the law extends to the urban marriage and which almost inescapably establishes the fact that the existing legal classifications are out of tune with the social realities and needs of this African community-in-transition. For even in spite of this extra padding and reinforcing, the foundations of urban marriage are far from sound.

Many factors tend to contribute towards this. There still is the basic imbalance between the sexes in most of the major urban centres (Bloemfontein and Port Elizabeth are among the exceptions with a fairly balanced male-female ratio), The basic situation has undoubtedly improved, from a nation-wide figure of 45.5 urban females per 100 urban males in 1936 to 63.5 in 1951.

This figure is, however, somewhat deceptive because it includes *all* age groups. A breakdown will show a slight preponderance of urban females over males in the under 15 age group. But in the age groups relevant to this study (15 years and over) the ratio is even more unfavourable than the overall figures indicate. With regard to the over 15 population, the figure for the Johannesburg Metropolitan area was 58.3 females to 100 males in 1951 (49.8 in 1936); in Pretoria, 66.8 (42.2 in 1936); in Durban, only 38.1 (23.9 in 1936). Cape Town Metropolitan area, which showed a fair 90.8 in 1936, dropped to a dismal 41.5 in 1951.

At the age of serious courtship (20-24) the overall urban ratio in 1951 was 54.2 females for every 100 males. Taking the age group of 15-34 years, within which 97-98 % of urban women are said to manage to find a husband, and comparing it with the more widely spaced age group (20-44) in which the great majority of men are presumed to marry, the figure drops even further to 46.2 women per 100 men.

In short, although up to date nation-wide figures are not yet available it is not unreasonable to suppose that (with a few exceptions) the position in our major cities still is that, within the effective marrying age brackets, there are approximately two men for every woman.

This need not, of course, constitute an unsurmountable marriage barrier to half the urban males. The urban areas are not watertight compartments, and there is the surplus of women in the corresponding age group in the rural areas, of which especially the migrant urban dweller can and does avail himself.

But the reversed sex ratio in the rural areas (and apparently in some of the smaller non-industrial urban centres) creates a parallel problem to that of the urban areas, with the result that both in women-starved urban society and men-starved rural society the uneven sex ratio strikes particularly hard at the very age groups within which, normally, men and women should be engaged in the building of their married life and the rearing of their children within the fold of a stable family unit. This factor alone cannot fail to have an adverse effect on moral stability and marriage security.

The situation may be aggravated by the tendency for black couples to marry at a later age than they used to marry. Here lies an interesting comparison between black and white society. In 1937, 30.9% of the European men married under the age of 25; 37.9% between the ages of 25-29; 31.2% at 30 years and older. The comparable figures (concerning mainly urban areas) for black bridegrooms in 1937 are 19%, 37.4% and 43.6%.

The figures for brides of both races in that year were:

Married	*White*	*Black*
Under 25 years old	62.2%	64.4%
Between 25-29 years old	22.0%	18.2%
At 30 years and over	15.8%	15.4%

Already at that time, therefore, the black bridegroom tended to be older than this white counterpart, though there was little difference between the average ages of black and white brides.

Twenty years later (1957) the median age of the *white* bridegrooms *dropped* sufficiently to allow nearly half (46.5%) to be married under the age of 25, but the age of the *black* bridegrooms had *risen* so much that just over half now married at 30 years and older.

The rise of the median age of African urban marriage may be partly due to economic pressure. If so, the figures would support an assumption that while the struggle to make ends meet has eased for white couples it has become more severe for black couples, One must here take into account the natural ambition among blacks to share in an ever-extending range of Western consumer goods and also the disproportionally heavy expenses which, mainly on socio-psychological grounds, are lavished on a 'proper' town wedding.

We may probably draw a further conclusion from our figures. The rise in the age of African marriage is comparatively greater for males than for females. Both sexes, however, have become wage earners and both can be expected to contribute to the expenses of their marriage and to the family income. The growing gap in their respective median age at marriage suggests that the men are less anxious than women to accept the responsibilities of a formal marriage; the sizeable number of illegitimate children in urban society (40-60 % and more, by some estimates) shows, however, that they have no such reservations as regards the privileges of a conjugal relationship. Indeed, reports of a booming trade in love medicine and magic seem to indicate that love making is a thriving cult in which there is little respect for the institution of marriage.

The result is, according to some social workers, that practically every girl has one or more children before marriage, a state of affairs that is found even in the best homes and apparently condoned by a society which has come to accept this as a norm. African urban society is not unique in this respect, and it would be wrong to judge the problem of extra-marital children according to the standards recognized in Western society. For, apart from the fact that 'illegitimacy' (the term in this respect is an akward one) carries no, or hardly any, social stigma in the new Bantu society, it does not necessarily carry the implication of social neglect or lack of parental care for these children. In fact, there is clear evidence that this phenomenon draws the ties of blood closer together; but this process takes place largely within the *maternal* kin-group. The children are either cared for by their mother, with the help of their maternal grandmother or other maternal relative, or they are sent to their maternal grandparents where they are treated as children-at-home. With pre-marital and extra-marital birth having become an integral part of the social pattern (and there is little doubt that, for the time being at least, it will remain so) we may expect a continuing trend towards this so-called matrifiliation of the family structure in modern Bantu society. This constitutes a significant modification of the hereditary patrilineal and patrifiliated basis of our southern Bantu, in spite of (and perhaps partly because of) a highly flourishing modern *lobolo* institution.

Urban lobolo

It is against a background of an emerging individualism born of a crumbling traditional culture and a largely shattered kinship structure, of a moral instability partly conditioned by the grossly unbalanced sex ratio at the ages of courtship and marriage and of severe economic stress – paradoxically accompanied by a steep *cash lobolo* – that we have to approach the new function of *lobolo*.

Personal responsibility for at least part of the *lobolo* is an idea which even in the rural areas had developed for some time, probably due to the introduction of cash items in the marriage transaction. But where the traditional family structure is still extant, these personal contributions do not seriously challenge the basic idea that the *lobolo* as such emanates from the groom's kin-group and that the latter remain the responsible party.

It is in the urban area, where the responsibility for *lobolo*, now predominantly a cash item, tends to, and often has, become the exclusive personal concern of the groom and where the wider kin-group is a remote and ineffective unity, that family responsibility is becoming a fiction in matters of *lobolo*, and a mere formality (if at all) with regard to the overall contract of marriage. Urban investigators therefore report that the function of *lobolo* is no longer the traditional one and that marriage has become the concern of the individual partners rather than of their respective kin-groups.

But in spite of its transformation, the thing called '*lobolo*' exists as an urban phenomenon. The very fact that it not only flourishes while customary marriage as such is dying in town, but that it has successfully transferred its roots to such foreign institutions as the Christian and civil marriage is proof of its need.

What is this need?

In a transitional society, desperately trying to find a familiar symbol of its own identity in a world full of confusion, its *symbolic* value is perhaps most significant. Miss Brandel quotes a remark by a qualified African observer in Johannesburg: 'When *lobolo* has not been paid, they do not really know whether they are married or not', and she adds: 'In a union without *lobolo*, the partners are lost in a network of confusing and only half-understood conventions of a vaguely western type, and there is no precedent of time-honoured and custom-sanctioned behaviour' (1958: 48).

The very fact that this symbol has lost its traditional substance, which enabled it to constitute an enduring guarantee of marital productivity and stability, renders it unsuitable for the dynamics of its original function. For, in a cash-needy society, a cash *lobolo* is usually dissipated before it can be used in turn by the bride's family for the same, family-productive, purpose. It has therefore lost its character of dynamic continuity. What then is its present function as a symbol?

It undoubtedly still contains the element of what Jeffreys calls 'child price', and it continues to fulfil the only socially generally recognized means of vesting paternal rights to the child on behalf of the *lobolo*-payer. But if the woman has started a family without the help of a legal husband (as seems to be rule rather than the exception), this premarital family unit is likely to be matri-linked; and if the husband joins this family as a latecomer, his *lobolo* may cover his wife's subsequent offspring as by right, but any claim to her previous issue (even if he is the genitor) can be resisted by her family. Moreover, the insistence on a high cash *lobolo* in a cash-poor community without a wide kinship set-up tends to delay marriage, and together with this delay militates against patriliny while strengthening the maternal family ties. Indeed a paradoxical function of the urban *lobolo!*

But there are more facets to the new *lobolo*. There is the information that, excepting an apparently small minority, the women themselves, including educated ones, insist that *lobolo* be paid for them, if only as tangible evidence of the husband's regard for them and his willingness to sacrifice for them. This reveals a woman's personal urge for self-recognition, common already among tribal brides, but with the difference that its appeal in the urban area is specifically addressed to the man himself.

There is also the observation that the cash *lobolo* is regarded as a financial compensation for her parent's expenses in educating the bride, which is corroborated by the statement in a recent urban study that 'the amount paid invariably depends on the standard of education attained by the girl'.

This economic argument has considerable validity, the more so when one reads that, in some cases, a husband may be absolved from his *lobolo* obligations, provided he undertakes to maintain also his wife's widowed mother.

Yet I doubt if economic security is as fundamental a consideration in the town *lobolo* as it is sometimes made out to be. A significant clue to the possibly deeper urge may be found in the observation that a proper town marriage must involve a wedding feast, a generous display of wealth and hospitality, that the bride's people are largely responsible for this, and that a considerable portion of the newly received *lobolo* may be directed towards defraying its cost and that of her trousseau.

Here the emphasis shifts from economic gain to the means of establishing social status and of publicizing the high standard of respectability (rather than the legality) of the marriage. Here *lobolo* (as a contribution to the wedding feast) fulfils a social and psychological function rather than an economic or even legal one. In fact, the need for formal legality may be found to be of secondary importance. One qualified observer bluntly stated that even a church marriage without a feast 'would cause more ridicule and talk than if the couple has just lived together without ceremony at all'. And if the cost of a festive, generous wedding party is too high, it is considered preferable merely to live together as man and woman and have children, while postponing the legal confirmation of this arrangement until this can be done with the festive display which alone would make it meaningful. For the *lobolo* to serve this end implies a change in its character and original function.

Even more striking is the information that a considerable number of wage-earning girls themselves make a substantial contribution towards their own *lobolo*, for this purpose handing over part of their savings to the men they thus hope to marry in proper fashion. In fact, as Miss Brandel has noted, in some cases the whole *lobolo* (R160-R300) emanates from the bride herself, though officially it is the groom who pays it to her father. This is no longer an extension of the scope of the *lobolo*, but a contradiction of it. For it cannot possibly mean that the bride pays this with the intention of securing for her husband (and husband's family) his paternal rights to her children. Rather the contrary seems true. With this tremendous gesture she serves three purposes: to attain, in proper fashion, the enhanced status of a married woman; to fulfil her obligation towards her own family and so secure her right to fall back on their support when she needs it; to assert her independence as a wage-earner, wife and mother, should the man fail her as a husband and father of her children. For he would indeed be a bold man who, having received *lobolo* for his wife from her own hands, would pursue a claim for its return or for his right to the children should the marriage later fail.

In line with this development is the case of the wage-earning woman who personally refunded the *lobolo* her husband had paid to her family, in order to gain her independence and secure on behalf of herself and her family, parental rights to her children.

Queer perversions indeed of the original concept of *lobolo*! And yet they fit into the overall unsettled picture of African urban society, the heterogeneous composition of its conjugal institutions and the uncertainty of its norms, and the acceptance of pre- and extra-marital children as part of the recognized social pattern.

Urban 'customary unions' and the application of the law

I now return to the question which I posed earlier in this paper. If those urban marriages which are termed customary unions upon closer examination do not conform to even a flexible interpretation of the basic principles of Bantu customary law, what law must be applied to them in our courts?

Section 11(1) of the South African *Native Administration Act* provides the courts, as far as I can see, with a choice of only two alternatives: the common law (including statutory Native law) and customary Bantu law; and no other.

In cases where these urban so-called customary unions are confirmed by civil or Christian rites there is, legally at least, no problem as regards the basis of marriage itself, for the common law will apply. (In terms of the Act they are then, in fact, no longer 'customary unions', but 'marriages'.) But if there is no such common law confirmation, and these 'customary unions' are not Bantu law marriages, and if my interpretation of *Section 11(1)* is correct, we arrive at the perplexing conclusion that the courts have no law to apply and therefore have no basis upon which to act, because *Section 11(1)* does not authorize them to apply a third category of law which is neither common law nor Bantu customary law. (From this conclusion only the urban areas of Natal are probably excluded, because the provisions of the Natal *Code* with regard to the 'essentials' of the customary union remain applicable also to the new urban unions.)

If this is considered to be a point of merely academic interest (which I doubt), the following is not.

The South African and Southern Rhodesian Legislators have created a dual system of law, with common law and Bantu customary law as its principal components. These components are applied, and are meant to be applied in the main, either singly with regard to restricted issues or in combination with one another on a wider field of legal interest (e.g., marriage). That this choice exists and that law courts have some discretion in the matter is to the Legislator's credit, for it is based on an awareness of the fact that wholesale application of the common law to a tribal community is as socially unjust as would be the wholesale retention of customary law in a society which is emerging from tribalism. What our Legislators failed to see was that, in spite of a measure of flexibility implied in this choice of laws, the system is nevertheless too narrowly conceived and too rigidly framed to serve the changing needs of present-day African society, in which social norms and institutions are developing which do not necessarily conform to either common law or customary Bantu law.

A more liberal application of *either* the common law *or* customary law will therefore not meet the situation. To give only two examples: for the tendency towards matrifiliation, the common law and our rigid Western concept of 'illegitimacy' are no remedy; to the modern concept of *lobolo,* Bantu customary law can give little or no quidance.

But the problem is of more than merely academic interest. In 1936 already, a thoughtful first-hand urban study by Dr. Eileen Krige reported that the European courts of law had proved quite incapable of coping with the situation, and from my own researches I have the unhappy impression that, especially among the emerging class of educated and wage-earning women – the mainstay and principal hope of whatever stability there is in modern African family life – there is a strong feeling of social and legal insecurity and little confidence in the existing complex apparatus of law. There is much confusion and despair and, what is worse, a growing indifference to a legally sanctioned marriage as an effective frame within which to raise a family.

For law to be an instrument to guide the orderly development of social institutions, it has to be flexible (which need not be 'uncertain'), attuned to social reality – a fluid quality – and it needs to be applied specifically to individual cases in their social context by a judicial organ which retains close contact with society. If the law and the courts do not have these qualities, they are apt to confuse rather than guide.

There is enough evidence to show that the law, in respect of the changing pattern of African marriage, is losing touch with the reality of the present situation, and I have submitted that its flexibility is not much more than a too restricted choice between prescribed alternatives, neither of which may always reflect social reality. It has therefore from time to time been suggested that the Legislator make new laws to meet the changing situation. If this means yet another near-exhaustive set of statutory provisions prescribing specific remedies for general application to 'the Bantu', then the results will be just another straightjacket, ill-suited to the dynamics of social change. For legislation means generalization of norms; and the very thing we can *not* do at the present fluid stage of African development is to generalize.

How, then, could the Legislator, here and across the Limpopo, help to bring order in the present near-chaotic situation regarding African marriage? I submit that a constructive contribution would involve the clear recognition by the Legislator of the fact that indigenous society is changing, but that this change is neither uniform in pace nor in pattern, and that it inevitably creates social problems of a multiplicity and diversity with which no legislation (by nature a slow and cumbersome process) can hope to deal adequately and in detail.

If these were to be the broad premises of the new statute law, it follows:

a. that the legal *guiding* principles for dealing with the situation should be laid down *only in outline*, related to the major issues involved; and

b. that the specific *application* of these principles should be left to a qualified and *effective* judicial apparatus specifically charged with the task of examining each case in relation to its particular social context.

Point *a.* would at any rate imply that the basis of the law to be applied will have to be widened, so as to include newly emerging, popularly accepted and stabilizing norms which do not now form part of the recognized systems of the common law or of customary Bantu law; point *b.* implies that the discretion of the appointed judicial bodies will have to be an even wider one than the present law allows and that their personnel should include social workers or other qualified observers of modern African life.

It would also mean that the responsibility for formulating applicable, case-measured law would be largely shifted from the Legislator to the judiciary, which would now have the task, not only of *applying* suitable legal norms, but of *searching for them* where they are likely to be found: in the living reality of modern African society.

The changing roles of African women*

In the tribal areas of Southern Rhodesia the casual visitor is struck by the constant industry of women in their dusty kraals and often delapidated thatched huts, their toiling in the fields, or fetching water in pots and gourds often from a considerable distance away. It seems a pretty hard life for the rural housewife, with little time for relaxation and recreation, especially when compared with the life of their menfolk. No wonder that those whose knowledge of tribal society is derived from casual acquaintance with it believe that women in traditional society are chattels and their existence a form of slavery. When one then observes in the new neatly laid-out urban settlements that all or most of the outward signs of domestic drudgery and hardship are absent, it is only natural to expect that a greater freedom, happiness and dignity has come in the life of the African women in the town.

Perhaps it is the bright appearance of the new African townships, the thousands of neatly-spaced cottages, which gives rise to this expectation. It is true that we still have a few urban slums, but both government and municipalities in Southern Rhodesia are making tremendous efforts to provide adequate and attractive accommodation for the steady stream of Africans to the urban areas. In a small city like Bulawayo, for instance, since 1954 two new townships for a total of nearly 6,000 tenant families have arisen, one of these under a large government-sponsored scheme. And in this scheme, next door to the town's industries, Africans will be the owners of the properties they occupy.

You have to be on the spot to realize what this means to a fledgling country in which, not so many years ago, the urban African was only a bird of passage, paying a short visit to town in order to earn some cash. The new townships have helped to change that, and the home-ownership schemes

* BBC Third Programme talk, 1956. First published in *The Listener*, 4th Oct. 1956, Vol. 56, No. 1436, pp. 496-497; reprinted in Prudence Smith (Ed.) *Africa in Transition*, Reinhardt, London, 1958.

make this change irrevocable because they give the urban African a sense of stability and security such as only ownership of a house and piece of ground can give.

In this new environment the women go about their household chores in a leisurely manner, cook the family meal over the little wood-stoves that are provided for them, tap water from standpipes and tend their vegetables and flower beds in the little gardens while keeping an eye on their children playing about in the sunshine.

The contrast with the rural domestic scene is there for anyone to see. It is therefore often a shock to find that, in spite of the improved domestic facilities, the nicely furnished interiors and the opportunities for leisure and recreation, the urban housewife herself does not generally think that her position and status have much improved. Indeed, it is especially the better-educated, better-to-do minority, the wives of teachers, ministers of religion and clerks, who voice the complaint that, in general, the position and status of the housewife in urban society is probably worse than it is in the tribal communities.

What then is their main difficulty? Surprisingly enough they do not immediately blame the shortage of money and high cost of living, or the government or city council, or Europeans generally, which the African male has chosen as his favourite scapegoats. With quiet outspokenness they blame in the first place their menfolk and husbands for 'holding them down' and preventing them from playing their full and legitimate part in this new life. And here, perhaps in an oversimplified manner, they have indicated the crux of what may well be the toughest problem which urban African society has to solve.

To explain this I must first return to the traditional social pattern, in which the life of an individual, man, woman or child, is wrapped up in an intricately woven, carefully balanced and very widespread fabric of kinship relation. In this 'web of kinship', as Professor Fortes calls it, a person's social position is more or less nicely balanced between relatives (by blood or by marriage) who are superior and those who are subordinate. This is not merely a matter of formality, of taking care to use the correct form of address. It involves a code of behaviour and a pattern of social order in which every person meeting another person within this web of kinship is either expected to extend service, obedience or courtesy to the other, or is entitled to receive it. Depending on the particular type or nearness of the relationship, these social obligations are discharged with varying degrees of strictness or with varying measures of familiarity. The point to remember is that these relationships are so wide-spread that they involve most of the people with whom a person regularly comes into contact in the neighbourhood.

Now, when we, as Europeans, think of the position of women in any society, we are inclined to see them mainly as wives of husbands or as mothers of children, thereby overlooking all the other relationships in which they may find themselves. Moreover, in the types of tribal society which exist in Southern Rhodesia the position of a woman as a wife and mother is *weaker* than in any other kind of relationship (although any anthropologist will probably tell you that even this position is not nearly weak as a paper analysis would allow). But it is when we turn to the other relationships in a woman's life that we find her social and even legal status growing to a remarkable extent, more indeed than we ever credited to our own womenfolk before they won the battle of their emancipation.

The age-old institution of marrying a wife upon the promise or delivery of a sizeable bridewealth to her family is, in spite of all anthropological writing, still widely regarded by Europeans as a form of 'buying a wife'. Yet this institution gives her as effective a security against marital abuse as could be devised, for a cruel husband not only runs the risk of losing his wife but he also impairs his claim for the return of the bridewealth he has given for her. Moreover, it places a woman in a strong position in regard to her brother and brother's wife. In Mashonaland, for instance, a normal bridewealth is so high that few fathers could afford one for their sons were it not for the fact that the daughters of the family, by marrying into other families, provide the necessary marriage cattle for their brothers' wives. The kinship system takes full account of this by making the woman *vamwene* ('keeper') of her brother's wife. She is the obvious arbitrator in her brother's marital disputes, she is by law the executrix of his estate when he dies and she is the respected confidante and *vatete* ('female father') of his children.

It is, however, as the mother of married daughters that a woman attains her strongest position: that is, as a mother-in-law to her sons-in-law and their families. In this relationship her position does not rest only on considerations of a social and legal character. Among the Mashona and kindred tribes it receives powerful support from the deeply rooted mystical concepts of fertility and procreation. As the mother of a young wife she is seen as the immediate link with the matriline of ancestresses from which the power of procreation is derived. Her favour or disfavour towards her daughter's family-in-law may spell the difference between a fruitful and a childless marriage. It is obvious then that this family will treat her with the utmost respect and even servility.

Nor are these relationships expressed merely in the services and courtesies which are extended to her. Prescribed by law, and further enforced by the fear of mystical retribution, a number of material benefits are due to her. The most important of these is the 'motherhood beast', a cow or heifer payable by her son-in-law upon or after her daughter's marriage. The motherhood beast can be retained by the woman, a significant difference from the actual bridewealth, which is a floating asset of the bride's *paternal* family, or from some other gifts of small livestock which are earmarked for immediate ritual sacrifice. The motherhood beast forms the beginning of a sometimes very considerable maternal estate which falls outside the control of the woman's husband or her paternal relatives.

These few examples illustrate that in tribal society there are relationships in a woman's life which, in a very real sense, compensate the comparative weakness in which she finds herself as a wife and mother in the domestic environment of her husband's family.

All this still applies at the present day in most of the rural communities in Southern Rhodesia. For even school education and a spreading Christianity have made no serious inroads upon it. Wherever the traditional fabric of tribal society has remained more or less intact, a woman will find not only the children of her own brothers and the husbands of her own daughters who pay homage to her, but a multitude of others who, on the strength of this classificatory kinship system, are placed in similar relations to her and therefore obliged to treat her in a similar respectful manner.

As long as the web of kinship is intact. And here lies the great and inevitable difficulty of the women in the new urban communities. For, in this heterogeneous town population, flocked together from half-a-dozen different countries and scores of different tribal backgrounds, a woman may find a few scattered relatives, but no kinship system. There are the loose and often frayed bits of tribal culture from many origins, a few traditional concepts commonly shared. But these do not nearly add up to a recognized code of behaviour or etiquette, let alone a cohesive pattern of social order.

A large proportion of the urban population consists of single men, who are still birds of passage and no respecters of respectable women. The rest is made up of a multiplicity of small family units, in which a woman is first and last the wife of a husband and the mother of his children. In other words, in this as yet unformed urban society the otherwise balanced pattern of a woman's social relationships is virtually monopolized by the one kinship relationship in which she is traditionally weakest. Moreover, on this husband-and-wife relationship the hand of tradition weighs perhaps even more heavily in town than in tribal society. First, because most town people still maintain individual contact with their rural background, and this impedes the acceptance and growth of a new social concept in which man and wife are equal partners. Secondly, because the short history of African town life has also seen the emergence of a new and daring class of easy-going women who take advantage of the ill-balance between the sexes by leading a relatively comfortable life as prostitutes; or, slightly more honourably, as short-term companions of men whose wives are at their rural homes. With masculine inconsistency many men secretly admire these glamour girls (the so-called 'spares' – delightful term!), but they dislike even taking their own wives and daughters out in public, to dances or cinemas. For there is the fear that their reputation might be associated with that of the light-hearted creatures who frequent these places.

And so, in spite of more time for leisure and the cultural and recreational facilities around her, the faithful wife of a self-respecting husband is even more strictly tied to her neat cottage in the township than she ever was to her rural homestead. This makes it difficult for her to widen the circle of friends which she might make among the strangers in her neighbourhood. In fact, what the student of rural African society regretfully misses in the townships is the congenial aspect of fairly large and happy parties of neighbouring housewives gathered for a common social or economic pursuit. There is no denying the loneliness, confused disillusion and, sometimes, bitterness of hundreds of women who are aware of the possibility of a full and rich urban community life, but seem unable to attain it.

This, then, appears on the reverse side of the promising picture presented by the neatly planned townships out under the bright African sky. It is, I think, an inevitable part of the labour pains which must be suffered with the birth of this new society.

What can we, as administrators, do about it? Very little, I am afraid. It is not the sort of problem that is solved by legislation or by-laws nor by the domestic guidance offered by helpful welfare workers and European ladies' societies, however useful these efforts may be from other points of view. What we can do, and what we are doing, is to unlock the doors which might bar a woman from entering public life. But it would be foolish to force her out into the open. What we can do, and are doing on an increasing scale, is to give her advice and guidance on how to run her household, how to look after her children, how to make her home attractive with simple and inexpensive means. We do this to give her confidence in an environment which must often be strange and confusing to her. Also because we hope that it will give her husband a new pride in his home, wife and family. And we try to encourage the kind of cultural activity in which both men and women, and preferably married couples, participate. For we think that this will foster a sense of equality and mutual respect between the sexes. Useful efforts, which, here and there, may bear a little fruit. But they cannot solve the problem, for the real change must come from within.

Perhaps it has started already: the wife of an African M.P. sharing her husband's public duties; a minister's widow staunchly taking care of her late husband's parish; a circle of young housewives meeting to discuss the problems of their urban community; a hesitant effort by factory girls to form their own workers' union; a cultural society encouraging women to become members; the married couples singing side by side in a newly formed choral society. Isolated instances, all of these. But they may be the early symptoms of a growing awareness that, with the loss of a widely active kinship system, the relationship between husband and wife must make room for a new concept of marital and social partnership. Within this single frame they must now seek to balance the relative weakness and strength which formerly derived from multiple kinship relations extending far beyond domestic life. This is the type of marriage relationship counselled by the Christian Church, but as the Church has found, it does not come by simple bidding.

Works cited or consulted

THE CASE OF THE TROUBLESOME FATHER

Gluckman, M., 1940, 'Analysis of a Social Situation in Modern Zululand', *Bantu Studies* Vol. 14, March & June (reissued in *Rhodes-Livingstone Papers No. 28,* Manchester U.P., 1958).

– 1955, *The Judicial Process among the Barotse of Northern Rhodesia* (2nd ed. 1967), Manchester U.P.

Holleman, J. F., 1952, *Shona Customary Law,* Oxford U.P. Cape Town (2nd impr. Manchester U.P., 1969).

Schapera, I., 1938, *Handbook of Tsawana Law and Custom,* Oxford U.P. London (2nd ed. 1955).

THE CASE OF THE IRATE HEADMAN

Cardozo, B. N., 1921, *The Nature of the Judicial Process,* Yale U.P. New Haven.

Gluckman, M., 1955, (above).

Holleman, J. F., 1950, 'An Anthropological Approach to Bantu Law', *Rhodes-Living-stone Journal* X, 51-64.

Nader, L., 1969, 'Styles of Court Procedure: To make the Balance', in *Law in Culture and Society* (ed. L. Nader), Aldine Publ. Co., Chicago.

Osborn, P. G., 1964, *A Concise Law Dictionary,* 5th ed., Sweet & Maxwell, London.

Shorter Oxford Dictionary, 1964 (3rd rev. ed.), Oxford U.P., Oxford.

Van Velsen, J., 1969, 'Procedural Informality, Reconciliation, and False Comparisons', in *Ideas and Procedures in African Customary Law* (ed. M. Gluckman), Oxford U.P., London.

MARRIAGE BRIDEWEALTH AND WOMEN IN AN AFRICAN SOCIETY

Barnes, J. A., 1951, *Marriage in a Changing Society,* Rhodes-Livingstone Papers No. 20, Oxford U.P., Cape Town.

Bohannan, L., 1959, 'Dahomean Marriage: a Revaluation', *Africa* XIX, 273-87.

Cripps, H., 1947, 'Should Lobolo be restricted by Legislation?', *NADA* XXIV, 41-44, Salisbury.

Gluckman, M., 1950, 'Kinship and Marriage among the Lozi of Northern Rhodesia and the Zulu of Natal', in *African Systems of Kinship and Marriage* (ed. A. R. Rad-cliffe-Brown and D. Forde), Oxford U.P., London.

Holleman, J. F., 1952, (above).
– 1953, *Accommodating the Spirit amongst some North-Eastern Shona Tribes*, Rhodes-Livingstone Papers No. 22, Manchester U.P.
– 1969, *Chief, Council and Commissioner*, Van Gorcum, Assen/Oxford U.P., London.
Krige, E. J. & J. D., 1943, *The Realm of a Rain-Queen*, Oxford U.P., London.
Morkel, E. R. R., 1949, 'Native Administration and some Customs and Beliefs', *NADA* XXVI, 40-42, Salisbury.
Phillips, A. (ed.), 1953, *Survey of African Marriage and Family Life*, Oxford U.P., London.
Reyner, R. H., 1948, *Zulu Woman*, Columbia U.P., New York.
Southern Rhodesia, 1951, *Report of the Secretary for Native Affairs and Chief Native Commissioner for the Year 1950*, Govt. Printer, Salisbury.
Schapera, I., 1938, (above).

CASH, CATTLE OR WOMEN: A CONFLICT OF CONCEPTS IN A DUAL ECONOMY

Daniel, J. B. McI., 1964, 'The Swazi Rural Economy', in *Experiment in Swaziland* (ed. J. F. Holleman), Oxford U.P., Cape Town.
Holleman, J. F. (ed.), 1964, *Experiment in Swaziland: Report of the Swaziland Sample Survey 1960*, Oxford U.P., Cape Town.
Hughes, A. J. B., 1962, 'Some Swazi Views on Land Tenure', *Africa* 42(3), 253-78.
– 1964, 'Incomes of Rural Homestead Groups', in J. F. Holleman (ed.) 1964.
Mitchell, J. C., 1957, 'Aspects of African Marriage on the Copperbelt', *Rhodes-Livingstone Journal*, Sept., 1-30.
Southern Rhodesia, 1961, *Report of the Mangwende Reserve Commission of Inquiry*, Govt. Printer, Salisbury.
Union of South Africa, 1955, *Summary of the Report of the* (Tomlinson) *Commission for the Socio-Economic Development of the Bantu Areas within the Union of South Africa*, Govt. Printer, Pretoria.

AFRICAN MARRIAGE AT THE CROSS-ROADS

Ashton, E. H., 1952, *The Basuto*, Oxford U.P., London.
Brandel, M., 1958, 'Urban Lobolo Attitudes', *African Studies* 17(1).
Hellmann, E., 1948, *Rooyard, a Sociological Study of an Urban Native Slum Yard*, RhodesyLivingstone Papers No. 13 Oxford U.P., Cape Town.
Hellman, E. (ed.), 1949, *Handbook of Race Relations*, Oxford U.P., Cape Town.
Henriques, F. M., 1953, *Family and Colour in Jamaica*, Eyre & Spottiswoode, London 1953.
Holleman, J. F., 1952, (*above*).
Hunter, M., 1936, *Reaction to Conquest*, Oxford U.P., London.
Janish, M., 1941, 'Some Administrative Aspects of Native Marriage Problems in an Urban Area', *Bantu Studies* XV(1).
Jeffreys, M. D. W., 1951, 'Lobolo is Child Price', *African Studies* 10(4), 145-84.

Junod, V. I., 1954, *New Social Groupings in Southern Bantu Urban Areas,* unpubl. M. A. thesis, University of London.
Kaplan, S., 1945, *Household Composition, Kinship and Marriage in an Urban Location,* unpubl. B. A. Hons. thesis, University of Witwatersrand.
Krige, E. J., 1936a, *The Social System of the Zulus,* Longmans, London.
- 1936b, 'Changing Conditions in Marital Relations and Parental Duties among Urban Natives', *Africa* IX, 1-22.
Krige, E. J. & J. D., 1943, (above).
Levin, R., 1947, *Marriage in Langa Location,* University of Cape Town, School of African Studies, stencilled comm.
Longmore, L., 1959, *The Dispossessed, a Study of Sex Life of Bantu Women in and around Johannesburg,* London.
Marwick, B. A., 1940, *The Swazi,* Cambridge U.P.
Marwick, M. G., 1958, *The Modern Family in Social-Anthropological Perspective,* Inaugural Lecture Univ. of Witwatersrand, Johannesburg.
Mathewson, J. E., 1959, 'Impact of Urbanization on "Lobolo" ', *S.A.B.R.A. Journal,* 10(3).
Mitchell, J. C., 1957, (above).
Natal University Institute for Social Research 1955 *The Baumannville Community, a Study of Family Life of Urban Africans,* Durban.
Phillips, A. (ed.), 1953, (above).
Phillips, R. E., 1938, *The Bantu in the City,* The Lovedale Press.
Ngcobo, S., 1947, 'The Urban Bantu Family as a Unit', *Journal of Race Relations* XIV, 97-101.
Schapera, I., 1938, (above).
- 1941, *Married Life in an African Tribe,* Faber, London.
Seymour, S. M., 1953, *Native Law in South Africa,* Juta, Cape Town.
Simons, H. J., 1958, 'The Status of African Women', in *Africa in Transition* (ed. P. Smith), Reinhardt, London.
Stafford, W. G. and Franklin, E., 1950, *The Principles of Native Law and the Natal Code,* Shuter & Shooter, Pietermaritzburg.
Stayt, H. A., 1931, *The Bavenda,* Oxford U.P., London.
Whitfield, G. M. B., 1948, South African Native Law (2nd ed.), Juta, Cape Town.
Van Tromp, J., 1948, *Xhosa Law of Persons,* Juta, Cape Town.

Bei Fragen zur Produktsicherheit wenden Sie sich bitte an:
If you have any questions regarding product safety,
please contact:

Walter de Gruyter GmbH
Genthiner Straße 13
10785 Berlin
productsafety@degruyterbrill.com